COMMUNICATION AND MEDIA
Studies in Ideas, Initiatives and Institutions

Communication and Media

Studies in Ideas, Initiatives and Institutions

ANGELA WADIA

KANISHKA PUBLISHERS, DISTRIBUTORS
New Delhi-110 002

KANISHKA PUBLISHERS, DISTRIBUTORS
4697/5-21 A, Ansari Road, Daryaganj
New Delhi-110 002
Phones : 2327 0497, 2328 8285
Fax : 011-2328 8285
E-mail: kanishka_publishing@yahoo.co.in

Communication and Media:
Studies in Ideas, Initiatives and Institutions

First Published–1999
Edition–2010

PRINTED IN INDIA

Published by Madan Sachdeva for Kanishka Publishers, Distributors, 4697/5-21A, Ansari Road, Daryaganj, New Delhi-110 002, Typeset by Sunshine Graphics, Delhi, and Printed at Rajdhani Printers, Delhi.

Preface

It has been said that great ideas one day become great institutions. The same is true of media and communication in the modern world. With the advent of information technology over three decades ago and the opening up of the skies, as it were to human endeavour, the age of communication and social revolution through the media dawned in a glowing sunrise on the future of mankind. However, as all good things have terrible uses, the forces of manipulation and exploitation too have raised their ugly visage. Since the days of Marshal Macluhan, the guru of the media, and the prophetic vision of Arthur C. Clarke in terms of satellite technology, communication and media have changed the evolution of mankind into less defined, more speculative and, perhaps, lessened human values. The concern of educators, sociologists, child development experts and parents over the ill-effects of television on impressionable children are well-founded. Yet, communication and media remain the very cornerstones of human progress and development—both as human endeavour and as institutions.

The present publication on *Communication and Media: Studies in Ideas, Initiatives and Institutions* examines in profile the key concepts that are behind the greatest moving force in human history and makes realistic projections for the future in terms of information technology, data management, multinational objectives and individual initiatives. That mass media and communication have assumed the proportions of social institutions is a well accepted fact of the century. However, the articles, papers, reviews and excerpts contained in the present publication bring together the thoughts, concepts and propositions of leading and not-so-well-known professionals in the field of communication and media, in a well-defined effort to present to the reader and student the framework of an agenda, the blueprint for a plan of action, the springboard for further research. It is hoped that the volume will serve as valuable supplementary reading for all students of communication and media.

EDITOR

Contents

1

New World Information and Communication Order

Perspective

The main media of modern communication are the sound radio, television, the film and the Press, apart from the traditional media which operate in a feeble form mainly in the rural areas. The sound radio and television are the most modern and the other media cannot compete with them in speed and vividness. But the Press or print medium has still its hold; it has a permanent form; people like to preserve, read and read what they hear on the radio or see and hear on television. What applies to one medium about its role in developing countries applies to other media, in spite of their differing techniques, and while the traditional media are important in developing countries and can be further developed, it is with the message that we are more concerned here and not with the medium and its techniques.

In what is known as mass communication, news is an important ingredient. But what is news? There are three theories about the origin of the word, news, but whatever its origin, it means something new. But the old saying of an American journalist that if a dog bites a man, it is not news, but if a man bites a dog, it is news, is not valid down. For a man to bite a dog is not normal; it amounts to sensationalism. Men do not bite dogs to make news. There is news even in normal happenings. There is news when something new happens; it means that change is news. "What news on the Rialto," says a character in "The Merchant of Venice." In developing countries, there is news, not the sensational news of murder and other crimes, of which there are always reports in developed countries. There is more social and economic change in developing countries, and that is the more important news, not political developments alone. The only worth while sensationalism is the sensation of social and economic change.

For developing countries, development is the main thing, and though it is not sensational in the ordinary sense, the changes, big or small, that take place all-round are news, and lack of change also is news. The most lasting changes are always slow and quiet. History, which is a more permanent and unhurried form of recording happenings, is no longer the history of the follies and crimes of mankind, as Gibbon saw it or as Herodotus had recorded it in a crude form from contemporaries. The main task of the present-day historian is to present the social and economic development of countries, the background against which kings, proconsuls, Presidents and Prime Ministers prance. Britain won an empire spectacularly, though in a fit of absent mindedness, but emphasis is now given to how Britain developed not only politically but socially and economically and in science and technology.

News Means Change

In developing countries, the media, which record history in a hurry, find that socio-economic development provides the greatest amount of news. There are no wars or landings on the moon to report, and as chroniclers and interpreters, media men will find much of interest for readers to speak or write about. For this, they require more and more means of communication, more and more newspapers, more and more radio and T.V. stations, more films. The development of the means of communication is also important, but the stress has to be laid on the content for progress means change, news means change every day, some part of society is always changing, and as there is greater awareness of the importance of communication to society, ministers become less important than common man.

The media are now not well organised in developing countries where they are more important for results than in the developed countries, where they serve curiosity or the need for entertainment more. In developing countries, there is need for more and more information and for more and more explanation. If society as a whole has to share in communication, society must have a share in the ownership, control and management of the means of communication; but it is the opinion of experts that in developing countries, where the sound radio and T.V. are under state control, they need not be converted into corporations, till the proficiency of those who run the media is raised to a high level. The state can run those media more purposefully, if it has social needs in view than private media with profit motive and uncertain aims. The political opposition can be given its due share even with state-run media, and that is a small part of their coverage. The film is to some extent under state control and the Press is mainly in the private sector, with the newspaper industry owned by other industries in this country. But the needs of communication between various segments of the community and participation in communication by the maximum number of people must be kept in view.

In the objective of a world information order is implicit the need for a national information order, and for that vagaries of private-controlled sources of information have to be corrected as much as the prejudices and bias of state-controlled media. The social aims are important, whether they are served by the state or by organisations of society. There must be a more even flow of information between the several countries of the world, and between the several areas of a country itself and between different sections of society. In the nation-building process in which developing countries are absorbed, the infrastructure of communication is necessary, but that must be used for better and closer communication.

The News Pool

The emergence of the News Agencies Pool of the non-aligned countries, which are almost all developing countries, was an effort to build a new world information order as a part of a new international economic order. The present imbalances should be removed and the domination by Western news agencies of dissemination of information from all regions of the world must be checked. This has meant a struggle as in the case of development. The News Agencies Pool of the Non-Aligned countries has meant a diversion from the talk of the more developed among the develeoping countries like India building their own strong international news agency structure to compete with the Western news agencies, but India, Yugoslavia and other countries have co-operated in the effort of the developing countries to help each other in the dissemination of information. This has meant correction of imbalances to a certain extent but not to a sufficient extent. The Pool has shown several insufficiencies, like lack of transmission facilities, lack of news media within certain countries, and lack of sufficient development itself within some countries. Unless each country is engaged in the task of ensuring sufficient and even development within itself, there is little information to transmit except occasional change of regimes.

If India's coverage of Asia is considered, it is still thin in quality, most of the coverage is about external relations, even India's close neighbours like Burma, Thailand, Indonesia, and Ceylon are not sufficiently covered. Nepal is, but for good neighbourly reasons, much cannot be covered, and from Pakistan there can be only diluted news. The case of African countries is worse, not to speak of the Caribbean countries. Much of the Asian and African news even now emanates from Europe or America, not from Asia or Africa. To report Asia or Africa is different from reporting Europe or America. It requires more sympathy and understanding, less of sensationalism and more of the dull news of development.

The cult of personality has added to the difficulty or reporting non-personal themes of development. There is need for leadership in developing countries more than in developed countries, but the personal is not as important as changes among the lives of the people. We are all men and women of destiny, said Jawaharlal Nehru, and the millions are more important than what some persons do. The so-called investigative reporting has also meant investigation of crime and corruption, which should be uncovered, but in concentrating on the Malkan Singhs, the magazines and other publications concentrate more on the romantic and sensational aspects of crime or corruption, not on its social and economic causes. The lives of the people at large are in the background, unless there is mass rape or mass murder, but what is behind it all escapes the journalist, if he is a mere haphazard chronicler in a hurry, not a social scientist in less hurry. There is blood, sweat, toil and tragedy in life, in the jhuggies or slums or pavements, and something must change there, if there are to be no social explosions. The media in countries like India are missing the lava and bruistone of the lives of the people, the real though silent revolution in their minds. There should be more facts, more analysis, less of sensationalism and vulgarisation.

COMMUNICATION TECHNOLOGY FOR THE PEOPLE

One could, of course, write at length on the technological possibilities in communication, from a global point of view, and could get into very futuristic scenarios like having a wrist watch communication system with which you can speak to anybody, any time you want. But we will refrain from that exercise in as far as it relates to our own situation. Basically our understanding of communication is that it is a sub-set of what is implied by the word interaction. Clearly if there is no interaction between elements of a system, then there is no structure. Indeed if there were no interaction between humans there would not have been any society. Interaction is what leads, sometimes, to new configurations, even creative configurations, and that is the essence of development. So, basically, communication has to have that particular capability—of being interactive—if it has not to degenerate into an activity or filling sacks, (notwithstanding the fact that even filling sacks is not that easy), then it won't be a creative enhancing, activity.

The developments which are occurring at the moment, around the world, and even in this country, in the areas of technology of communication are exceedingly exciting. We are—thanks to the synergetic developments in the field of electronics, space, computers, printing technology, in all kinds of things—we are getting to a stage when there is a possibility that one might be liberated from the very tyranny of technology. This, because large technological systems have always implied that you were forced to do somethings a certain way. Old technological systems usually carried not only the messages of what you can do with this technology but also a certain value system. You were forced to do somethings in a certain way, the way they had been done earlier for a set purpose. They were a sort of pre-programmed and that is why people have had an abhorrence of this large mechanical technology because it forces society to go certain ways. But what is happening now has a new feature and we have to recognise it. It is a feature such that the sub-systems of technology are so flexible that they can be put together in many different ways into systems which can begin to have desired value orientations.

There has been a lot of discussion about questions like centralisation and decentralisation. There has always been a fear that when you increase the reach of a communication system, as one is beginning to do by the use of satellites, you will automatically—you are destined to—also increase the tendency for centralisation. Because larger reach implies that a few wise people sitting in one place can dispense wisdom to a large number of others and there will be a temptation, therefore, to use the system only in that particular way. This can have an homogenising effect and it can have an indoctrinating effect. It can certainly lead to some kind of common sharing, some kind of growth, but it will not encourage creativity and it will not lead to enhancement of society, and you could say that such a system, in principle, ultimately, in the long run, may be something which may not be very nice.

In the beginning it would be wonderful to bring news and views even if only from one place, but if it is only one place which supplies news, wisdom and everything that has to be learned, we know that society will not be enhanced. But one might then say: well this is it, we have access to a technology which seems to be very efficient, which reduces costs of reaching many people and, therefore, even if this technology will go in that way we have no choice, we are just prisoners. On the other hand, if we use this technology in association with lot of other small technologies and use a little, small, degree of creativity, both in organisation and in terms of using other technologies, "we can overcome." We definitely can overcome what we consider to be rather undesirable aspects of this particular technology. But this will be possible through positive action alone, it will not be possible if we use it the way everybody else is using it—if we use it in the easiest way it comes. We will mention some of these things later.

Demystifying Technology

Now let me come to the Indian scene. Normally we have the tendency, in our country—an under-developed syndrom. We think that for practically everything we need to go and get consultancy or at least see how other people are doing things, and then we think that this is the only legal, allowed, way of doing things. But I suggest to you that at the moment the situation in our country, if only we will use our advantages, is far different. We are in a very different situation. A few days ago we all heard the news about the launch of SLV-3. Lot of congratulations have been offered to the Project Director and space scientists on this achievement. We feel proud that we are the sixth nation to be able to launch satellites. We also seem to feel that there is some kind of magic or trick people have discovered which enable us to put a satellite up there. But let us look at it just from communication point of view.

If you open up the work done in connection with the launch of SLV-3 (and this is just one of the things that I am talking about; there are many things in the country which are happening), look at various element involved. It involves the most reliable communication electronics, computer control of communication, digital communication, recording of messages, retrieving of messages, fast analysis of information, control systems. It involves anything you can think of in principle in the technology of communication, in various bands interference-free in all aspects, antennas, feeds, transmitters, receivers, radars, computer systems, what have you. If we open the guts of this SLV achievement, and others, then we would find that we have in many places—not only here, but in many places—at least a few people who have demystified technology, who can put things together for a purpose. So we can also learn to put things together for another purpose, if only we will define that purpose. We are not defining purposes well enough, in time, in order to let our people loose on solving problems and delivering goods. There is nothing else. There is no other mystery about launching SLV-3 or doing anything else even more challenging. These are the aspects which we have to consider. So I suggest that in terms of understanding the subsystems which go into communication systems of all types—I have mentioned a few—that we have enough people, we have reasonable technology, at least for systeming; we may not have all the components. So time has come for us to think freely about what kind of a system we would design, which would be best for our own country. And I am not talking only of broadcasting. I am talking of telecommunication, broadcasting, printing various other things which could be done. In terms of satellite broadcasting and satellite communication, as you are well aware, there is very good experience in the country, in making all the hardware, ground stations. I hope we will also be making our own operational communication satellite—I wish we had taken a decision to do it by now. But we would be making them soon. In terms of ground-based space-related systems of various types—to mention a few things which are not very well-known—we have developed, through experimentation, systems for very high bitrate communication, time division multiple accessing, spread spectrum multiple accessing—which allows you to work with very small terminals, in any emergency area, secure communication, all kinds of techniques of various types, ship-born communication, small portable terminals, almost man-pack kind of terminals for working with communication satellites. And not only satellites. Clearly the same technology is available for micro-wave-linking, for transmitters, for radio links, for various things of this sort.

Different Emphasis

Now why am I saying all this? What relevance it has to a different emphasis, somewhat different emphasis, on choosing and developing our communication systems? Let me give one example. When sattelites first came on the horizon in the West, in the affluent countries, they already had a very good, very well-developed infrastructure for communication through microwave-links, cables, etc. Practically every city, every town and every home was in a way connected to a central exchange and through the exchange to each other, though the trunk lines may have been somewhat crowded. So, it made a lot of sense for them to put large ground stations in a few places, so that one part of the network could be connected to another part of the network very far away, very quickly. So everybody who could get to this ground station then could go to a very distant part of the world via satellite and then through the local network get to anybody else. It made a lot of sense to work with these large ground stations in that situation.

Same approach was followed for international communication through INTELSAT, requiring large ground stations; practically every country has such an overseas station now for communicating with other countries. And what has become possible now is that if you are in a capital city in any country in the world you can talk to another capital city—no matter how underdeveloped communications are in your own country. You can talk to them with equal facility. Lot of people in capital cities have been internationalised and, in some sense, I think, removed at least in developing countries, from the rest of their population even further. But the ground links in developing countries around the world have been very poor and so most of the population in these countries has not been helped. Many countries have set up their own satellite systems or leased transponders, and again set up a few rather large ground stations, which has not helped the people very much because only those ground stations can talk to each other or those abroad but everybody else is left out.

Now I suggest if we were to think about a proper communication system for a country like ours or other developing countries, we would try to go differently. We would try to see how we can turn into an advantage our every adversity. We would recognise the fact that we do not have a very good terrestrial system at the moment, that we have bottlenecks in exchanges, that even our telegrams now begin to be sent by mail because they have to go through so many different nodal points that the message gets distorted and they get stuck. So I would think, as an example, that here is an opportunity where we would sit down seriously and say, "All right, we have had a great deal of metropolitan communication, it is inefficient, we have to improve it, and shall keep working at it. But we have had essentially no communication from the hinterland or between one part of the hinterland to another. Is it possible that this might be the first country where, in some parts, even for whole of the country, all mail will become electronic and all parts of country will be treated equally, without getting into horrible delays and bottlenecks?"

How can we do it? It appears impossible, even ridiculous. But if you do a small sum, as some people have done, you find that using a very small part of the INSAT capacity itself you could serve thousands of telegraph offices in the country and infact also provide telex service to many, many different types of areas. And they could really become well connected with each other, without going through any of the cluttered exchanges. Such studies have been done, perhaps without a detailed cost benefit analysis. May be, it is a useless idea, may be it will not work, but this is the kind of thinking we have to do at once. It would be fantastic to have all the distant and difficult parts of the country treated so equally and so well. Because we have to get the people in this country really moving and interacting with each other. Once you set up roadways and once you set up canals and rivers between different parts of the world, different segments of society the interaction starts. People living along the banks of a river always learnt from each other, interacted with each other far better than the people living away from the river. People living on the side of a road always communicate better with each other than with others. So we have to set up three new roadways and this will be the stimulus, the catalyst, for starting a new type of interaction. It is true that many of these things are not revenue-earning in the beginning, these are thin routes and so it may not be easy to justify such services on the basis of normal cost-benefit analysis or from the point of view of rate of return kind of analysis which we normally do. But I would suggest that economists and social scientists should try another type of justification for such projects, keeping in mind the long-term societal gains which will be far greater than the near time gains which you get in terms of return on capital. I am not even saying that we be extravagant, to the extent that we become bankrupt; I am saying, let us use some of the facilities (like the satellite) which we have justified otherwise for purposes of this type. As a beginning, I hope after a while we will learn to justify them in their own right. These are some of the socio-economic—futuristic—aspects you can look at.

Plan for Communication Needs

This is about telecommunication, and there are a whole lot of other things in telecommunication you can think about and do. Today I read in the newspaper about a discussion about having a National Electricity Grid with the Super-Thermal Power Station to be interconnected via a satellite communication network. This will make it possible, centrally, to adjust the power output of different station connected to the same grid, responding to the demand. It could also provide channels for telemetry and management. It needs a fairly good, reliable, communication system and I think it is a good idea. Now I do not know who suggested this. This has been talked about a great deal in academic groups everywhere. But somehow we do not originate these things ourselves. Perhaps we are getting a loan, or a grant from somebody outside and he has asked: "What is your communication system?" I would say that if it is going to be done if it is going to be needed. Then today there should be a study group set up to plan for it so that when it is to be established, a year or two from now, we will be able to supply it ourselves rather than say, there is not enough time available. So let us get a foreign consultant and a turn-key job from outside. There are a lot of things of this type which we have to plan for in terms of communication needs five years from now, 10 years from now, 25 years from now, on which we must start work, start building capabilities. I feel very upset that years and years after we started manufacturing telephone instruments in the country, somebody says that since 35 per cent of telephone faults are due to the faults in the instrument, let us import the technology for making telephone instruments. We have our own "momentum wheel" functioning in the APPLE Satellite for over a year. A momentum wheel is perhaps the ultimate in precision mechanical design in which electrical signals are supplied and signals are taken out and which have been functioning for a couple of years in the lab. Yet we cannot make a good telephone dial which will make correct contacts and we have to go out to get know-how. It is important to talk about these thing because if we are taking about futuristic systems, we are talking about making proper use of what is already developed in the country—in terms of manpower and basic know-how, no matter in what context it has been developed.

I believe there is no other place in the world which has such wonderful challenges for a communication enthusiast and one exciting thing is that we have developed the requisite capabilities to convert these challenges into accomplishments if only we move ahead with self-confidence. It is not given to many countries very often in their history to be in such a position as we are now.

Technical Role

There has been a great deal of talk, in which many people here have been involved, about the need for a better information exchange between developing countries. After having taken part in, and led, the very successful NAM meeting in New Delhi I am wondering whether India should not think in terms of playing a certain technical role in this matter. Quite often our information with the rest of the developing countries is exchanged—news, developmental information, all such interaction—through the metropolitan countries, through their news agencies, many times the messages being rooted via London or Paris or wherever. It is a pretty demeaning business to have to go through these gate-keepers and that is one reason there is not as much interaction between developing countries as there could be. A year and a half ago, while I was in New York, an Indian friend, a computer scientist from TIFR, had come to my office after being at a Conference in Canada. He and a colleague had a proposal which I will elaborate presently, which has a quality of freshness and appropriateness that it appeals to me a great deal.

We say that we have so few telephones in a country like ours and we must increase the number of telephones. Yes we should. But the average investment per telephone, including exchange equipment, wires, cables, etc., is about 10,000 Rupees which is 5-10 times the per capita income of an Indian. So, to think in terms of every Indian family having a telephone within next five years; or 10 years or 20 years, I think, is rather unrealistic. Sure many of us in Delhi will have telephones, and in Bombay and other big cities; but if you think of the whole country, think of the future of communication in our country, if you want to involve everybody, it cannot be based on telephones for a long time. That is the situation. Whether you make them in India or import them the cost per telephone is about the same—$ 1,000 or Rs. 10,000. But does it mean that we, and many other developing countries, should do without the support of efficient communication systems, needed for connecting people in different parts of the country and for many other essential operations? For literates, and those who can get their messages converted into text, telegraph or telex communication is something which might be very useful, certainly for communication between agencies, institutes, across countries, government administration, development activities, banks, airlines, all sorts of things. But normally, these services are also constrained, because they require proximity to existing lines, which are not widespread, and are subject to congestion when passing through city exchanges. So the suggestion was the following.

Normally, we work with a satellite which is situated at an altitude of 36,000 km over the equator which is stationary. It revolves around the earth at the same angular speed with which the earth itself rotates. So for us on the earth it is like a fixed point, six earth radii away over the equator. If you put a satellite very close to the earth, like the Rohini which was launched by SLV the other day, then it goes around the earth once in an hour and a half. If you were to put it a little higher; at two to three thousand km altitude, then it will take a little longer, 110 or 120 minutes, to go around the earth. Now, you can choose various orbits, at various inclinations to the equator.

If I were to choose an orbit over the equator the satellite will spend all its time over the tropical countries, most of which also happen to be developing countries. I put a very little transponder, a low power transponder, with a narrow band width, and since now I can borrow all sorts of other technological elements, I also put a storage, a memory, and a microprocessor—a small computer. The solid state memories are cheap now, and they are becoming cheaper. I could put one megabyte for storage which would correspond to many many pages of typed text.

The microprocessors are also light weight and inexpensive, and their cost is also going down. What is envisaged then is a satellite system which would work somewhat like this: it will come over longitude 80 degrees and say to the station at a longitude 80 degrees. This will be a very tiny station with an antenna, like a fixed TV antenna, non-traking. Send a message and say I have this message for you which will be recorded at this station. The station will have the recorded message for different addresses, setting in its memory and will transmit them in a burst. The satellite will load these in its memory and go on. The interesting feature is that it will come back within a couple of hours after delivering and collecting messages all around the earth. So what we have is an orbiting postman carrying a bag of post around the world, coming back every two hours, which can serve thousands of stations, distributed largely in developing countries. If you can get an answer back from anywhere in these communication difficult parts of the world, within a few hours, you have done something really remarkable. You have developed a possibility of adding entirely new dimension to global communication: you are building a new roadway across the sky, a new river across the wilderness, and you will start developing new contacts, new connections between those who are touched by this roadway and are on the banks of this new river.

Implications of this for interaction between developing countries, in terms of developmental information exchange, political implications, are tremendous. You could put up satellites in inclined orbits: you can also talk to developed countries, northern and southern countries, if you want. Then you can have contact twice a day with all parts of the world.

Telecommunication is Important

Sometime ago I worked out a little system for the United Nations itself and made a proposal to the Secretary-General. The United Nations system has problems of communicating with stations which are in developing countries, for peace keeping operations, for U.N. offices every where, and yet it spends about 40 million dollars a year on its communication. Looking at different types of the communication traffic, one can work out that the cost for a one page message may be a fifth to a sixth of the present costs and one will be able to reach which places cannot be reached now with good efficiency. The total investment might be recouped within a few years. Indeed one hardly needs a big new budget allocation. I understand the proposal is under study. The point I want to emphasise in the possibility of entirely new approaches if the systems are tailor-made for meeting the bread and butter needs, both nationally and internationally.

As far as India is concerned, we may not need such a satellite at this time for our national requirements because we have already invested in our own satellite, the INSAT. However, we might think of using some of the capacity of the satellite in a similar spirit, namely, use, store and forward techniques to cover the whole country with efficient telegraph, telex services. The storage and micro-processor in this case would be at the ground stations.

These are the kind of possibilities which do exist for a country like this, with our established capabilities, both nationally and internationally, if we reorient our priorities, concerns and goals and begin to think afresh and freely. In this group, dominated by mass communicators, I might emphasise that tele-communication is exceedingly important for many, many purposes. All of us who have tried to confirm a reservation on a railway train, leave aside an inter-connected train, know the difficulties in this regard. Clearly railway reservations, aeroplane reservations, all kinds of things for a society like ours, depend very strongly on communication and we cannot escape the need for a reliable communication infrastructure. We will have to get into the total gamut, even if our own variety, and have storage systems, access systems, and the related channels for us to be able to function.

Proper of appropriate technology cannot be an archaic technology if you are going to run trains, if you are going to run aeroplanes; or else stop them, don't have aeroplanes or trains and don't come to seminars from a thousand kilometres away. If you want them then it is a necessity to run them efficiently and it is possible to do that and it is possible to configure systems in the country which will be able to do that. If we only give advance notice and set task teams and put them down to work, you will give challenges to people to fulfil themselves; technically but you will also involve them socially to do something for the future of the country, even the future—which Dr. Seth drew our attention to—which will arrive 7,000 days from now when this century runs out.

Now let me come back to the question of broadcasting. I mentioned early in this talk the dilemma we will face with the opening of this new chapter of satellite broadcasting. We have had some time to think about it, because India was one of the first countries to get excited about the potential and the possibilities of satellite broadcasting. In fact, in a way, the very first country. In 1975-76, we conducted the SITE experiment, termed by Arthur Clarke as the greatest communication experiment in history. I have to emphasise that it was an experiment, for learning, even though it had life size dimensions. Nobody expected to change the face of India with one year of TV broadcast, when everything else going on has not changed the face of India terribly much. I do not want to discuss my personal involvement and that of many others in that historic, almost inconceivable exercise except to say that in this country we have had a great deal of excitement about the possibility of being able to reach our people far away, wherever they are with talking, moving imager; we have had this excitement because we thought that this is something which is going to be used for—at least provide the possibility of using it for—development, for education, for various other things, for essentially, for the first time, not discriminating against people who live far from the urban centres which is not true of many of the new technologies, normally metropolitan technologies, which get invented. We all realise that our excitement, or this proposal, is and was, rather simple-minded. You have to do a great deal more, in addition, to make this technical possibility bear fruit, to give it essence and value.

Need for Sharing Experience

We certainly can reach the electromagnetic signal to all parts of the country, irrespective of their distance from urban centres, irrespective of whether they are close to a microwave line or not, or close to a presently existing transmitter or not. Of course, reaching the electromagnetic signal in itself does not provide access, in the absence of receivers. Nor does the signal necessarily carry value or relevant communication. It is remarkable, of course, for people to be able to share the same images, to feel a sense of identity, to be able to see how the countrymen elsewhere look like, and behave. But, clearly, the real value of this enterprise will depend a great deal on whether you *really* share things with each other, whether you bring images from many many places, and the images and experiences come with equal validity from everywhere to everywhere because only that is real sharing. I mentioned in the beginning the problem that a medium of long range interaction like a satellite—carries with it the inherent danger that it can become a medium of centralisation, even indoctrination. The real challenge lies in finding ways of moving this medium away from a centralising role and towards becoming an integrating medium, a medium which knits together, on an equal basis, lot of decentralised activities. I suggest, indeed that decentralised activity in a large country like this, without a mechanism for integration or this knitting together is not a viable proposition. It is not a viable proposition, because it will lead to parochialism, it will lead to dissentions, it will lead to becoming petty, to being engrossed in thing which are not supportive of each other. So to support decentralisation which has inherent value, you need, an integrating system. And so if we can work towards decentralisation plus integration and not just centralisation, we have the ideal system. Is it possible?

Why Decentralisation

First why I believe that decentralisation has value (and mind you, I have already said decentralisation in isolation without integration will not be viable, will not be productive), is because you deal with the integrity of things; you touch each other, you touch each other through your total personality, things which matter, the smiles and sounds. It is essentially the element of communication philosophy which enters into decentralised communication. There are felt problems to be dealt with. There are nuances to be communicated—nuances drenched in local custom, local shared experiences, are irrelevant nothings which say a great deal. Also education cannot be conducted only centrally, it is a process of give and take. If you are discussing intimate problems which are locale-specific, for example, if it is going to rain only around Delhi, and rain very hard, then you need to spend a lot of time telling the farmers around Delhi that if the crops are ripe, please leave them standing till the rain passes over because they would not be damaged as much as they would be if you cut them and let them lie in the field. You may have to say it many times a day in different ways. But this is not of importance to Tamil Nadu which is drying up. There are many things of this sort which certainly have to be dealt in a decentralised way and you have to give lot of them. You have to work with people. Then you may go out with cameras, you may have to talk to them, bring back the material and retransmit it. You have to say with the important issues so that people and problems get closely involved. But then you must also open your windows to the rest of the country.

Everybody should be able to open their windows to everybody else, so that the learning, the understanding and the beauty of decentralised experience is shared across the country, and we become whole, a totally, in this marvellous beautiful country of ours which has so much diversity and so much richness. And all this is possible now. I was suggesting that tyranny of technology has gone. You have seen these little cameras operating here. We call them (because long time ago some one outside gave them this name), as news-gathering cameras. I suggest that the technical quality of most of these simple cameras and simple systems that go with them is quite acceptable if what they record is of interest. They are not only newsgathering cameras, they are also programme-making cameras. They are cameras which you can carry freely wherever you go and allow you to record programmes wherever you go. We have seen lot of programmes made with similar cameras during Asiad and NAM and we found them to be quite acceptable. There may be some loss of technical quality as compared to the very expensive studio cameras but this is more than compensated by the fact that you see reality in the raw; you interact with people; you get their reactions and that is compensation enough. Further, you get away from the need for very massive systems, large studios, enormous places.

MYTHS AND REALITY

The experience of the developed world of adopting hightech has not been altogether rewarding. Perhaps realising this at one point some communication thinkers did talk of interpersonal communication, appropriate technology and uses of traditional channels of communication. But somewhere along the way that voice got lost in the clamour for more and more sophisticated communication technology. And more importantly these choices had to be justified, therefore, all kinds of myths were built around what these technologies could actually do. The author tries to expose these myths and suggest a possible alternative approach.* As he wrotes: "One cannot take up the task of defending the implications of high technology. We could not be true if we tried to show that high technology has always improved my life style or that of my neighbours. I grew up in the worked-out coal fields of western Pennsylvania where I watched, without knowing the fancy economic theories or literature behind it, the exploitation of my family and generation after generation of other immigrants by corporate America and its attachment to high technology. I now live in a suburb and work in the fourth largest city in the United States. There, I become frustrated trying to breach the self-imposed isolation of neighbours who live in electronic cocoons; fighting the invasions of privacy and freedom imposed upon me by computerised telephone, postal, banking and other data banks; hoping to escape the ever-present noise pollution caused by bigger and louder radio sets and the always-on, inane television programmes; watching once proud citizens become more dependent on and more adorating of high technology, in the process "unlearning" commonsense and other human capabilities. I am incensed as people are convinced to pay higher prices for less efficient service and poorer-made products, end results of high technology, and as these people become less critical because they have been indoctrinated to believe there are no alternatives, that one cannot fight high technology. It is with these feelings what I proceed to write this paper."

Nearly a decade ago, with some optimism and much naivete, I wrote a few papers on the changes in the thinking about

* This section is based on a paper presented by H. Cess, communications expert, at an international seminar.

communication patterns and the needs of rural people. In one of them, I, perceived that:

> More emphasis has to be placed on interpersonal communication networks and folk media, on adapting formal mass media to villagers' problems, on using smaller media, on reopening ancient lines of contact between Third World nations, and on re-evaluating the development paradigms associated with these people.[1]

Almost simultaneously, the marketing of the Information Age hit the world full blast. Instead of discussing appropriate, intermediate or smaller media and technology, the push was on for a telephone in every home, a micro-computer in every village (eventually every home?) and satellite and cable linkups everywhere.

With this promotion of new technology came a number of myths—some old, some new, some rewordings of those supposedly debunked after the Development Decade. This paper will look at these myths, re-raise some unanswered, and may be unaswerable questions and re-suggest a few alternatives.

Myths

1. *New information technology will lead to the development of a global village.*

Perhaps Eurich struck down this myth best in his quote:

> Whoever talked of an electronic neighbourhood must surely have lost every awareness of true neighbourhood, of the feeling of familiarity—even of feeling itself.[2]

He went on to say that a village consists of...

> Close personal observation, building on personal experiences, direct contact, creating a common ground by exploring numerous everyday questions and problems, and thus the dominance of individual behaviours....

On the other hand, a global village, according to Eurich, is linked only by:

> Theoretical chance of more or less anonymous, momentary contacts by telephone or by television; ignoring altogether those factors which impede communication, personal contact and community.[3]

Submerged here is the sub-myth that availability and affordability of new information technology are universal, or can be; that microcomputers are affordable to local groups in developing countries; that a microcomputer network will offer unprecedented low-cost instantaneous communication; that developing country groups will have most of their technical information needs covered with microcomputer and satellite hookups.

As Darrow and Saxenian wrote, this is not to be the case; in fact, they described as "nonsense" the many writings that said micro-computers, through satellite hookups, will solve the problem of getting information to poor country villages. They used the interesting and far-fetched analogy that:

> In a poor country, using a microcomputer linked by satellite to an information system halfway around the world is rather like buying a copy of Shogun printed on a strip of paper three miles long and having a flock of carrier pigeons fly across the country, with it. It's not very practical.[4]

Nor will cabling a developed country, such as West Germany at a cost of US $ 15 billion, create a global village; instead, it will provide an artificial closeness that will have the opposite tendency of alienating and isolating people.

2. *New information technology will serve international understanding, peace and brotherhood.*

It has not so far. With such a large proportion of the new information technology used to enhance thermonuclear arsenals, to spy on other nations and to exploit poorer nations' resources (sometimes before they even know they have the resources), it is difficult to imagine this myth being taken seriously. Yet, it is. The basis seems to be that new information technology will augment trade and commerce, which, in turn, will increase understanding, which will lead to a better and safer world. The Maitland Report said as much:

> An expanded world telecommunications network would benefit both developing and industrialised countries. The process of improving and expanding networks in developing countries will create a major market for telecommunications equipment. A more comprehensive world system will increase international traffic to the advantage of the operators. Where information flows so does commerce. More world trade and other contacts will increase understanding. An expanded telecommunications network will make the world a better and safer place.[5]

It would seem that if larger, industrialised countries are determining the terms of that trade, to the detriment of less developed nations, the understanding that results is hesitant, temporary and often fraught with pentup frustrations.

Norbert Wiener, as early as 1945, worried about new technology getting into the wrong hands. He had two main concerns: its exploitation by the military to wage war and its misuse by industry to deskill and disemploy workers. Wiener did not see these as separate maladies, but part of the same structure.[6] He may have been proven right a long time ago, for having gotten into the wrong hands, information technology that could have helped world understanding, has often been used to spread misinformation, hatred and fear.

3. *New Information technology will lead to increased independence and promotion of democratic ideals.*

The evidence seems to indicate the opposite tendency—that with more information technology, the have nots, whether individuals or nations, become even more dependent upon those that have, and that the computer is a convenient subverter of democratic values, through its ability to concentrate and control information. Dordick, discussing critical issues of new technology, addressed this issue in two of his five speculations:

(*a*) Information will become an economic good with a price tag out of reach of many people, causing a growing gap between the information rich and information poor.
(*b*) Use of computers by government will centralise power and increase the authority of the technocrats.[7]

Numerous examples of the latter point have been given over the years. To cite one, when the Palapa satellite was launched in 1976 in Indonesia, it was criticised as a tool of the government and military for centralisation of power. On an international level, Shipley *et al* described the tendency of transnational companies to increase their control of the markets of developing countries, resulting in centralised decision-making, loss of cultural autonomy and national sovereignty and the inability of such nations to compete with the transnational companies through indigenous growth of their informatic industries.[8]

Others have been concerned with the lack of cultural autonomy on the part of developing countries, which, once dependent upon the hardware of new information technology, must also import the software, which often is relevant, dangerous or inappropriate for indigenous values or morals. There was also a fear that continued importation of media programmes, for example, could lead to extinction of local cultural forms.

Tied to all this is a tendency toward homogenisation. Shipley *et al* said the worldwide oligopoly in information access and processing imposes upon cultures "limited styles or methods of organising information." They said those cultures might prefer "to operate under different premises had they the economic leeway or capability to develop suitable alternatives."[9]

Roszak has discussed a number of traits of new information technology that hinder democratic growth. As a surveillance machine, information technology, according to him, continually invades the privacy of individuals—weak legislation to the contrary. Data are being filed on individuals at a tremendous pace; in the United States, for example, five government agencies alone hold two to four billion overlapping files on the American public. According to Roszak, security and law enforcement agencies usually have the greatest appetites for information. The type of information being filed, Roszak contended, is beneficial for the "professional eavesdroppers...the snoops, the sneaks, the meddlers," and contains the "dross of daily life: every phone call, every cheque passed, every airline ticket." He asked, "Of what use is this to a healthy culture and a vital political life?"[10]

Using United States elections as his example, Roszak showed how new information technology, used for polling purposes, can be honed to sell candidates much like commodities are sold, all detrimental to the democratic process. Biasing elections in favour of those who can spend the most for the best polling services, Roszak added, leads to a dismal style of politics that grows more and more obsessively focussed on imagery, sloganeering, rhetorical legerdemain—in fact, on the hukestering skills of the market-place.[11]

In the United States, pollsters are pitted against pollsters, computers against computers, and often the only issue is the reliability of the polls, according to Roszak, so that one is led to believe that politics is about "opinions—not the forming of opinions, but their tabulation:"[12]

Roszak sees even a greater danger to democratic principles in the United States, and to the survival of the species worldwide. Because control over the world's thermonuclear arsenal is increasingly in computerised systems, and as these systems are programmed to make quick decisions, he believed that in the United States, the constitutional power of the President and Congress to declare war has thus been removed.

Labelling computers "psychotic machines," Roszak further warned of the augmented tendency toward automatic programming of programmes:

> Machines that run by incomprehensible programmes are approaching a kind of technological madness. They are on their way to becoming disintegrated intelligences, split and fragmented, a psychotic stew of assumptions and standards that can no longer be given a rational order,[13]

Summing up about this myth, two additional quotes are given: the first by Dallas Smythe, the second, again by Roszak. Smythe, pleading that acceptance of Technology (with capital T) is not inevitable, said:

> It seems that for communications scholars to push hightech equipment as being potent with democratic tendencies is like physicians prescribing medicines for the cure of disease in the absence of any solid ground for believing that they will not make the disease worse.[14]

Roszak is even stronger in his condemnation of the myth of new information technology leading to democratisation:

> It is the coming of the Information Age, dawning upon us like a change of season. But no matter how high the promise of that age is pitched, the price we pay for its benefits will never outweigh the costs. The violation of privacy is the loss of freedom. The degradation of electoral politics is the loss of democracy. The creation of the computerised war machine is a direct threat to the survival of our species. It would be some comfort to conclude that these liabilities will result from the abuse of computer power. But these are the goals long since selected by those who invented information technology, who have guided it and financed it at every point along the way in its development. The computer is *their* machine; its mystique is *their* validation.[15]

4. *New information technology is promoted as the salvation of the Third World masses.*

Despite claims by governments that high technology leads to social benefits for poor Third World masses, Hamelink, among others, believes something different happens—that it is used as a support system for expanding the transnational business of a few countries, and that it reinforces the existing social structures rather than transform them.

The information technology itself is controlled by a few countries which reap most of its benefits. United States companies, for example, dominate the world market in computers (81 per cent in 1979), integrated circuits (80 per cent in 1978) and telecommunications (52 per cent in 1978).[16]

Hamelink said that the idea of mutual interests between North and South countries is an ethical fiction, that global problems are not solved with global solutions, but are identified and solved according to the interests of the most powerful actors. Most often these actors are in the North and their interests are very different from those of the South.

Commercial, rather than humanitarian, interests motivate those dispensing the new information technology. One writer pointed out:

> The whole idea of an 'information society' seems to be an invention of a marketing department of a computer manufacturer in order to sell electronic hardware; or a new attempt by powerless economists and politicians to boost up a dying industrial civilisation.[17]

In the hands of governments and transnational corporations, the technology is unlikely to do much to serve the masses. Instead, it probably widens the gap between the have and have nots, elites and masses and the rich and the poor.

These myths relate to what new information technology supposedly can accomplish. The final myth deals with the type and degree of use of new information technology for effective results.

5. *More Information made available through bigger communication systems is a goal to be sought.*

The basic premises here are that the more information available, the better society will be, and that bigger is better. On a personal level, how am I better off when I spend extra time in the chain-owned supermarkets trying to determine whether six ounzes of a tinned vegetable at 24 cents is a better deal than nine ounzes at 37 cents for so many grams at still another price? How is a society better off that collects and stores information on my phone calls, banking transactions and airline tickets? How am I better off when unwanted commercial information inundates all parts of my life-polluting my telephone, mailbox, lawn, media, public transportation and the natural resources? Of course, I'm not. In fact, much of the information that reaches me seems to come with conditions attached that attempt to take away more of my decision-making powers.

Eurich said that through new information technology, the "development of society is being reduced to the marketing function, with the negation of self-determined action. Man made passive has to function as a machine." Adding to that, he showed that the information technology requires:

> Large-scale networks and central storage and control systems; it ensures the dominating position of those who install it, but not the emancipation of those at the receiving end who are, at some time, forced to use it.[18]

I believe a question I asked in 1981 is even more appropriate today, and that is: Is it possible that the transnational corporations and certain governments are purposely overloading the information process toward the ultimate goal of mental and social paralysis for their own benefit? Is it not possible that an information overload can lead to less understanding, passivity, more confusion and generally, the Big Blur?[19] I believe it can, and does. Illich said something similar, in that, "the machine-like behaviour of people chained to electronics constitutes a degradation of their well-being and of their dignity,"[20] and Eurich, in a much longer quote, expanded upon the more-information-is-better myth. Exposing another myth in the process (that an informed society is a communicative society), he called for a communicative society that is suited to human nature—that has integrity, coherence and identity, not just more information. "We need space to exercise our basic human right to imperfection," he said, adding:

> This right can be obliterated by the mass media's omnipresent and wellnigh perfect images, allowing individuality to degenerate and give way to a conditioned reflex to mass, public rituals and generalisations.[21]

Eurich said the number of things, of people, of relationships should be kept small, for, "if the mark is exceeded, then the ability of an individual or an organisation to function at the optimum is jeopardised."[22] According to him:

> Indeed, the mass media, by giving us more people, more things, more images, hinders real communication; it reinforces the blockages; it may even be the cause of these blockages.[23]

Eurich's comments are meant to expose the myth that better results are obtained by bigger media, or that medica can bring about results at all. Apparently, the notion prevalent two decades ago, and amply refuted since (that development can be stimulated by mass communication) is on the rise again. The tools and actors are different, the notion the same, according to Jayaweera. In the 1960s, the prophets came from the social sciences promoting television and radio as development tools; in the 1980s, the prophets are technologists and engineers pushing satellites (and computers). "The more penetrating, the more widespread, the more efficient the delivery system, the more easily the ultimate development goals can be realised" is the thinking, he said, adding it is doomed to failure as the theories of the 1960s.[24]

Jamison and McAnany and Schramm, among many others, have shown that media size does not make a development campaign successful.[25]

Other myths relating to new information technology abound, but time does not permit elaboration upon them. Let me conclude this section with brief mentions of just two more.

6. *Information technology is neutral.*

It isn't, anymore than the individuals who created it are neutral. It has the capacity to support and carry values, as well as to destroy them. It comes, according to Jayaweera, in a socio-economic-cultural-political package, and "by its very inner dynamic it seeks to integrate its users into the larger system of which it is the expression and the tool."[26]

7. *New Information technology worked in the industrialised world, therefore, it will work in the Third World.*

Often times, hucksters of new information technology dump

this gadgetry upon Third World countries without looking at cultural-economic-political differences between the sending and receiving countries, and without having solid evidence that it ever worked in the sending countries, except for the benefit of a select few.

Questions

This is the easy part. The number of questions about new information technology left unanswered almost requires computerised programming to make sense. The foregoing myth have questions built into them, a few of which are:

1. Is not technology being promoted for liberation purposes, when in fact, it is being used as a vehicle of mass control?

2. What are the implications of telecommunications and transborder data flow for the development process? How can Third World countries use and supply the telecommunications technology, equipment and data in national development, and at the same time remaining competitive in international markets?

3. Since information is a basis of power, how can there be a minimisation of the political, economic, social and legal advantages that industrialised nations and multinational corporations enjoy over other countries and institutions?

4. In cases where telecommunications is used for development purposes, whose development is being enhanced? Who determines what is good for a nation's development?

5. Is it likely that transborder data flows through telematics will decrease imbalances between developed and Third World countries, reinforce self-reliant development and serve as a tool for economic co-operation among developing nations? Or, is it more reasonable to assume that because of the apparent avarice and greed of the controllers of telematics, that transborder data flows will act as powerful extensions of economic and cultural imperialism that existed for generations in Third World societies?

6. Do not transnational corporations, through the implementation of telematics, preserve the existing division of labour in the world? In other words, are not the Third World countries kept in a slave-master relationship, where they continue taking out the garbage, doing the dirty work?

7. Is not new information technology homogenizing peoples and cultures, obliterating diversity and richness of culture for which Third World nations are known, and creating what P.C. Joshi referred to as "cultural nihilism"?

8. How can information technology be changed from its emphasis on crass commercialism and manipulation to promotion of humanitarian goals?

9. Who can be the sane and objective watchdog in the field of telematics?[27]

10. How and to what extent can communication be channeled into a country from abroad, be subjected to the law and values of the receiving country?

And a few additional questions raised by Bella Mody:

11. Does the receiving country have the financial resources and technical infrastructure to sustain the technology?

12. Is the design and development of the technology going to deal only cosmetically with the symptoms of underdevelopment or is it going to tackle root causes?

13. Is the option going to promote dependency or imitation in hardware, programming, organisational structure or professional values or will it encourage domestic innovation?

14. Will the technology benefit the poor more than the rich?[28]

And three raised about computers by Joseph Weizenbaum:

15. "What pressing problems (is) this inundation of technological fixes supposed to attack?"

16. "Just what are the responsibilities of the mere technicians, or of engineers, of scientists, in the information society?" "If the programmers of these systems...are not responsible for the consequences of actions based on what these computer systems tell policymakers, and if policymakers are excused from responsibility on the ground that they merely relied on 'what the computer said,' then who is responsible?"

17. "What limits ought we, the people generally, and scientists and engineers particularly, impose on the application of computation to human affairs?"[29]

Alternatives

This part is not intended as a preaching down, all-the-answers-are-available-and-I-have-them diatribe. Instead, the aim here is to re-look at some alternatives that need more exploration.

Although the temptation is to throw out most high technology and start all over, this may not be realistic. But a call for a search for the appropriate information technology is in order, defining appropriateness much as Hamelink and Hoover have. Believing appropriate information technology may mean a blend of the latest and best with "primitive technology," Hamelink wrote:

> In meeting specific needs under specific conditions, the combination of the most complicated with the simplest, the largest with the smallest, are possibly the most adequate.... Development, however, may demand that advanced knowledge be exploited for the upgrading of primitive technologies. It may also invite the application of super technology in order to subvert the rich man's use of it.[30]

The difficulty, of course, is making certain that the "super" technology is used in conjunction with "primitive" technology, and that the latter is not thwarted at best, or extinguished at worst. The obvious goal should be to adapt high technology to local needs, without irreversibly harming local cultures and values. Stewart Hoover, in an unpublished report on the Caribbean, defined appropriateness in communication technology as the "extent to which a device can be appropriated and used, not left to its own momentum and direction."

Thus, appropriateness should be defined from the bottom up—whatever works at the grass-roots level as defined by the people at that level, perhaps including horizontal communication flows, inter-personal communication networks and folk media usage. In a number of cases, however, appropriate technology is equated with low or small technology. Smythe, distinguishing between high technology, and low technology with a decided preference for the latter, said low technology includes characteristics of:

> Simple, relatively inexpensive, requires no exceptional skills to use, and is available from many countries

> (mimeograph, POT...plain old telephone service—audio cassettes, and local radio broadcasting). These equipments can be and have been examples of tools which in the service of needs, whereas 'high tech' equipment determines needs.

On the other hand, according to Smythe, high technology is equipment with one or more of the following characteristics: "complexity, cost, training by professionals before ordinary peasants can use it...; and originating messages on a mass production basis from outside the community (TV, satellites)."[31]

Delegates to a 1985 conference in Mexico also equated low technology with appropriateness. A Brazilian economist said his country has an elaborate computerised data bank "but nobody uses it," and called for more use of mails, copying machines, blackboards and radio. An Argentine columnist educator said the tendency in his country was to focus on the instruments of transmission and gloss over the fact that there is nothing of value to transmit, while a Venezuelan physician said 40 per cent of all information technology bought in that country is inappropriate to local needs and is never used.[32]

Probably useful in thinking about alternatives is the schemata proposed by E.F. Schumacher in his classic, *Small is Beautiful*—that systems be kept small, simple, cost efficient and non-violent. Although Schumacher used these concepts in describing his ideal economics policy, they can be (and have been)[33] applied to communication. I would add a fifth concept: *Slow (or slower) is beautiful.* No doubt this is a preposturous request for governments in a hurry to catch up (with what, it is undetermined) and transnationals scurrying to monopolise markets. But, whoever is entrusted with determining the people's need for, or use of, communications and information technology must slow down and disengage themselves from the informatics bargain basement sale that is going on. They need that time to make rational, safe, useful and broadbased decisions. Although national communication policies might be the way of doing this, unfortunately, too often they have been concocted in a hurry, by bureaucrats, government officials and outside consultants (many with heavy vested interests), with very little input from the village level. Breathing space is definitely needed.

Finally, development of technology and communications for human growth should be kept as free as possible from government and big business interests. The sceptic in me does not allow for the belief that elites who make up these agencies promote their techno-phobia to relieve poverty, starvation or other human misery. More efforts such as "Live Aid," "Farm Aid," or the Amnesty International fundraiser, though huge in scale and having some connection to government and business should be encouraged because the developers and participants have at least a spark of concern for the plight of fellow humans.

Despite my claim that "slow (slower) is beautiful," I contradict that now by pleading that resistant action be taken quickly—that time is running out—as development in information technology feeds upon itself to proliferate for the benefit of those who wish to replace the human potential with high-tech machinery.

It is fitting that I conclude with a quote from Mahatma Gandhi, concerning culture·

> I do not want my house to be walled in on all sides and my windows to be stuffed. I want the cultures of all lands to be blown about my house as freely as possible but I refuse to be blown off my feet by any.[34]

We too must refuse to be blown off our feet by any technology.

INFORMATION TECHNOLOGY AND THE THIRD WORLD

The strong oligopoly in the production of information technology makes importing countries dependent upon a very small number of suppliers. The importing countries also usually lack the expertise for the assessment and integration of information technology. At the same time there is a drive among Third World nations to create some form of informatics capacity. This is happening usually in a totally uncontrolled manner guided by *ad hoc* decisions. It is imperative for Third World countries to have policies that give protection against foreign economic impositions with its implied political and cultural agenda. At the same time there should be an effort to build an infrastructure harnessing available resources to enable future self-reliance. In the strict sense technology should not be equated with technical equipment but should refer to knowledge. Properly speaking technology is the total body of knowledge pertinent to the generation, innovation, and maintenance of human artefacts: tools, machines and systems.

Artefacts are the vital interface between human beings and their environments enabling them to bridge the gap between their native insufficiencies and a demanding and complex milieu.

Adequate coping with the environment is crucial to human survival.

Coping involves the manipulation of three essential resources: matter, energy, and information.

Information technology represents the body of knowledge that is essential to the development of the artefacts with which the resource information can be manipulated. This manipulation encompasses: producing, processing, storing, transmitting, and consulting.

Information technology is the aggregate of scientific/technical disciplines basic to the production of devices (tools/machines) and systems for the capture, transportation, storage, processing and retrieval of voice, text, numerical and pictorial information.

Devices are such pieces of equipment as keyboards, disk drives and telephone terminals. More often than not these devices operate as systems. The telephone, for instance, functions in a system configuration—forming a net-work through the interconnection of a terminal, a transmission medium, and a switching technique.

In this sense one could differentiate between equipment technology and system technology.

Table 1.1 is a non-comprehensive, illustrative survey of artefacts (devices and systems available to manipulate the resource information).

A characteristic feature of information technology is its pervasiveness. Increasingly information technology produces the essential infrastructure of an un-precedented large variety of social activities. This is due to the increasing significance of the resource information in fields such as industrial manufacturing, air transportation, financial transactions, private consumption, military logistics, corporate management. In all these areas there is growing dependence upon the specific type of knowledge information technology represents.

Table 1.1

Operations	*Information Technology Devices/Systems*
CAPTURE	remote resource sensing satellites radar systems electronic camera VCR systems videodisks optical character recognition
TRANSPORTATION	coaxial cable optical fibre cable micro wave link communication satellite cellular mobile radio laser beams facsimile transceivers videophone electronic teleprinters modems multiplexors
STORAGE	memory chips magnetic film/tape/drum holography laser emulsion micro film
PROCESSING	integrated circuits computer software peripheral equipment
RETRIEVAL	high definition television teletext videotex pay television systems on-line databases, databanks

Information technology produces, innovates and maintains industrial products as well as industrial production methods

basic as well as luxurious commodities
material as well as immaterial goods.

Information technology blends in unprecedented ways work methods and life styles.

This implies that information technology is not restricted to a limited social niche, such as medical or weapons technology, but pervades society at large affecting all people at all times.

Information Technology: The Economic Stakes

Information technology as an industrial production sector is part of a larger information industry that also encompasses information services and leisure. Tables 1.2 to 1.7 shows the structure of the information industry.

Total market is estimated at $ 30 billion. Since there are no disaggregate data of the audio-visual sector for the consumer electronics market (which in total comprises such products as electrical shavers, hairdryers, kitchen tools and may amount to several hundred million dollars) the estimate is very rough. Sources for the video cassette recorder market suggest some 10 billion dollar sales for 1984.

Table 1.2

INFORMATION INDUSTRY

Information Technology | Information Services | Leisure

Information services comprise i.e. data transmission, processing services, publishing, advertising, news production.

Leisure comprises i.e., music, film, television, video. The information technology sector comprises various sub/markets.

Table 1.3

INFORMATION TECHNOLOGY

Telecommunication Equipment	Dataprocessing Equipment	Semiconductors	Consumer Electronics

Calculating from a number of sources (Datamation, Fortune, OECD, Arthur D. Little, Input, Business Week, and InfoCorp.) the sales of information technology products can be estimated for the year 1984:

—Telecommunication Equipment: $56 billion
—Dataprocessing equipment and software products: $175 billion
—Semiconductors: $28 billion
—Consumer Electronics: $ 30 billion

The total world market for information technology products in 1984 amounted to $289 billion.

By way of comparison: the world market for automobiles in 1984 can be estimated at $ 313 billion.

Table 1.4

TELECOMMUNICATION

Terminals	Transmission Equipment	Switching Equipment
14%	30%	31%
$ 7.8 billion	$ 16.8 billion	$ 17.4 billion

In addition markets for private systems (10 per cent) and mobile systems (9 per cent) generated respectively $5.6 billion and $ 5 billion.

Table 1.5

DATAPROCESSING EQUIPMENT

Mainframe Computers	Mini Computers	Personal Computers
54%	23.4%	22.6%
$ 72 billion	$ 31 billion	$ 30 billion

In addition markets for peripheral equipments (e.g. printers, keyboards, VDU's) and software products generated respectively $ 25 billion $ 17 billion.

Table 1.6

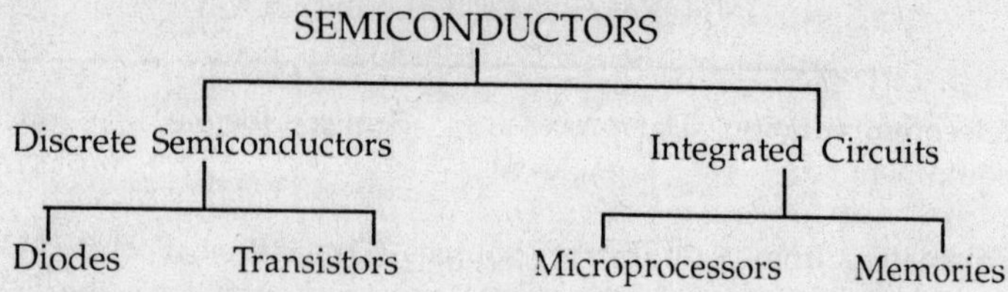

Total market can be estimated worldwide at some $ 22 billion. In addition there is a market for the equipment with which chips are manufactured such as photo aligners, logic testers, wafer steppers, and electronic beam machines.

Table 1.7

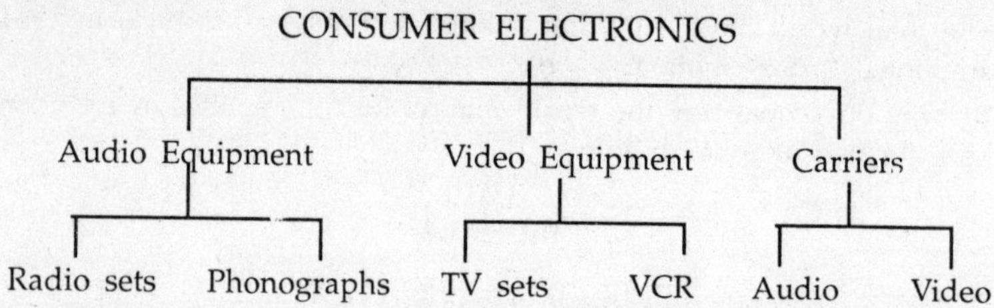

The corporations responsible for the overall information technology market represent together worldwide sales of some 489 billion dollars which represents 13 per cent of the total sales of the world's 1000 largest industrial companies in 1984.

A crucial characteristic of the information technology industry is concentration. Taking the data processing equipment market as an illustration, one observes that an already oligopolistic market (14 companies controlling over 3/4 of all sales) is moving rapidly towards further industrial concentration. Merger activity is on the increase in its various sub-markets (cf. the merging in 1986 of Sperry and Burroughs) and among trade analysts there is a general expectation of "shake outs."

Strong indications to support this come from the computer manufacturing sector and the software market. Only a decade ago the manufacturing of computers was nicely divided into clear segments: mainframe manufacturers and minicomputer manufacturers. The personal computer has changed this: blurring established niches and creating an all-out competition of all manufacturers against each other in the struggle to grab a share of the most profitable market segment: the office automation. Central to current office automation is the electronic work station: the PC as desk-top computer.

This has forced all manufacturers to produce and market personal computers. The largest mainframe manufacturer IBM has been a late entrant on the PC market (since 1981) but is rapidly expanding its market share (already over 25 per cent) and setting—once again—standards for the rest of the industry. With IBM there is a large variety of companies struggling for survival. Some of them are entering into joint ventures to improve competitive positions, some concentrate on specialised small users, others produce computers that offer more than the IBM PC and yet are compatible with it (APPLE).

As the demand grows for the provision of complete, integrated office systems only those manufacturers will survive that can deliver a comprehensive package. It is not unlikely that in the next three to four years only some four companies will prove to offer a sufficiently large array of products and maintain customer credibility.

The advent of the personal computer has contributed largely to the rapid growth of the software market. In 1981 total sales of software in the USA amounted to US $ 2.7 billion. By 1984 this was over US $ 10 billion.

The fastest growing part of the software industry is in the sales of software for personal computers: and average 44 per cent annually.

This growth has made small software firms into very large corporations and has attracted thousands of new entrants. The boom may however not last too long for most of them. As customers become more demanding and competition increases, the need for large investments put serious restrictions on the market. Software firms need to spend enormous amounts on the advertising of their products. The launching of a new product can no longer be done on a shoestring budget. Also the costs of developing a new product are increasing whereas the prices are sliding down. Moreover, the leading computer manufacturers are now also marketing software for their personal computers. Only a few firms can ultimately survive in this environment.

Information Technology: The Third World

Most of the world's information technology products are installed in the industrial market economies of the North. Information technology is almost totally generated in the North. In terms of international trade in information technology products and services, the USA and Western Europe are by far the largest exporters and importers. Most of this trade takes place within and between Western Europe and North America. These trading patterns are corroborated by an increasing number of know-how exchange arrangements between the leading information technology companies across the Atlantic. There is, however, an increasing interest in the developing countries to improve and expand their information technology capacity.

At the 1978 Intergovernmental Conference on Strategies and Policies for Informatics (SPIN) the majority of participants claimed, "Informatics is an instrument ideally suited to promote economic and social development." Informatics was, also by representatives from developing countries, seen as "an undisputed factor of progress." In the same year, 1978, a survey by the inter-governmental Bureau for Informatics showed that out of a sample of 43 developing countries, 34 had "imperative" or "incitement" policies for the utilisation of informatics in public administration.

More recently, March 1985, the IBI held a meeting of African personalities on informatics and sovereignty. This meeting which took place in Yamoussoukro (Ivory Coast) issued a declaration on the contribution of informatics to the development of Africa. The Yamoussoukro declaration states "that one of the main keys to solving Africa's development problem lies in mastering the rational management of information in all its forms. It would be highly desirable for our countries to revise their priorities in this respect and establish a major objective (more than 1 per cent of their GNP) for an efficient informatisation which has become indispensable for the economic and social development of the Continent. Like all the other advanced technologies, informatics needs an economy of scale and critical mass before it can develop in an endogenous and viable manner. It is, therefore, not only a positive factor for regional and continental integration but also an essential condition for the survival of

Africa within the community of nations in the twenty-first century".

The growing interest in developing countries is also evidenced by the spread of capacity in information manufacturing in a number of countries, such as Brazil, India, South Korea, and Malaysia.

In India, for example, there has already been a significant growth in the domestic information technology industry as Table 1.8 shows:

Table 1.8

GROWTH OF INDIAN INFORMATION TECHNOLOGY INDUSTRY
(US $ million)

Sector	*1973*	*1983*	*Growth Rate*
Consumer electronic	53.3	275	17.8%
Communication equipment	48.3	225	16.6%
Computers	18.3	274.2	31.1%

As can be concluded, from the table, the fastest growth was in the subsector of computers.

In 1984 India had 15 companies manufacturing 8 bit computers and 15 firms manufacturing 16 bit computers.

In the 1985-1990 technology development plan it is foreseen that the growth of computer demand reaches US $ 862.5 million. The plan is aimed especially at India's capacity to become an exporter of software. For 1990 software exports are projected to reach US $ 258 million.

Also the telecommunication capacity will be significantly improved in order to facilitate such services as packet-switched telex and videotex.

It also has to be observed that the Third World is gaining importance as an import market for information technology. During the 1970s for example average annual computer imports grew in Africa with 44 per cent, in Asia with 14 per cent, and in Latin America with 38 per cent. This trend continues in the 1980s.

Large import markets, are Brazil, Mexico, Venezuela, Argentina, the People's Republic of China, Saudi Arabia, Hong Kong and Thailand.

These imports imply, however, a number of problems. The strong oligopoly in the production of information technology makes importing countries dependent upon a very small number of suppliers. The importing countries usually lack the expertise for assessment and integration of information technology.

Importing countries are often sold obsolete technology.

Also in cases where developing countries export information technology products there are some problems to be noted.

The share of the developing countries in imports by the OECD countries in such areas as office machines and semiconductors has considerably grown over the past years.

It has to be observed, however, that such imports came predominantly from a limited number of countries which very narrow ranges of specialisation in specific products. Moreover, this production was mainly a result of foreign investments. Electronic exports from developing countries reflect the general pattern of direct foreign investment: largely directed to a selected number of countries that are chosen for their political stability, economic incentives (tax privileges, low wages), and linguistic convenience (mainly anglophone countries). Exports from these few countries are in majority resulting from the investments of large transnational electronics manufacturers in offshore production and assembly operations by their subsidiaries. A large proportion of this international trade consists effectively of intra-firm transactions. The result of this situation seems to be that the core of information technology know-how remains under the control of transnational corporations and that developing countries are allocated a minor role in a globally integrated production process.

Electronics technology usually becomes obsolete within three years. This means that also in cases where local plants take over, the products come late on the market and can only compete on less advanced levels of the technology. Additionally, the competitor from the South may, as South Korea experienced, find export markets in the North closing down, due to recession and protectionism.

Information Technology: Inadequate Policymaking

Despite these problems there is undoubtedly a strong drive in many developing countries to create some form of informatics capacity. It may not be advisable for developing countries to completely ignore this advanced technology, it would seem however that its introduction minimally asks a careful weighing of costs and benefits. Today the introduction of informatics in the Third World happens usually totally uncontrolled or guided by *ad hoc* decisions. The present state of policy making and planning for informatics seems rather inadequate. In the main, emphasis is still on equipment procurement and too little interest is given to the control of imports, the creation of independent assessment capacity, and the steering of social impact.

No country has yet drafted a coherent policy in the field of information technology. This may be due to the relatively recent explosive development of the field, an unclarity as to where in public administration the responsibility for information technology resides, and the degree of technical complexity that demands a very specialised expertise. Moreover, in several countries the dominant climate of privatisation and deregulation militates against public policy formation. Also Third World countries are increasingly affected by an economic recipe suggested by donor countries (such as the USA, the UK, France and the Netherlands) and donor agencies (such as the World Bank, the IMF, and the African Development Bank) that implies the retreat of the state in favour of various forms of privatisation. Third World countries have begun to return state companies in diverse sectors of their economies to private ownership. This "more market, less state" policy has also reached operations dependent upon information technology, such as tele-communication services.

There appears to be a general anxiety about missing the "information revolution" and as a consequence the majority of policy decisions relate to the spending of public funds on the acquisition of the latest generation technology.

This means that often the decisive factor in such resource allocation is "technology opportunity": since the technology is available it should be purchased and utilised! Such policymaking allows social development to be driven by technology, rather than adapting technology to social priorities. This is corroborated by the fact that in many cases the actual decision-making is open to few actors only. Information technology decision-making can be adequately described with the "scrambled-eggs" model which refers to breakfast sessions during which small cabals of industrial and government representatives seal the vital deal: without proper assessment or elaborate consultation, or comparative shopping, and more often than not against a suspiciously high price!

An illustration of the "scrambled eggs" model is provided by the Mexican national satellite case.

After three years of negotiations among a restricted number of agencies (such as the government executive, the secretariat for Communication and Transport, and the commercial TV company Televisa) a public announcement was made on March 24, 1983, that as from 1985 Mexico would have a national satellite system called Morelos. On June 1, 1983 the secretariat for Communication and Transport announced that the Morelos system—initiated and operated by the federal government—was contracted to Hughes Communication International for the manufacturing of the satellite, to McDonnell Douglas for the rocket and to NASA for launching. The approximate costs for placing and operating the satellite would be US $ 140 million. The Morelos system would be used for television, radio, telephone, telegraph, telex, and private data networks.

Characteristic of the whole process was:

- there was no comprehensive analysis of needs and possible applications;
- there was no full consultation with all the potentially involved parties (such as the future users and those affected by uses);
- there was no precise calculation of the additional costs of operating the earth segment of the system;
- the Mexican technicians would have to be trained abroad and would remain low-level operators;
- other offers were not made public and the choice of Hughes was not publicly justified;
- the price was too high: a comparable system could have been procured on a competitive market for less than 100 million dollars.

Among the other problems affecting information technology policymaking in Third World countries is the complication that the desire to become technologically self-reliant (as for example in India) may at the same time imply the need to import foreign technology. Certainly if a country aims at a domestic technological capacity with export potential, it will be crucial to acquire the best technology that is available on the world market.

Lagging behind the current technology frontier would seriously impair the export potential. The imports, however, could in turn impair the development of local innovative capacity. This is compounded by the tension between the long-term goal of technological self-reliance and the short-term demands from users. Users of information technology will expect efficient, reliable and cheap services which can only be supplied through imported technology and this obviously adversely affects the long-term policy.

This is a very real policy problem which is further aggravated by the fact that information technology policymaking is usually fragmented and unco-ordinated between various public agencies, such as informatics authorities, post and telecommunication parastatals, information and broadcasting ministries, and industry and technology departments.

Information Technology: The Need for Policymaking

Information technology policymaking in Third World countries is particularly urgent in the light of two vital issues that the international environment poses to the Third World.

The International Division of Labour

Before 1950 the international system knew a division of labour in which—according to the doctrine of comparative advantage—the South contributed the raw materials and the North manufactured the industrial end-products. Around the early 1950s a remarkable shift occurred. The concurrence of sky-rocketing industrial wages in the North and the emergence of such techniques as containerisation and satellite communications brought considerable industrial investments to the low-wage countries in the South. Again, following comparative advantage it was now thought that while the North—with its knowledge advantage—would lead in hightech, the South—with its cheap labour—would lead in labour intensive industrial production. A 25 per cent share for Third World countries in global industrial manufacturing was even projected on this basis. This new international division of labour is, however, since the 1970s under threat. The low wage advantage is eroded by the higher productivity level achieved in the North through the application of computer technology. Automation makes labour costs a less important factor *vis-a-vis* investments in advanced equipment and top management. Although the picture is far from clear, there are some indications that industries that would have been expected to move South remain in the North. The electronics industry itself, heavily involved in off-shore operations, seems to be planning new generations of plants in the North.

The question this raises is whether Third World countries are well advised to bank on an industrial export led development policy. In the light of a possible global industrial restructuring this may be a dubious proposition.

A related problem is that an information technology-led development may add to an already massive unemployment and may produce goods that are internationally not competitive or that find protectionist markets.

Concentration on high-tech exports, unless sufficiently diversified, may also lead Third World countries in the old colonial trap of the mono-culture. The dependence on the manufacturing of chips, for example, in a world market that is externally controlled and unstable, is as problematic as dependence upon coffee or copper.

The Trade in Services

From the early 1970s the international economy shows a trend towards the increasing role of the trading of services. Transnational Service Corporations expand the size of their operations and for several of the large market economies the export of services grows rapidly. In 1980 the IMF estimates the global export of services to amount to US $ 350 billion which equals 25 per cent of all exports of goods.

Exporting services lead to trade surplus in some market economies, notably the USA where this offsets the trade deficit in goods trading.

Important factors in this development are the transnationalisation of industrial production (demanding the support of various services, such as finance, marketing, advertising, transport, and insurance) and—in particular—the progress in computer—and telecommunication technology and their convergence. Among the characteristics of services is the difficulty to trade them since they are tied to location and time. Moreover in services economies of scale are not achieved through more production units at one place, but by decentralising. Here "telematics" makes a decisive difference. Computer-communication networks facilitate the decentralisation of operations since dispersed units can easily be co-ordinated through such networks. They also make services trade-able: transactions become possible simultaneously at different locations.

The implication is that internationally traded services become in fact transborder data flows and are as such dependent upon the access to telematics networks. Restrictions on international computer-communications can now be seen as non-tariff trade barriers.

At present, an important debate on the role of services takes place around the preparations for the next world trade round of GATT (General Agreement on Tariffs and Trade—the organisation that since 1947 supports the removal of international trade barriers). Several Western countries (particularly the USA have proposed to adopt the trade in services on the agenda of the meetings that start September 1986. Several Third World countries, headed by India and Brazil, want to exclude services from the agenda.

For countries that export services it makes good sense to plead for the application of the liberal GATT—regime to services. Their surplus in this trade has become a critical factor to their economies as the case of the USA demonstrates.

The Third World countries, however, argue that liberalisation would only benefit the strong market economies. They face increasingly large trade deficits in services and fear that non-protectionist trade will lead to more imports and a weakening of their own service sector. Moreover, they claim that the industrialised countries would first have to remove all their restrictions on the imports of goods from Third World countries.

The issue demanding more reflection is indeed whether Third World countries stand to gain or lose with liberalisation versus protectionism in trading services. One could argue that since the bulk of trading in services takes place between the OECD countries, a liberal regime would hardly affect the Third World anyway. In addition it would seem likely that decreases in service exports to Third World countries would imply also decreasing OECD imports from those countries.

It is also important to observe that despite the growth in service exports these are stil outweighed by the foreign sales of services. The argument in favour of liberalisation states that more direct investments in such scales could largely compensate the current reduction in international credit supplies to Third World countries. The counter-argument says that exactly this implies the free establishment of foreign entities within Third World economies thus stifling the growth of their own infant service companies. Moreover, it is argued, that in the near future direct foreign investments will diminish as a consequence of the application of telematics. In any case, foreign investment in such services as advertising, market research, data-processing, and fast food restaurants is considered a threat to further cultural erosion which undermines national sovereignty. Related to this is the complication that since services are basically information handling and/or dependent upon information technology their liberalisation versus a protectionist policy is basically also a decision on degree to which international information flows should be free or subjected to restrictions.

Epilogue

Current Third World policymaking in the field of information technology cannot adequately deal with the imminent issues of industrial restructuring and trading of services.

The implications of these issues demand both a re-active and active policy. Re-active policy in the sense of creating a modus of protection against foreign economic imposition with its implied political and cultural agenda. Active policy in the sense of the construction of domestic infrastructures and the harnessing of available resources to maximum levels of self-reliance.

If policy fails to achieve this—as it does today—Third World countries will be further integrated in a world market that perpetuates their dependent development.

A minimal programme for information technology policymaking would entail the following steps:

1. Before public policy can be formulated on any issue, it needs to be recognised as a "public problem," i.e. it needs to be put on the institutional agenda: the action agenda of the official policymakers.
2. Policymaking has to be based on a serious (and relatively reliable) database that enables a minimal level of resource assessment: an inventory of locally available resources, a projection of needs for imported resources, and a scenario for resource development.
3. Policymakers (the executive, the legislators, and the judiciary) will need to have a minimal idea of what information technology is, does, and costs. This needs the establishment of scientific advisory boards, awareness and training courses.
4. The development of basic technical expertise is needed for pertinent judgement on comparative shopping, selective procurement, and long-term cost projections. This needs the establishment of technology assessment boards.
5. The institutional location and accountability for information technology decision-making needs to be defined and/or clarified. This implies the identification of the agencies to be involved and the construction of mechanisms for their co-ordination.
6. The various direct and indirect forms in which social actors other than the official policymakers can participate in decision-making on information technology need to be explored and developed.

Such participatory mechanisms could range from information about decision-making to citizen review boards and national referenda.

Global Implications: International Relations

The recent communication explosion is the beginning of a new era in the history of mankind. This era is characterised on the one hand by the rising aspirations and expectations of millions of people living in the Third World and, on the other, by the emergence of new forms of domination and colonialism. The recent advance in the field of science and technology has led to an entirely new kind of political dispensation which is going to change relations among nations and peoples. Revolution in science and technology and the intensifying ideological struggle have brought about a colossal increase in the role played by information media in international relations. It has also brought about unprecedented transformations, changing the very social, cultural, economic and political fabric of the world.

The communication explosion witnessed particularly after the revolution in the field of electronics affected the very "base," of society, that is, the modes of production and of exchange and has tremendously expanded the power and size of the "superstructure" comprising the media institutions and value systems. This has enormously strengthened the forces that believe in manipulating the consciousness of people by waging psychological war. This psychological warfare has assumed dangerous proportions with the use of new technologies, which are a threat to the social and cultural environment of man.

The collapse of the colonial system, the emergence of a large number of independent states and the expansion of a new world community along with the growth of consumerist societies are the dominant features of the present day world. However they cannot be allowed to gain strength unhindered. Therefore, the powers of domination and subjugation have acquired new teeth from the communication explosion and have unleashed a barrage of information in order to manipulate and influence the "base" and "superstructure" in the developing world to suit their own ends.

The intensifying ideological struggle throughout the world reflects the rapidly growing role of the modern means of communication which have become key instruments of ideological manipulation in the new era. All political streams, all groups of states, individual countries and their organised forces are busy mobilising their resources to expand and improve the information systems at their disposal.

The media were allowed to grow without restraint, patronised by the market economy elite as one of the most lucrative industrial ventures of the future. Despite the economic trauma and tumult faced by the advanced world and the persistent difficulties encountered by the developing countries, the information industry registered rapid growth. The advance of science and technology has created a powerful weapon in the modern mass media. This weapon can be used for speeding up progress, strengthening peace, promoting co-operation and understanding or for exploiting people, stirring up hatred and speeding up the arms race. Unfortunately, today this powerful weapon has been nurtured and monopolised by commercial and colonial interests.

A colossal concentration of the mass media in the hands of the transnational corporations enable these forces to exert a negative influence in international affairs and indulge in information imperialism in Asia, Africa and Latin America. Through these means they seek to justify confrontation and the arms race. In short, it has resulted in the intensification of propaganda over the last decade. These have been the characteristic activities of the giant information and propaganda conglomerates.

Direction of Development

It is hardly surprising that, with the increase of international news flow, we find the world population covered by a blanket of propaganda. There is a positive correlation between the total mass media content and the total propaganda outpouring. Even a casual observer of the media cannot fail to notice that man's mind—nationally and internationally—is being subjected to a ceaseless and clever bombardment of messages. These messages are calculated to influence and control. Information is treated as a weapon of low intensity warfare—people's perception of a situation drives man from the conscious and the rational to the irrational and the obscure. Never before in history have the basic educational and cultural needs of humanity been so widely appreciated. But while the resources to satisfy these requirements are physically available, they are directed to other ends. This reflects the dominant direction communication development has taken.

The following figures give an idea of the extent of the "communication explosion" that is occurring today. At present, there are more than 1.3 billion radio sets in the world. There are more than 30,000 radio stations, around 500 million TV sets, about 150 news agencies operating in the world, and tens of thousands of periodicals and some 1,700 different new books are being published every day. According to UNESCO 12 satellites of the Intelsat system are owned by the USA, 10 of the 15 largest information companies have headquarters in the USA. A small group of transnational and mostly American companies control approximately 80 per cent of the dailies of industrial and developing capitalist countries as well 90 per cent of radio and 95 per cent of television stations. On a global scale the U.S.A. controls 60 per cent of the international market of television programmes while American television broadcasts only one per cent of foreign programmes. The four largest Western agencies—UPI, AP, Reuters and Agence France Presse—supply information to 140 countries of the world, totalling about 40 million words a day.

Data concerning the scale of the United States' ideological expansion into foreign countries are in sharp contrast to the figures of the import of cultural products and informations from abroad by the United States itself. According to available data, not more than 3 per cent of the information disseminated inside that country is derived from foreign sources. An analysis of the news items which Western radio stations and news agencies send to the developing countries today shows that 65 per cent of the information is related to the USA and only 8-10 per cent is devoted to the developing countries. What is more, the coverage given to the developing countries is largely determined by their impact on the political and economic interests of the West. The information about these states is generally sensational and scandalous and often prejudicial to the interests of the developing countries. At the same time there is hardly anything relating to economic and social problems.

Introduction of new technologies has further strengthened the hold of powerful states over information which is being used to impose an alien ideology and culture upon the Third World countries and confining their role to that of passive recipients of information. The domination of certain powers in the sphere of information is resulting in proliferation of Western consumer ideology and way of life over traditional and national values.

Nature of Information Imperialism

The essence of this phenomenon lies in the fact that the powerful countries, taking advantage of the extremely underdeveloped conditions of the local mass media, are pursuing in the developing world a policy of ideological expansion; they are imposing their own information on the countries of Asia, Africa and Latin America, usually distorting the picture of the world, in the socialist countries and even in the developing countries themselves.

In the sixties the U.S. Administration set its priorities as defence, foreign affairs and communications. In a paper titled "Winning the Cold War: The U.S. Ideological Offensive" it was said that, "to a significant degree what America does will shape the emerging International Communication system...to a very large degree other countries will imitate our experience and will attach themselves to the institutions and systems we create. Given our information technology and information resources, the United State clearly could be the hub of the world communication system."

A report of the U.S. congressional committee concerned with "Winning the Cold War" and "ideological operations and foreign policy," elaborates the new approach: Certain foreign policy objectives can be pursued by dealing directly with their governments. Through the use of modern instruments and techniques of communication it is possible today to reach large or influential segments of national populations—to inform them, to influence their attitudes, and at times, perhaps, even to motivate them to a particular course of action. These groups, in turn, are capable of exerting noticeable, even decisive, pressure on their governments.

What lends sophistication to the still youthful American imperial structure is its dependence on a marriage of economics and electronics, which substitutes in part, though not entirely, for earlier "blood and iron" foundations of more primitive conquerors. The developing nations stand practically defenceless before the rampaging Western commercialism.

The information activity of the USA abroad is to a considerable extent aimed at changing the local traditions and customs and adapting them to the needs of American business, the mass advertising of goods and the ideology of the consumer society. This situation has led to the swallowing up by the giant American monopolies of the communication systems operating within the United States as well and has turned the Press, television, radio, cinema, literature and entertainment industry into an extension of the advertising agencies.

What is less apparent, though no less real, are negative characteristics of the electronic imagery that is being introduced in poorer communities across the globe. Whereas public service broadcasting is hardly visible, a tidal wave of commercial material is flowing over the earth. Everywhere local culture is facing submersion from the mass produced outpouring of commercial broadcasting. Television in the United States is tailored almost exclusively to fit the market needs of consumer goods producers who sponsor and finance the programming. The programme material is assigned especially to secure and hold mass audiences in thrall to the delight of consumerdom.

The values and concepts of the "consumer society," which are built into the news, advertising and entertainment programmes coming from the West contradict the fundamental interests and goals of the developing countries. Such Western influences not only are in contradiction of these countries' traditional ways of life and cultural identity, but also provoke will more serious conflicts between the rich and the poor, between wishes and possibilities and lead to a still greater stratification and dissociation between the masses and the "elite." Whereas the developing countries should be mobilising all their resources for the implementation of effective national policies, the Western mass media offer programmes that have been conceived for the purpose of ensuring a greater consumption of Western goods. Such activity has not only a political character, as it serves the strategic interests of the USA abroad, but it also causes direct economic harm to the developing countries by orienting their economies against their own national interest, contrary to their national needs.

Western television and cinema programmes, writes M. Masmoudi of Tunisia, are instruments of cultural domination. They provide the developing countries with information which is harmful to their cultures, contradicts their own system of values and jeopardizes their objectives and their efforts for development. The transnational corporations are the key instruments to give a thrust to cultural colonialism. The communication apparatus which these industrial giants have at their disposal provides the methodology without which the new colonial surge would be ineffective, coming as it does on the heels of political liberation in so many former colonial territories.

If free trade is the mechanism by which a powerful economy penetrates and dominates a weak one, the "free flow of information," the designated objective incidentally of UNESCO, is the channel through which life styles and value systems can be imposed on poor and vulnerable societies. The Third World countries are more vulnerable to the cultural invasion but it is not strictly confined to them. West European countries are also feeling the brunt of this cultural invasion. Canada, whose sky is overloaded with American radio and television waves, is the worst sufferer.

Canada: A Case in Point

Canada's media-expert Comor submitted back in 1970: Canada is in contact with the United States along a great and undefended border; and by the process of osmosis America is destroying not only our television, but our values and our very culture.... American television has made the development of a Canadian cultural identity almost impossible.... Through its own faulty development, American television had negatively influenced the development of a worthy native television in Canada. American television has destroyed television as an art. Canadians are often told that their potential enemies are Russia and China. In my view, the United States is a much more dangerous enemy. Never before had the undefended boundary presented such an open door to cultural annexation. In Canada, where 60 per cent of the population watches American television programmes, a mass movement developed, particularly in the 70s, against the cultural and information domination of the United States.

The West European allies of the U.S. are also affected by the electronic invasion. Since the early post-war period when the USA monopolised the Western mass media it persistently resorted to a propaganda offensive against its NATO allies. As soon as big business in the United States was ready for another leap and the US claims for world domination were becoming more persistent, Washington invariably attempted to force its concept of free flow of information upon the rest of the world. The very recent and continuing case is that of Nicaragua which is facing a massive electronic and information invasion. Seven years into its revolution, Nicaragua was suffering a veritable torrent of foreign radio and television signals penetrating its borders. This electronic war of ideas was incessant and as damaging to Nicaraguan morale as the Contra military radio and as the economic blockade imposed by the United States government. However, despite this the Nicaraguans were to some extent able to turn the tables on their enemies. In a world linked by instantaneous communication Nicaragua was caught in an electronic war with foreign powers possessing superior broadcast resources and bent on winning the hearts and minds of the Nicaraguan population. Today, though, Nicaragua is a society in revolution, caught among the legacy of a brutal dictatorship, the pain of armed struggle and the travails of wrenching and continuing social upheaval, central to this process were radio and television, the great mobilizers, agitators and propagandizers of change. This in recent times is an example when facing a formidable power a liberation movement could use modern channels of communication to advance its cause. Nicaragua could do it only because of the determined political will of her people and leadership.

The export of television software is one of the main channels of the global ideological expansion. The study "Television Traffic: A One-way Street?" prepared by Finnish scientists shows the scale of this expansion: 160 American companies export upto 200,000 hours of TV programmes a year. The annual profits made by these companies from these exports amount to 200 million dollars. Great Britain is the second biggest exporter (30,000 hours), then come France, the FRG and a number of other developed countries. Many developing countries import between 30 to 70 per cent of their TV programmes mainly from the USA, England and France.

Information colonialism is already posing a serious threat to the countries and communities which are striving for their own road of development. American TV products are setting the tone for television programming throughout the world. Popular music may not have an immediate effect on the political attitude of the audience but it ensures the entry of Western ideas and concepts.

The Third World is heading for a state of electronic seige. What is the way out? The question has been well debated in various forums. Movements for a New International Information and Communication Order and greater exchange of information among the developing countries in the form of Non-Aligned News Pool are steps in the right direction.

But there is not yet an adequate policy frame for an interface between communication and nation-building and between different modes of communication. Communication has yet to emerge as an important policy instrument, integrating economic, social, educational and cultural planning. The economics and sociology of communication are still unexplored fields in India. As a result there is not enough theoretical support to communication planning, which is the technocrat's domain. These remarks made in the context of India, are applicable to a majority of the Third World countries.

The communication system is more responsive to elite pressure which is turning the communication revolution into an instrument of consumerism and of a cultural counter-reformation. Widening the rural-urban and the elite-mass hiatus, it is also taking us away from national integration. There is not an adequate response from the political system to these distortions and to the exploding mass pressure for a new information order. Just as Gandhi distinguished between "mass production" and "production by masses," we can also draw a distinction between "mass communication" and "communication for and by the masses." The former was mechanical and manipulative, the latter was creative and participatory. Gandhi's communication style evolved in the context of national mobilisation based on mass mobilisation.

The struggle between different world outlooks and an honest competition of ideas shall go on as an objective process. However, in this sphere of information we must act and act as quickly as possible, to rid ourselves of these influence of "psychological warfare," which has consistently generated hatred among men and nations.

In conclusion one can quote Schiller: The technology of modern communications must be won from its current custodians. It should be generally apparent, although it is not, that the aims and practices of the commercial market are not always in step with the social requirements of the human commonwealth.

References

1. John A. Lent, "Mass Media, Folk Media and Rural Masses in the Third World," presented at International Studies Association, Washington, D.C., February 24, 1978.
2. Claus Eurich, "Communication Polluting Speech", *Development: Seeds of Change*, 1, 1985, p. 75.
3. *Ibid*.
4. Ken Darrow and Michael Saxenian, "Worshipping a False God?" *Development: Seeds of Change*, 1, 1985, p. 67.
5. *Missing Links*, Executive Summary, 1984, p. 6.
6. Quoted in Theodore Roszak, *The Cult of Information: The Folklore of Computers and the True Art of Thinking*, New York, Pantheon, 1986, p. 178.
7. Herbert Dordick, *Critical Issues for National Computerisation Policy*, Singapore, AMIC, 1983, Dordick's other points were: 3. Computerisation will lead to long-term unemployment across all sectors of society, 4. Traditional education may be unable to cope with demands for new careers and for retraining workers for new jobs, 5. In the long run, unemployment will have to be redefined.

   For treatments on the benefits of new information technology, see works of Pool, Bell, Simon Saunders and Hudson. Some of this work is in: Tom Forester, editor *The Microelectronics Revolution: The Computer Guide to the New Technology and its Impact on Society*, Cambridge, Mit Press, 1983; Michael L. Dertouzos and Joel Moses, eds., *The Computer Age: A Twenty-year View*, Cambridge, Mit Press, 1983; and Robert J. Saunders, Jeremy Warford and Bjorn Wellenius, *Telecommunications and Economic*

Development, Baltimore, Johns Hopkins University Press for World Bank, 1983.

8. Carrie Shipley, Dwayne L. Shipley and Rolf T. Wigand, "Corporate Transborder Data Flow and National Policy in Developing Countries," in Brent Ruben, ed., *Information and Behavior*, Vol. 1. New Brunswich, Transation Books, 1985, p. 455.
9. *Ibid.*, p. 471.
10. Roszak, *op cit*, p. 187.
11. *Ibid.*, p. 190.
12. *Ibid.*, p. 192.
13. *Ibid.*, p. 206.
14. Dallas Smythe, "Needs Before Tools? The Illusions of Electronic Democracy," Presented at International Communication Association, Honolulu, Hawaii, May, 1985, p. 34.
15. Roszak, *op cit*, p. 209.
16. Cees Hamelink, "High-Tech Transfer: Selling the Canoe without the Paddle," *Development: Seeds of Change*, 1, 1985, pp. 28, 34.
17. Gerard Blanc, "Beware of the Information Age", *Development: Seeds of Change*, 1, 1985, p. 79.
18. Eurich, *op cit*, p. 74.
19. John A. Lent, "Telematics in the Year 2000: Some Moral Questions", *Democratic Journalist*, 11, 1982, p. 29.
20. Ivan Illich, "Silence Is a Commons", *Development: Seeds of Change*, 1, 1985, p. 80.
21. Enrich, *op cit*, p. 76.
22. *Ibid.*
23. *Ibid.*
24. Neville Jayaweera, "Communication Satellites—A Third World Perspective," *Media Development*, 4, 1983, p. 13.
25. Dean T. Jamison and Emile G. McAnany, *Radio for Education and Development*, Beverly Hills, Sage, 1978; Wilbur Schramm, *Big Media, Little Media*, Beverly Hills, Sage, 1977.
26. Jayaweera, *op cit*.
27. Lent, "Telematics," *op cit*.
28. Bella Mody, "Technology Options for the Third World Countries: Do We Have the Freedom to Choose?" *Media Asia*, 11, 2, 1984.
29. Joseph Weizenbaum, "Once More: The Computer Revolution," in Dertouzos and Moses, *op cit*, pp. 440, 449 and 457. Same chapter is also in Forester, *op cit*, pp. 550-570.
30. Hamelink, *op cit*, p. 36.
31. Smythe, *op cit*, p. 34.
32. Fred Hechinger, "Technology and the Third World", *New York Times*, March 12, 1985, p. C-9.

33. Lent, "Mass Media. Folk Media....," *op cit.*
34. Quoted in J.S. Yadava, "New Communication Technologies and Developing Societies," New Delhi, Indian Institute of Mass Communication, 1983.

Further Reading. The literature on new information technology is almost boundless. Among many other readings done in preparation for this paper, these were instructive: *Development: Seeds of Change,* 1, 1985, including Ponna Wignaraja's "The Democratisation of Communications," and Armand Mattelart's "Peddling Images World-Wide," Raquel Salinas Bascur, "Information in the Third World: Adjusting Technologies or Strategies?" *Media, Culture and Society,* 7 7(1985), pp. 355-368; Cees, Hamelink, *Cultural Autonomy in Global Communications,* New York, Longman, 1983; Hamelink, *Transnational Data Flows in the Information Age,* Lund, Student-literature, 1984; Jorg Becker, *Information Technology and a New International Order,* Lund, Student Literature, 1984; Herbert Schiller, *Who Knows: Information in the Age of the Fortune 500,* Norwood, N.J., Ablex, 1981; Jorg Becker, "Information Technology and International Politics in the 1980s", *Media Development,* 1983, pp. 8-12; Dan Schiller, "Pathways to Digitisation in International Telecommunications," presented at International Conference on the Information Society, Seoul, Korea, June 12-14, 1986; Carrie L. Shipley, "Information Access Inequality in Rural America: Concepts, Trends, and Policy for the Information Age," *Communications,* 11:3, 1985, pp. 129-145; Klaus Balukopf, "Cultural Mutation Brought on by New Technologies," *Communication,* 11:3, 1985, pp. 37-49.

2

Communications as Sociological Force

As long as there has been human communication, there have been persons, organisations, and places that have served as centres for the input and output of information. The traveller, the scholar, the teacher, the merchant, and the gossip have been such persons. The bazaar, the social club, the government, in our time even the barber shop and beauty parlour, have been such organisations. The rocks along the Oregon Trail on which names and messages were scratched, the stone on which the Roman Senate inscribed its decisions, and the college bulletin board have been such places. All these have shared the ability to attract information and distribute it widely.

When mass media came into being—that is, when we learned how to insert a machine into the communication process, and print or film or broadcast the signs of communication—the principal differences between the new media and the more traditional media were in scale and in operation. Between the rock on the Oregon Trail and sixteenth-century printing there is a quantum jump in the power to multiply and distribute messages. Between the travelling minstrel and a network news operation there is a quantum jump in the ability to scan environment and distribute information about it. Between the village gossip and the news or documentary film there is a quantum jump in the ability to share "what really happened."

The enormity of these differences, the startling power of the mass media to leap space, telescope time, and make information portable and preservable, gives them a kind of social impact that the more traditional media never had.

A second difference is that the mass media require an organisation to operate them. Behind a newspaper or a news broadcast stand thousands of professionals and technicians. The making of a book or magazine or film requires a large capital investment, sophisticated equipment, and many highly trained persons working skillfully together. Consequently, the mass media have taken on many of the characteristics and social constraints of other large social institutions and organisations. As DeFleur makes clear in the paper immediately following, they form a social system which is tightly integrated with the whole of the American economic institution, and closely related also to the political system.

Looked at from the media side, therefore, communication through mass media channels seems considerably different from communication through the more traditional channels. Looked at from the university classroom, the two processes seem different, too, because students of communication note at once that there is a fundamental difference in feedback from receiver to sender of messages. In personal communication, feedback is usually quick and extensive; in mass communication, usually slow and weak. But when the process is looked at by the members of society at whom mass communication is chiefly aimed, these differences seem less sharp and less significant.

Communication flows constantly through society, touching every member. Some of it comes through personal channels, some through mass media. To a user, it makes really very little difference through what channel it arrives; he is concerned, rather, with what use he can make of it and how much he can rely upon it. Any message from the mass media enters into a flow of communication that is already in progress. In most cases, therefore, it does not retain its identity. It is picked up and relayed through personal channels. It is reinterpreted, retold, redirected. If it represents any significant suggestion for change, it is sure to be discussed and debated. If the discussion is of broad enough interest, it is likely to be continued in the media—an interview, quotation, statement, letter, public speech, panel discussion. If anyone in the audience decides to make a significant change as a result of the communication that has come to him, he is likely to return to the media for reassurance and confirmation.

Thus mass and personal communication interact and supplement each other. The rural sociologists studying diffusion of innovation discovered that different kinds of communications are more likely to be used at different points in the adoption process: for example, the mass media to bring about awareness, personal channels during the period of evaluation and decision, and both mass and personal communication when confirmation is desired.

We have not included in this volume an article on the two-step flow of communication, although that is perhaps the best-known concept of the relationship of mass to personal channels. We made this decision because the theory is presently in flux, and a succeeding theory has not yet clearly emerged. A reader who wants a summary of late thinking on this topic can look at Everett M. Rogers' volume, *Communication of Innovations: A Cross-Cultural Approach* (Glencoe, Ill.: The Free Press, 1969).

The concept of the two-step flow arose out of a classic study of the 1940 Presidential election by Lazarsfeld and others, which was published in 1944 as *The People's Choice.* The research team found, somewhat to their surprise, that almost no votes seemed to have been directly influenced by the mass media. Rather, the evidence appeared to indicate that "ideas often flow from radio and print to opinion leaders and from these to the less active sections of the population."

This two-step flow model was highly useful, both in sparking a number of field research studies and in casting doubt upon the long-held "hypodermic needle" or "bullet" theory of mass media effect. The two-step model turned attention to the importance of personal influence, as distinct from media influence, and to the interactive process among communication channels.

Therefore, the concept of a two-step flow has proved fruitful; but the more research that has been done, the clearer it has become that the model as stated is too simple to represent reality. Later campaign studies showed that many voters do not seek any personal advice at all. Many nonleaders are not followers of opinion leaders. The process of personal influence itself is much more diffused and complicated than the model suggests. There is no very general dichotomy between leaders and followers, and leaders have others who influence them, who in turn have others, and so forth. Opinion leadership, as Rogers has pointed out, is a continuous variable. Rogers, Katz (who has written perhaps most definitely about the two-step flow), and others including the present authors have concluded that the two-step flow model must be reconceptualised in terms of an "*n*-step" or "multi-step" flow, in which there are many relay points from channel to channel and a much more complex pattern of influence than was previously assumed.

In other words, the communication institutions we call mass media sometimes reach a member of the audience directly with their information and ideas, sometimes second-hand, or third- or fourth-hand, and sometimes in a form considerably different from the original. In some situations the media may have a direct effect, but more often the effect of mass communication, if any, must derive from whatever the media contribute to the ongoing flow of personal communication, and their interaction with the patterns of influence, norms, and learned behaviour that exist in society.

But even though the process of effect may be complicated, and effects often hard to prove, still it is hard to doubt the potency of the media as social institutions. In the following pages Lasswell analyses their functions from a political base, but in a way that makes it easy to generalise far beyond political process to the functioning of the social system as a whole. The last four papers, in different ways, deal with the significance of the fact that so much of society's information now necessarily comes through the mass media. McLuhan postulates an effect from the nature of the medium, regardless of the content; he argues that it makes a difference in human life whether environment is seen through personal communication, or print, or television. Boorstin, Rivers, and the Langs, however, are concerned more with content, and with the performance of media personnel, than with the physical nature of the medium *per se*. They recognise the social constraints upon media performance, but they are not happy with the clarity and balance of the picture of environment being provided through media channels. The enormous power and responsibility delegated to a social institution when it is assigned to act as the eyes and ears of society becomes clearly evident.

Communication in Society

This is one of the classic papers which contains well-known formula for describing communication (who says what in which channel to whom with what effect), and also his analysis of the functions of communication in society. Unlike DeFleur, who saw "low-taste" material as central in the social communication system. Lasswell did not even mention entertainment as a primary function of communication. Later commentators have added that to his list, however. They have also suggested that contributions to the economic system would be a primary function of mass media in a country like the United States.

A convenient way to describe an act of communication is to answer the following questions:

Who
Says What
In Which Channel
To Whom
With What Effect?

The scientific study of the process of communication tends to concentrate upon one or another of these questions. Scholars who study the "who," the communicator, look into the factors that initiate and guide the act of communication. We call this subdivision of the field of research *control analysis*. Specialists who focus upon the "says what" engage in *content analysis*. Those who look primarily at the radio, Press, film, and other channels of communication are doing *media analysis*. When the principal concern is with the persons reached by the media, we speak of *audience analysis*. If the question is the impact upon audiences, the problem is *effect analysis*.

Whether such distinctions are useful depends entirely upon the degree of refinement which is regarded as appropriate to a given scientific and managerial objective. Often it is simpler to combine audience and effect analysis, for instance, than to keep them apart. On the other hand, we may want to concentrate on the analysis of content, and for this purpose subdivide the field into the study of purport and style, the first referring to the message, and the second to the arrangement of the elements of which the message is composed.

Structure and Function

Enticing as it is to work out these categories in more detail, the present discussion has a different scope. We are less interested in dividing up the act of communication than in viewing the act as a whole in relation to the entire social process. Any process can be examined in two frames of reference, namely, structure and function; and our analysis of communication will deal with the specialisations that carry on certain functions, of which the following may be clearly distinguished:

1. the surveillance of the environment;
2. the correlation of the parts of society in responding to the environment;
3. the transmission of the social heritage from one generation to the next.

Biological Equivalences

At the risk of calling up false analogies, we can gain perspective on human societies when we note the degree to which communication is a feature of life at every level. A vital entity, whether relatively isolated or in association, has specialised ways of receiving stimuli from the environment. The single celled organism or the many-membered group tends to maintain an internal equilibrium and to respond to changes in the environment in a way that maintains this equilibrium. The responding process calls for specialised ways of bringing the parts of the whole into harmonious action. Multi-celled animals specialise cells to the function of external contact and internal correlation. Thus, among the primates, specialisation is exemplified by organs such as the ear and eye, and the nervous system itself. When the stimuli receiving and disseminating patterns operate smoothly, the several parts of the animal act in concert in reference to the environment ("feeding," "fleeing," "attacking").[1]

In some animal societies certain members perform specialised roles, and survey the environment. Individuals act as "sentinels," standing apart from the herd or flock and creating a disturbance whenever an alarming change occurs in the surroundings. The trumpeting, cackling, or shrilling of the sentinel is enough to set the herd in motion. Among the activities engaged in by specialised "leaders" is the internal stimulation of "followers" to adapt in an orderly manner to the circumstances heralded by the sentinels.

Within a single, highly differentiated organism, incoming nervous impulses and outgoing impulses are transmitted along fibres that make synaptic junction with other fibres. The critical points in the process occur at the relay stations, where the arriving impulse may be too weak to reach the threshold which stirs the next link into action. At the higher centres, separate currents modify one another, producing results that differ in many ways from the outcome when each is allowed to continue a separate path. At any relay station there is no conductance, total conductance, or intermediate conductance. The same categories apply to what goes on among members of an animal society. The sly fox may approach the barnyard in a way that supplies too meagre stimuli for the sentinel to sound the alarm. Or the attacking animal may eliminate the sentinel before he makes more than a feeble outcry. Obviously there is every gradation possible between total conductance and no conductance.

Attention in World Society

When we examine the process of communication of any state in the world community, we note three categories of specialists. One group surveys the political environment of the state as a whole, another correlates the response of the whole state to the environment, and the third transmits certain patterns of response from the old to the young. Diplomats, attaches, and foreign correspondents are representative of those who specialise on the environment. Editors, journalists, and speakers are correlators of the internal response. Educators in family and school transmit the social inheritance.

Communications which originate abroad pass through sequences in which various senders and receivers are linked with one another. Subject to modification at each relay point in the chain, messages originating with a diplomat or foreign correspondent may pass through editorial desks and eventually reach large audiences.

If we think of the world attention process as a series of *attention frames,* it is possible to describe the rate at which comparable content is brought to the notice of individuals and groups. We can inquire into the point at which "conductance" no longer occurs; and we can look into the range between "total conductance" and "minimum conductance." The metropolitan and political centres of the world have much in common with the interdependence, differentiation, and activity of the cortical or subcortical centres of an individual organism. Hence the attention frames found in these spots are the most variable, refined, and interactive of all frames in the world community.

At the other extreme are the attention frames of primitive inhabitants of isolated areas. Not that folk cultures are wholly untouched by industrial civilisation. Whether we parachute into the interior of New Guinea, or land on the slopes of the Himalayas, we find no tribe wholly out of contact with the world. The long threads of trade, of missionary zeal, of adventurous exploration and scientific field study, and of global war reach far distant places. No one is entirely out of this world.

Among primitives the final shape taken by communication is the ballad or tale. Remote happenings in the great world of affairs, happenings that come to the notice of metropolitan audiences, are reflected, however dimly, in the thematic material of ballad singers and reciters. In these creations far away political leaders may be shown supplying land to the peasants or restoring an abundance of game to the hills.

When we push upstream of the flow of communication, we note that the immediate relay function for nomadic and remote tribesmen is sometimes performed by the inhabitants of settled villages with whom they come in occasional contact. The relayer can be the school teacher, doctor, judge, tax collector, policeman, soldier, peddler, salesman, missionary, student; in any case he is an assembly point of news and comment.

More Detailed Equivalences

The communication processes of human society, when examined in detail, reveal many equivalences to the specialisations found in the physical organism and in the lower animal societies. The diplomats, for instance, of a single state are stationed all over the world and send messages to a few focal points. Obviously, these incoming reports move from the many to the few, where they interact upon one another. Later on, the sequence spreads fanwise according to a few-to-many pattern, as when a foreign secretary gives a speech in public, an article is put out in the Press, or a news film is distributed to the theatres. The lines leading from the outer environment of the state are functionally equivalent to the afferent channels that convey incoming nervous impulses to the central nervous system of a single animal, and to the means by which alarm is spread among a flock. Outgoing, or efferent, impulses display corresponding parallels.

The central nervous system of the body is only partly involved in the entire flow of afferent-efferent impulses. There are automatic systems that can act on one another without involving the "higher" centres at all. The stability of the internal environment is maintained principally through the mediation of the vegetive or autonomic specialisations of the nervous system. Similarly, most of the messages within any state do not involve the central channels of communication. They take place within families, neighbourhoods, shops, field gangs, and other local contexts. Most of the educational process is carried on the same way.

A further set of significant equivalences is related to the circuits of communication, which are predominantly one-way or two-way, depending upon the degree of reciprocity between communicators and audience. Or, to express it differently two-way communication occurs when the sending and receiving functions are performed with equal frequency by two or more persons. A conversation is usually assumed to be a pattern of two-way communication (although monologues are hardly unknown). The modern instruments of mass communication give an enormous advantage to the controllers of printing plants, broadcasting equipment, and other forms of fixed and specialised capital. But it should be noted that audiences do "talk back," after some delay; and many controllers of mass media use scientific methods of sampling in order to expedite this closing of the circuit.

Circuits of two-way contact are particularly in evidence among the great metropolitan, political, and cultural centres of the world. New York, Moscow, London and Paris, for example, are in intense two-way contact, even when the flow is severely curtailed in volume (as between Moscow and New York). Even insignificant sites become world centres when they are transformed into capital cities (Canberra, Australia; Ankara, Turkey; the District of Columbia, U.S.A.). A cultural centre like Vatican City is in intense two-way relationship with the dominant centres throughout the world. Even specialised production centres like Hollywood, despite their preponderance of outgoing material, receive an enormous volume of messages.

A further distinction can be made between message controlling and message handling centres and social formations. The message centre in the vast Pentagon Building of the War Department in Washington transmits with no more than accidental change incoming messages to addresses. This is the role of the printers and distributors of books; of dispatchers, linemen, and messengers connected with telegraphic communication; of radio engineers and other technicians associated with broadcasting. Such message handlers may be contrasted with those who affect the content of what is said, which is the function of editors, censors, and propagandists. Speaking of the symbol specialists as a whole, therefore, we separate them into the manipulators (controllers) and the handlers; the first group typically modifies content, while the second does not.

Needs and Values

Though we have noted a number of functional and structural equivalences between communication in human societies and other living entities, it is not implied that we can most fruitfully investigate the process of communication in America or the world by the methods most appropriate to research on the lower animals or on single physical organisms. In comparative psychology when we describe some part of the surroundings of a rat, cat, or monkey as a stimulus (that is, as part of the environment reaching the attention of the animal), we cannot ask the rat; we use other means of inferring perception. When human beings are our objects of investigation, we can interview the great "talking animal." (This is not that we take everything at face value. Sometimes we forecast the opposite of what the person says he intends to do. In this case, we depend on other indications, both verbal and nonverbal.)

In the study of living forms, it is rewarding, as we have said, to look at them as modifiers of the environment in the process of gratifying needs, and hence of maintaining a steady state of internal equilibrium. Food, sex, and other activities which involve the environment can be examined on a comparative basis. Since human beings exhibit speech reactions, we can investigate many more relationships than in the nonhuman species.[2] Allowing for the data furnished by speech (and other communicative acts), we can investigate human society in terms of values; that is, in reference to categories of relationship that are recognised objects of gratification. In America, for example, it requires no elaborate technique of study to discern that power and respect are values. We can demonstrate this by listening to testimony, and by watching what is done when opportunity is afforded.

It is possible to establish a list of values current in any group chosen for investigation. Further than this, we can discover the rank order in which these values are sought. We can rank the members of the group according to their positions in relation to the values. So far as industrial civilisation is concerned, we have no hesitation in saying that power, wealth, respect, well-being, and enlightenment are among the values. If we stop with this list, which is not exhaustive, we can describe on the basis of available knowledge (fragmentary though it may often be) the social structure of most of the world. Since values are not equally distributed, the social structure reveals more or less concentration of relatively abundant shares of power, wealth, and other values in a few hands. In some places this concentration is passed on from generation to generation, forming castes rather than a mobile society.

In every society the values are shaped and distributed according to more or less distinctive patterns (*institutions*). The institutions include communications which are invoked in support of the network as a whole. Such communications are the ideology; and in relation to power we can differentiate the political *doctrine,* the political *formula,* and the *miranda.*[3] These are illustrated in the United States by the doctrine of individualism, the paragraphs of the Constitution, which are the formula, and the ceremonies and legends of public life, which comprise the miranda. The ideology is communicated to the rising generation through such specialised agencies as the home and school.

Ideology is only part of the myths of any given society. There may be counter-ideologies directed against the dominant doctrine, formula, and miranda. Today the power structure of world politics is deeply affected by ideological conflict, and by the role of two giant powers, the United States and Russia. The ruling elites view one another as potential enemies, not only in the sense that interstate differences may be settled by war, but in the more urgent sense that the ideology of the other may appeal to disaffected elements at home and weaken the internal power position of each ruling class.

Social Conflict and Communication

Under the circumstances, one ruling element is especially alert to the other, and relies upon communication as a means of preserving power. One function of communication, therefore, is to provide intelligence about what the other elite is doing, and about its strength. Fearful that intelligence channels will be controlled by the other, in order to withhold and distort, there is a tendency to resort to secret surveillance. Hence international espionage is intensified above its usual level in peacetime. Moreover, efforts are made to "black out" the self in order to counteract the scrutiny of the potential enemy. In addition, communication is employed affirmatively for the purpose of establishing contact with audiences within the frontiers of the other power.

These varied activities are manifested in the use of open and secret agents to scrutinise the other, in counter-intelligence work, in censorship and travel restriction, in broadcasting and other informational activities across frontiers.

Ruling elites are also sensitized to potential threats in the internal environment. Besides using open sources of information, secret measures are also adopted. Precautions are taken to impose "security" upon as many policy matters as possible. At the same time, the ideology of the elite is reaffirmed, and counter-ideologies are suppressed.

The processes here sketched run parallel to phenomena to be observed throughout the animal kingdom. Specialised agencies are used to keep aware of threats and opportunities in the external environment. The parallels include the surveillance exercised over the internal environment, since among the lower animals some herd leaders sometimes give evidence of fearing attack on two fronts, internal and external; they keep an uneasy eye on both environments. As a means of preventing surveillance by an enemy, well-known devices are at the disposal of certain species, e.g., the squid's use of a liquid fog screen, the protective coloration of the chameleon. However, there appears to be no correlate of the distinction between the "secret" and "open" channels of human society.

Inside a physical organism the closest parallel to social revolution would be the growth of new nervous connections with parts of the body that rival, and can take the place of, the existing structures of central integration. Can this be said to occur as the embryo develops in the mother's body? Or, if we take a destructive, as distinct from a reconstructive, process, can we properly say that internal surveillance occurs in regard to cancer, since cancers compete for the food supplies of the body?

Efficient Communication

The analysis up to the present implies certain criteria of efficiency or inefficiency in communication. In human societies the process is efficient to the degree that rational judgments are facilitated. A rational judgment implements value goals. In animal societies communication is efficient when it aids survival, or some other specified need of the aggregate. The same criteria can be applied to the single organism.

One task of a rationally organised society is to discover and control any factors that interfere with efficient communication. Some limiting factors are psychotechnical. Destructive radiation, for instance, may be present in the environment, yet remain undetected owing to the limited range of the unaided organism.

But even technical insufficiencies can be overcome by knowledge. In recent years shortwave broadcasting has been interfered with by disturbances which will either be surmounted, or will eventually lead to the abandonment of this mode of broadcasting. During the late sixties advances have been made toward providing satisfactory substitutes for defective hearing and seeing. A less dramatic, though no less important, development has been the discovery of how inadequate reading habits can be corrected.

There are, of course, deliberate obstacles put in the way of communication, like censorship and drastic curtailment of travel. To some extent obstacles can be surmounted by skillful evasion, but in the long run it will doubtless be more efficient to get rid of them by consent or coercion.

Sheer ignorance is a pervasive factor whose consequences have never been adequately assessed. Ignorance here means the absence, at a given point in the process of communication, of knowledge which is available elsewhere in society. Lacking proper training, the personnel engaged in gathering and disseminating intelligence is continually misconstruing or overlooking the facts, if we define the facts as what the objective, trained observer could find.

In accounting for inefficiency we must not overlook the low evaluations put upon skill in relevant communication. Too often irrelevant, or positively distorting, performances command prestige. In the interest of a "scoop," the reporter gives a sensational twist to a mild international conference, and contributes to the popular image of international politics as chronic, intense conflict, and little else. Specialists in communication often fail to keep up with the expansion of knowledge about the process; note the reluctance with which many visual devices have been adopted. And despite research on vocabulary, many mass communicators select words that fail. This happens, for instance, when a foreign correspondent allows himself to become absorbed in the foreign scene and forgets that his home audience has no direct equivalents in experience for "left," "centre," and other factional terms.

Besides skill factors, the level of efficiency is sometimes adversely influenced by personality structure. An optimistic, outgoing person may hunt "birds of a feather" and gain an uncorrected and hence exaggeratedly optimistic view of events. On the contrary, when pessimistic, brooding personalities mix, they choose quite different birds, who confirm their gloom. There are also important differences among people which spring from contrasts in intelligence and energy.

Some of the most serious threats to efficient communication for the community as a whole relate to the values of power, wealth, and respect. Perhaps the most striking examples of power distortion occur when the content of communication is deliberately adjusted to fit an ideology or counterideology. Distortions related to wealth not only arise from attempts to influence the market, for instance, but from rigid conceptions of economic interest. A typical instance of inefficiencies connected with respect (social class) occurs when an upper-class person mixes only with persons of his own stratum and forgets to correct his perspective by being exposed to members of other classes.

Research in Communication

The foregoing reminders of some factors that interfere with efficient communication point to the kinds of research which can usefully be conducted on representative links in the chain of communication. Each agent is a vortex of interacting environmental and predispositional factors. Whoever performs a relay function can be examined in relation to input and output. What statements are brought to the attention of the relay link? What does he pass on verbatim? What does he drop out? What does he rework? What does he add? How do differences in input and output correlate with culture and personality? By answering such questions it is possible to weigh the various factors in conductance, no conductance, and modified conductance.

Besides the relay link, we must consider the primary link in a communication sequence. In studying the focus of attention of the primary observer, we emphasize two sets of influences: statements to which he is exposed; other features of his environment. An attache or foreign correspondent exposes himself to mass media and private talk; also, he can count soldiers, measure gun emplacements, note hours of work in a factory, see butter and fat on the table.

Actually it is useful to consider the attention frame of the relay as well as the primary link in terms of media and nonmedia exposures. The role of nonmedia factors is very slight in the case of many relay operators, while it is certain to be significant in accounting for the primary observer.

Attention Aggregates and Publics

It should be pointed out that everyone is not a member of the world public, even though he belongs to some extent to the world attention aggregate. To belong to an attention aggregate it is only necessary to have common symbols of reference. Everyone who has a symbol of reference for New York, North America, the western hemisphere, or the globe is a member respectively of the attention aggregate of New York, North America, the western hemisphere, the globe. To be a member of the New York public, however, it is essential to make demands for public action in New York, or expressly affecting New York.

The public of the United States, for instance, is not confined to residents or citizens, since noncitizens who live beyond the frontier may try to influence American politics. Conversely, everyone who lives in the United States is not a member of the American public, since something more than passive attention is necessary. An individual passes from an attention aggregate to the public when he begins to expect that what he wants can affect public policy.

Sentiment Groups and Publics

A further limitation must be taken into account before we can correctly classify a specific person or group as part of a public. The demands made regarding public policy must be debatable. The world public is relatively weak and undeveloped, partly because it is typically kept subordinate to sentiment areas in which no debate is permitted on policy matters. During a war or war crisis, for instance, the inhabitants of a region are overwhelmingly committed to impose certain policies on others. Since the outcome of the conflict depends on violence, and not debate, there is no public under such conditions. There is a network of sentiment groups that act as crowds, hence tolerate no dissent.[4]

From the foregoing analysis it is clear that there are attention, public, and sentiment areas of many degrees of inclusiveness in world politics. These areas are interrelated with the structural and functional features of world society, and especially of world power. It is evident, for instance, that *the strongest powers tend to be included in the same attention area,* since their ruling elites focus on one another as the source of great potential threat. The strongest powers usually pay proportionately less attention to the weaker powers than the weaker powers pay to them, since stronger powers are typically more important sources of threat, or of protection, for weaker powers than the weaker powers are for the stronger.[5]

The attention structure within a state is a valuable index of the degree of state integration. When the ruling classes fear the masses, the rulers do not share their picture of reality with the rank and file. When the reality picture of kings, presidents, and cabinets is not permitted to circulate through the state as a whole, the degree of discrepancy shows the extent to which the ruling groups assume that their power depends on distortion.

Or, to express the matter another way, if the "truth" is not shared, the ruling elements expect internal conflict, rather than harmonious adjustment to the external environment of the state. Hence the channels of communication are controlled in the hope of organising the attention of the community at large in such a way that only responses will be forthcoming which are deemed favourable to the power position of the ruling classes.

The Principle of Equivalent Enlightenment

It is often said in democratic theory that rational public opinion depends upon enlightenment. There is, however, much ambiguity about the nature of enlightenment, and the term is often made equivalent to perfect knowledge. A more modest and immediate conception is not perfect but equivalent enlightenment. The attention structure of the full-time specialist on a given policy will be more elaborate and refined than that of the layman. That this difference will always exist, we must take for granted. Nevertheless, it is quite possible for the specialist and the layman to agree on the broad outlines of reality. A workable goal of democratic society is equivalent enlightenment as between expert, leader, and layman.

Expert, leader, and layman can have the same gross estimate of major population trends of the world. They can share the same general view of the likelihood of war. It is by no means fantastic to imagine that the controllers of mass media of communication will take the lead in bringing about a high degree of equivalence throughout society between the layman's picture of significant relationships, and the picture of the expert and the leader.

Summary

The communication process in society performs three functions:

(*a*) *surveillance* of the environment, disclosing threats and opportunities affecting the value position of the community and of the component parts within it;
(*b*) *correlation* of the components of society in making a response to the environment;
(*c*) *transmission* of the social inheritance. In general, biological equivalents can be found in human and animal associations, and within the economy of a single organism.

In society, the communication process reveals special characteristics when the ruling element is afraid of the internal as well as the external environment. In gauging the efficiency of communication in any given context, it is necessary to take into account the values at stake, and the identity of the group whose position is being examined. In democratic societies, rational choices depend on enlightenment, which in turn depends upon commuincation; and especially upon the equivalence of attention among leaders, experts, and rank and file.

References

1. To the extent that behavior patterns are transmitted in the structures inherited by the single animal, a function is performed parallel to the transmission of the "social heritage" by means of education.
2. Properly handled, the speech event can be described with as much reliability and validity as many nonspeech events which are more conventionally used as data in scientific investigations.
3. These distinctions are derived and adapted from the writings of Charles E. Merriam, Gaetano Mosca, Karl Mannheim, and others. For a systematic exposition, see Harold D. Lasswell and Abraham Kaplan, *Power and Society* (New Haven, Yale University Press, 1950).
4. The distinction between the "crowd" and the "public" was worked out in the Italian, French, and German literature of criticism that grew up around Le Bon's overgeneralised use of the crowd concept. For a summary of this literature by a scholar who later became one of the most productive social scientists in this field, see Robert E. Park, *Masse und Publikum; Eine methodologische und soziologische Untersuchung* (Berne: Lack and Grunau, 1994).
5. The propositions in this paragraph are hypotheses capable of being subsumed under the general theory of power, referred to in n. 3. See also Harold D. Lasswell and Joseph M. Goldsen, "Public Attention, Opinion and Action," *The International Journal of Opinion and Attitude Research*, 1 (1947), 3-11.

3

Reorienting Communication: Form and Content

The concept of development communication has reached a major breakthrough in Asia during the last two decades or so. Although the process from a mere idea to an accepted concept was slow and full of constraints, the new concept has now been adopted by almost all the countries of the third world. Both, the policy makers and administrators had over looked for a long time that the problems like illiteracy, overpopulation, malnutrition, etc., simply cannot be solved by the mere process of buying technology, skills and instruments necessary for development. The people have to be informed and motivated to use these instruments.

And, this is what development communication is all about to inform, motivate and influence all sectors and levels of people of a developing country to use hitherto unfamiliar ideas, skills and instruments, thus adding the long neglected social component without which the process of development remains dormant. We have to make use of the vast potential that communication can provide today and tomorrow towards development. To try and find out a satisfactory parameter to 'what is' and 'what is not' development communication, let us first briefly discuss its two components, namely the development and the communication.

Development: What is it? Certain terms used synonymously to development are a change, growth, progress and modernisation. However, there can be changes without development, so we should rather say that development stands for all that is good, positive and favourable. It is a process of movement from a state of dissatisfaction to a state of satisfaction; it is dynamic and not static. Development is an all embracing concept, encompassing economic, social, cultural, educational and political aspects of the society. It is the sum total of all-round, balanced and planned growth.

Communication: What it means? Communication is at the root of all human activities. Human beings share knowledge, information and experience and thus understand, persuade, convert or control their fellows through communication. It is a two-way process, both vertically and horizontally, in a spirit of 'give and take' or 'send and receive.' Only after communicating with the people at their level, can we understand their problems in the right perspectives and assist developmental agencies in accelerating the pace of progress.

Thus both the development and communication are engaged in a symbiotic relationship, one helping another, complementing and supplementing each other in the process of fostering balanced growth and progress.

Development Communication

Meaning and Nature: The concept of developmental communication has gained prominence during the last two decades. However, its genesis can be traced to the introduction and application of agricultural extension, termed extension education during the later half of the 1940's and early 1950's in most of the developing countries. The need for bridging the gap between the haves and have-nots called for a new philosophy and approach in the efforts aimed at achieving the objectives. This necessitated rational decisions on the part of the people. Thus, the importance of communication as a tool to motivate and persuade people for eliciting positive response to various developmental ideas grew manifold. Accordingly, the use of agricultural communication became very popular, leading in due course to 'Rural Communication' for the sake of wider coverage and applications.

As defined by Nora Quebral (1975) the "Developmental Communication is an art and science of human communication applied to the speedy transformation of a country and the mass of its people from poverty to a dynamic state of economic growth that makes possible greater social equality and larger fulfilment of the human potential."

Rosario Braid (1979) redefined the concept and to put in his own words the "Developmental communication is an element of the management process in the overall planning and implementation of development programmes. In a broad sense it is the identification and utilisation of appropriate expertise in the development process that will assist in increasing participation of intended beneficiaries at the grass-root levels."

Development communication has emerged from practical life situations and, therefore, is an innovation of the developing countries alone. It implies desirable changes in the thinking and works of the people. To be more specific, it grows mostly out of people's participation and people's satisfaction. The ingredients of which are:

(a) a sense of feeling to have actively participated;
(b) a sense of pride in evolving solutions to the problems in hand; and
(c) sense of mental and physical achievements.

Development communication can use any channel or a combination of channels such as television, radio, print media, etc., to achieve the objectives of development. Thus, all these sources fall within the ambit of development communication. Starting with agriculture which forms the focal point, development of all other aspects such as health and sanitation, family planning, education, roads transports, etc., need greater efforts. Development communication is not only for the rural areas, issues such as drug addiction, crimes, accidents, conservation of water and energy are a few among the long list confronting the urban masses. It is in the sphere of involving people that development communication can and must play a positive role.

The Communication-process and its Goals: Irrespective of the urban and rural area, to be purposive and pragmatic, the development communication has to be practised in a planned and systematic manner. A balanced growth and desirable change in the behaviour complex of the people could result only from systematic co-operation. The following stages would constitute the process of effective communication:

* Analysis of the situation
* Identification of problems and fixing of priorities
* Consideration of resources
* Preparing a plan of action
* Action
* Evaluation

The development communication has to be goal-oriented. Its ultimate goal is a higher quality of life for the people of a society. We should not view the goal in economic terms alone but also in terms of the social, political, cultural and moral values that make a person's life whole, and enables a person to attain his or her fullest possible potential. The goal of development communication in a specific society will be influenced by the ends and values of that society.

Planning and Strategies of Development Communication

Planning is a human activity based on human attributes. It is a process for determining appropriate future action through a sequence of choices. In other words, it is a very general activity which encompasses an orderly sequence of activities designed to analyse and evaluate alternative actions for achieving carefully stated goals.

Definition and Purpose: The development communication can be defined as a deliberate, systematic and continuous effort to organise human activity for the efficient use of communication resources and for the realisation of communication policies, in the context of a particular society's developmental goals, means and priorities, and subject to its prevailing forms of economic, social and political organisation.

Modern societies are more complicated than older ones, with many problems to be solved and needs to be met with. Advance planning helps decision makers to effectively influence, develop and control the environment in order to attain better quality of life. Planning helps by identifying the logical consequences of events that are more likely to achieve a pre-determined goal.

Constraints and Complexities of Planning: Developmental communication planning is faced with many complexities. The elements of planning are not separate and distinct activities, but are dynamically interdependent on each other.

Planning, therefore, must take into account the developmental approaches and goals of the particular country in which the planning occurs. Such planning must also take into account of the country's political ideology and issues, extent social issues, the state of the communication system and theories being followed, and resources available since all these factors will affect the planning process and subsequent development effects.

The complexities involved may be illustrated in the following manner as in Fig. 3.1:

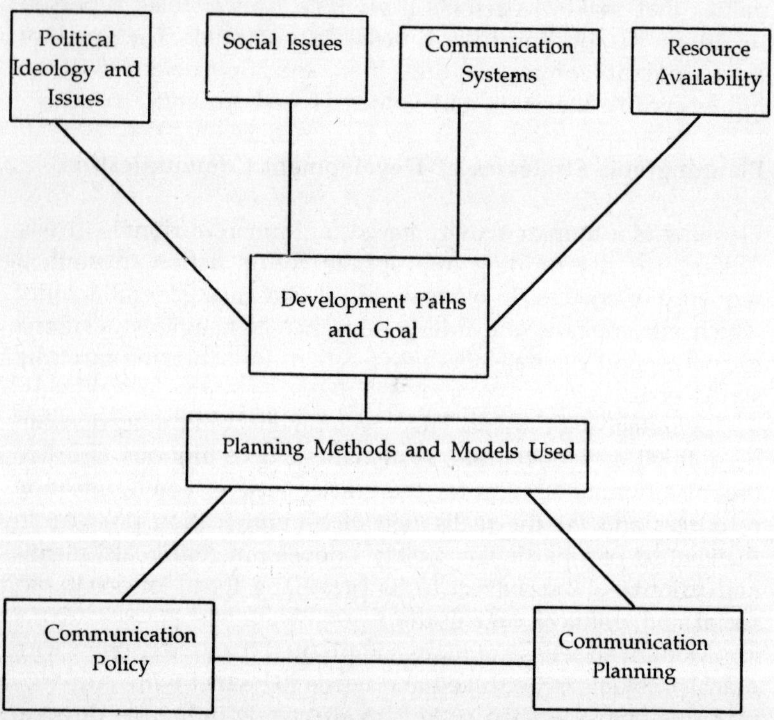

Fig. 3.1: Complexities of Developmental Communication Planning

Paradigm and Elements: The development path followed by a country, together with its national development goals, obviously influences development communication planning. This is particularly true when its objectives and channels are created to support achievement of the development goals of that country. For instance, if the national policy is to encourage local participation, then national or regional messages to that effect may not be as effective as providing local access to communication facilities.

Elements of developmental communication planning involves the following aspects:

* Identification of communication needs and resources, a critical analysis of the communication needs of each society, especially in relation to the existing social and communication, structures and the uses to which communication is applied.
* Goal specifications, a statement of goals in clear and measurable terms.
* Planning a development strategy, a combination of channels and messages to reach certain audiences in order to achieve certain goals. There may be a number of possible communication strategies which must be carefully analysed, including their benefits and costs, before selecting the appropriate one.
* Planning for implementation, a scheme for implementation of the chosen strategy which involves organising resources and time.
* Planning for evaluation, an essential aspect that seeks to establish mechanisms and allocate resources to determine how well the strategy is working, whether goals have been achieved and to identify the relationship between strategies and goal achievement.

Development Aids: Two essential requirements of developmental aids include *(a)* mass media and *(b)* the village level worker.

Mass Media: An extension worker desirous of bringing change for the masses must first reach the masses. One can reach them, teach them and create desirable behaviour changes through the mass media. The opportunities are there for all the media, old or new to participate in the grant endeavour of development.

In India, the mass media have to be rural-oriented, for 76 per cent of the population lives in rural areas. Despite the enormous expansion of communication facilities over the years, the reach of mass media is limited, especially in the rural areas and amongst the weaker sections of the society. This is mainly due to 5 mutually reinforcing factors:

* Low literacy rate
* Language barriers
* Low purchasing power
* Poor means of transportation for timely delivery of newspapers or maintenance of radio or TV sets.
* Lack of relevant information if purposive communication is the aim of media policy.

Radio and television technology offer great potential for the communication of anything man can hear or see more quickly and cheaply to a large audience at one time. Similarly, the print media can perform as a basic communication tool for the total population.

But there is lot of anonymity and lack of feedback. To realise the potential of mass media for social progress and development:

1. the media personnel have to alter their approach to suit the acceptance level of the people;
2. communication policies should be sufficiently localised in content, decentralised in set-up giving scope for upward articulation of feedback;
3. the little media should be fully exploited and made specific to the needs of the villagers; and
4. there should be an integrated approach to communication where the planners should be consulted at the beginning of the planning stage, and will continue to guide the planners.

Village Level Workers (VLW)

Development of mass media as instrument for getting

development messages across to the people has brought about a neglect of the human factor. Mere information via mass media cannot automatically bring about motivation, action and change.

For this purpose the Village Development Officer (VDO) can be an effective link for communicating at the grass-root level. He has that personal touch, knowledge of his environment and the ability to initiate a mutual, permanent and direct discussion with the villagers. The VLW contributes greatly to the developmental process by:

1. Collecting information about new ideas, techniques and practices from the central agency and disseminating it to the villagers. At the same time he initiates feedback about problems, needs and wishes of the people and provides this information to his agency for future activities.
2. Persuading and motivating villagers to try new ideas.
3. Trying to understand the socio-cultural barriers to acceptance and how to overcome them.
4. Arranging financial or technical support from the central agency or instructing villagers on how to prepare the needed instruments themselves.

The VLW opens the gates of communication of his village to the outside world. He can control the communicative channels going from the Extension Office to the village and *vice versa*. Thus his role is closely related to all that can be regarded as development in the villagers of the developing countries.

Researches in Development Communication

Development communication is a purposive, goal-directed, audience-oriented branch of human communication. The research areas in this field that need to be thoroughly worked out include the following:

1 What the communication media ought to be like, what they should do, and how to get desired results with them?

2. What are the crucial problems in development such as hunger, disease, illiteracy, etc?
3. What are the traditional channels of communication available, particularly in the rural areas?
4. What kind of satellite systems can be usefully shared for developmental tasks?
5. What have been the reasons for success or failure of developmental plans?

The nucleus of the government health strategy is the Primary Health Centre (PHC) and the Community Health Worker (CHW) who will be the first contact point between the villagers and the Government Health Organisation (GHO). This can be achieved not by barefoot approaches but by heavy reliance on advanced technological and managerial systems. If the rural health care programme is to succeed, the following are essentials:

* The programme should be conceived as an integrated package,
* Communication efforts should provide support,
* The programme should lay stress on the infrastructure, inputs, motivation through communication and training of personnel,
* Continuous evaluation and feedback is essential for the success of the programme.

Over 45 years of development experience in India has clearly indicated that it is not just economic modelling, legislative action or administrative reform that propels development. The key is motivation and that too at the mass level-mobilisation of commitment, involvement, participation and dedication of masses in planning and developmental tasks. It is in this area that the Indian Woman could be the most powerful channel for motivation and development. Her moral force in the house on parents, the husband, children and others is stronger than that in any other society in the world. She has the unmatched faculty of being able to inspire others to act as she wishes. The ethical force she exerts is enmeshed in our religious convictions. Her participation in custom and ritual is inseparable from our culture.

The study of woman ought to grow into a discipline of its own-right in which we should concentrate on the positive side of her faculties. The women resource has to be tapped so that it becomes an integral part of the planning and developmental process.

Communicating Indigenous Technology

In designing a communication system for sharing of indigenous technology, we should rely heavily on the traditional media, channels, particularly in rural areas, because,

* Despite modernisation and industrialisation, the rural people continue to rely on human and oral communication.
* The spread and effect of mass media on the bulk of the population which lives in rural areas is small.

What is required for development is not unregulated and so called free flow of information but optimal doses of communication which might act as a support to and nourish the development process. There is an urgent need for considerable research and action-oriented studies to design optimal, low-cost, human-oriented systems. A third-world communication model should be developed which will have the following characteristics:

* An advanced system like the satellite communication to interconnect points considerably far from each other and yet focussed on local needs culture.
* Focus on decentralisation and use of low-power technology.
* Overall emphasis on the use of communication for education and development.

Development Communication in India

India is a vast subcontinent with a population of over 860 million people, with 16 major regional languages and over a hundred major variations in dialect. The problem of communicating to such a vast populace with regional, sub-regional as well as local linguistic variations means giving attention to local and sub-regional communication strategies.

In India, of late, the planners have realised the value of communication as an input in the overall developmental-approach to the rural sector which today constitutes nearly 76 per cent of the population. The real problem is one of tailoring media to suit to the aspirations of the people, and mobilising media for development keeping in mind that illiteracy is the major barrier to communication. Some popular media in India include the followings:

* The radio has a wide coverage of agriculture and rural change programmes in Indian languages and dialects.
* The television devotes only 5 per cent of the time to rural programmes, the rest goes for entertainment, films, news, etc.
* The Hindi films are solely a means of entertainment for the masses, reinforcing existing values, projecting fatalism, fantasy and mythology.
* The reach of the Press is limited to urban and sub-urban areas as the rate of literacy is very low among the rural population.
* The government has a field publicity unit as well as a song and drama division which propagates development messages through the use of folk music of drama forms and film screening. But the staff is limited and is unable to cope with the vast demands of the population.
* The number of village level workers is also inadequate. Very often, the VLW's job is target-oriented rather than people-oriented.

Till now the approach to rural development has been specific with communication as a supporting unit. India has not yet fully exploited for developmental efforts the 'little media' such as tape cassettes, 8 mm films and slide shows. They can be made specific to the needs of the village population and are easily operable by VLWs.

It is hoped that in the years to come communication policies and planning in the country will be sufficiently localised in content, decentralised in set up, giving scope for upward articulation of feedback.

Failure of Development Communication Paradigm

During the past four decades, we in India have been working on the basis of theoretical framework developed essentially in the West. However, experience has shown that the reality is totally different. Some of the reasons for the total breakdown of the paradigm may include the followings:

* The developmental theory emphasises in maximising production of goods and increasing Gross National Product (GNP).
* However, what is required in developing countries is sufficiency leading to availability of food, housing, health care, safety, satisfaction and social justice.
* It has wrongly been accepted that development can take place only when the traditional society is swept away and, instead, the people accept a highly industrialised and urbanised society.
* It has been presumed that there is a direct correlation between communication infrastructure and development. However, for bringing about behavioural change at the local level, the media should reflect the cultural aspirations of the people.
* The communication sectors and channels, which matters, are all outside the purview of whatever policy mechanism exists.
* Communication has been confused with dissemination of information, whereas it is essentially based on management of feedback.
* Finally the Western thinkers have been of the view that the values embedded in the traditional culture are an obstacle to development and growth. But in India, modernisation, has taken place along with the retention of tradition.

All the above problems offer immense challenges in the field of development communication. Thus, there is great need to evolve a conceptual framework on which to base the future work in this field.

To ensure that the communication effort is relevant to and synchronious with the developmental effort, a national communication policy needs to be outlined. Although the agriculture sector is central to the new economic strategy, greater attention needs to be paid to other developmental sectors like village and small-scale industries, education, health and family welfare, rural infrastructure, post and telegraphic services and transport.

Efforts have to be made to reach the people through audio-visual and interpersonal means of communication with locally available and indigenous forms of communication like folklore, puppetry and little media.

Some policy suggestions worth consideration include the followings:

1. To evolve a comprehensive communication approach to deal with problems of mass education, development and economic growth through mass involvement and mobilisation of effort.
2. To identify the role of various communication media like films, T.V., radio, print, advertising and marketing in the development process.
3. To develop inventories of overall resources in the communication area.
4. To locate developmental areas where the impact of communications can lead to accelerated growth.
5. To determine the investment policy required for meeting the priorities.
6. To recommend the special linkages which need to connect the areas of education, culture and communication.
7. To examine how communication software and hardware systems can be improved with special reference to social change, cultural values and appropriate technology.
8. To develop appropriate computer software programmes for scholastic, scientific and social science studies.
9. To develop the role of communications in the management areas.

10. To suggest organisational, administrative, physical and legal measures required for planning, implementing, monitoring and evaluating programmes formulated for giving effect to the relevant components of a National Communication Policy.

The effects of public policy decisions taken today are reaped for many years into the future. Public policy analysis must, therefore, look to the future to seek the context in which to examine many of today's issues. Activities must have time reference that ranges from the present to 20 or more years into the future.

Conclusions

Development communication like the science of communication, has come to stay and owes its genesis to developing countries. It is relatively young field of study. It is dynamic, purposive and pragmatic in approach and can be utilised effectively in journalism, mass communication, public relations, communication etc. Furthermore, the development communication can use some of the communication channels available to advance development.

The communication spectrum extends from the most traditional forms of interpersonal and performing arts to sophisticated technology like satellites and computers. Despite the great advances, the communication systems and networks in most developing countries are far from adequate and still do not reach even the fringes of the large rural population. Any communication policy will have to be based on a two-way flow of information, the horizontal and vertical levels both requiring simultaneous approaches.

However, development communication is one of the means employed for speeding up the pace of progress. It is not a panacea for all ills, but is one of the most vital components in any developmental planning and its implementation.

Potential of Cable TV

"ISRO has been promoting the use of satellite based interactive audio-video networks and a few national and regional level experiments have been conducted in the use of such networks for education and training. The idea of creating an interactive network on a cable system is only a logical extension of this concept and Modasa Experiment is the first such effort in the country. Cable TV network is growing at an unusually high speed and so the telecom services, *inter alia*, half-inch Video Home System (VHS) and its multiple use has already spread faster than any other technological invention in the history. Such changes in the media scene, therefore, necessitated to examine the feasibility and effectiveness of using the existing cable network in an interactive mode for educational purposes.

An educational programme was conducted in collaboration with IGNOU from the cable feeding point convened into a studio-cum-teaching end. Among others, the Modasa Experiment has taught us new lessons on how community resources with little additional investment and careful planning can be utilised for imparting education by private entrepreneur even without any financial support from the Government. The future potential of this new communication technology is enormous, which needs to be harnessed for human resource development in the country.

Background

The applications of a technology, ultimately can become operational only when it is routinely available, easily affordable and simple to handle and operate upon. Hence, the conduct of experiments in close association with the user agencies and their preparedness to use and co-operate represent the vital links between in-house efforts and field utilisation of its outcome. ISRO has been promoting the use of satellite based interactive audio-video networks and a few national and regional level experiments have been conducted in the use of such networks for education and training. The idea of creating an interactive network on a cable system is only a logical extension of this concept. Modasa Experiment is the first such effort in the country conducted on a local cable network. The experiment was conducted during April 12-18, 1993, jointly by Development and Educational Communication Unit and Indira Gandhi National Open University to examine the feasibility and effectiveness of using existing cable network in an interactive mode for educational purpose.

Media Scene

Television came to India in 1959 as an experimental service to promote development. Regular telecasting started in 1965 with a daily one-hour programme with news bulletin in Delhi. Except metropolitan cities, other locations had to wait quite long for this medium till the country went for an operational satellite broadcasting system in 1982. The expansion since then has been rapid. As the TV sets increased there was more and more demand for entertainment, particularly films. Doordarshan could not meet this increased demand and watching video and film based cassettes on hired VCRs, therefore, became popular. Enterprising people started feeding the household TV sets through cable and thus cable networks mushroomed. Coverage of 1991 Gulf War straight from the battle front using satellite link further brightened the horizons for the cable network operation. With the arrival of: ZEE, STAR TV's Hindi channel, the rate of growth picked up and subscriber's list started swelling as never before in cities and even in smaller towns.

A number of market research organisations have estimated the penetration of cable TV. Important among these (as referred by Chandrasekhar, 1992) are the study of 1991 by MARG in four metro cities and another of NTS IV by MRAS covering a number of cities and towns. The NTS study appears to be more relevant in drawing general estimates on the coverage of cable TV. It points out that the proliferation of cable TV is high in western India, Maharashtra, Gujarat and parts of Madhya Pradesh. In non-Hindi states it is moderate and in Hindi states only marginal. Audience Research unit of Doordarshan (1992) has also conducted yet another cable TV coverage study. This also confirms the hard fact that there has been a significant increase in the number of cable connections and about six per cent households have STAR or cable TV connections.

Chandrasekhar (1992) refers that majority of these connections are single channel getting both VCR and STV programmes as per choice of the operator rather than multi-channel connections giving the choice to the viewer to shift any channel. One of the dominant reasons for not subscribing to cable TV is that it affects children's study. In the present context, there is yet another point to understand that by this time developments in both space and ground based communication has become visible: telephone infrastructure substantially increased, several new value added services became operational and; so is the large scale photo copying and computer networking. *Inter alia,* half inch Video Home System (VHS) and its multiple use has already spread faster than any other technological invention in recent history.

The spatial penetration of video is so remarkable that it has reached those places which Indian Cinema could not reach in 75 years. Within a short span of time the video cable network system has grown at a record speed without any support from any financial institution. This large population unemployed and partially employed look for escape from their day-to-day frustrations towards the fantasy land of video.

Distance Education Scene

In order to bring this large body of population in the mainstream of national development in the present day socio-economic and communication environment, the demand for education through the Open University System has been increasing. The requirements of this large body of population which remains outside the University System are very large and varied. IGNOU offers programmes of study that lead to degrees, diplomas and certificates to the disadvantaged clientage groups, who happen to be widely spread and are housewives, the unemployed and the working people. It, therefore, offers flexibility of place-pace and time of study, and adopts a multi-media approach. Self-instructional material is delivered at their place of residence, TV programmes are broadcast in the mornings, study centres remain open on all Sundays to further enable them to contact the teacher in person. However, the students at weekends have their family and other social commitments.

The heterogeneity among the student groups and diversity in their work activity, therefore, poses a real threat to sustain interest in studies and arrest their drop-out rate. This necessitated exploring the possibilities of utilising advantageously the development in communication technology for meeting the educational needs in the distance education system.

Cable TV network is growing at an unusually high speed and so the telecom and its value added services. Such changes in the media scene, therefore, also necessitated to explore the possibility of using this interactive network system for education. More so, the field experiences gained through such efforts can also help in designing a future satellite based interactive integrated broadcasting network system for the country.

As a prelude to incorporating interactive element of cable TV network in distance education, therefore, DECU-IGNOU conducted the experiment in the use of cable based interactive network system.

Objectives

The objectives of the experiment in general were:

1. To gain experience in the development, testing and management of the interactive network system.
2. To find out the advantages and limitation of a cable-based interactive network system when used as an instrument of academic counselling in the Distance Education System.
3. To examine the effectiveness of this system as an instructional and interactive tool.
4. To gain insights into the organisational and technical constraints and problems in operationalising the system on a large and wide scale.

The Experiment Configuration

The programme was conducted from the Cable feeding point converted into a Teaching End. A counselling—learning situation was simulated by locating a group of students. In order to further create an effective situation for group discussion, six (excluding one at the Teaching End) select group of students were located at different points on the network, while other students remained naturally scattered on the 3000 cable household locations. The programme was conducted through counselling/discussions supported by graphics, charts and actual situations and audio-visual aids. The mode of discussion was through public switched telephone system. These live participatory counselling sessions were recorded and later played back as 'repeat' for those students, who missed the actual programmes. Such students also had the facility to ask questions, but these had to be delivered to the Studio Centre by hand and the answer, however, to these questions were given the next day, on the network. Similarly the students who would not have access to a telephone were still able to ask their questions through hand delivery system (refer Modasa Experiment, 1993).

To make the system much more personalised, the Resource person gave assignments on Cable TV (CATV) network, to the students. The completed assignments were received through telephone as well as 'Hand Delivery' from the students. These, then on the next day were evaluated and performance discussed on the network system. All this was expected to compress the learning time and, therefore, might decrease dropout rate and improve performance of the students.

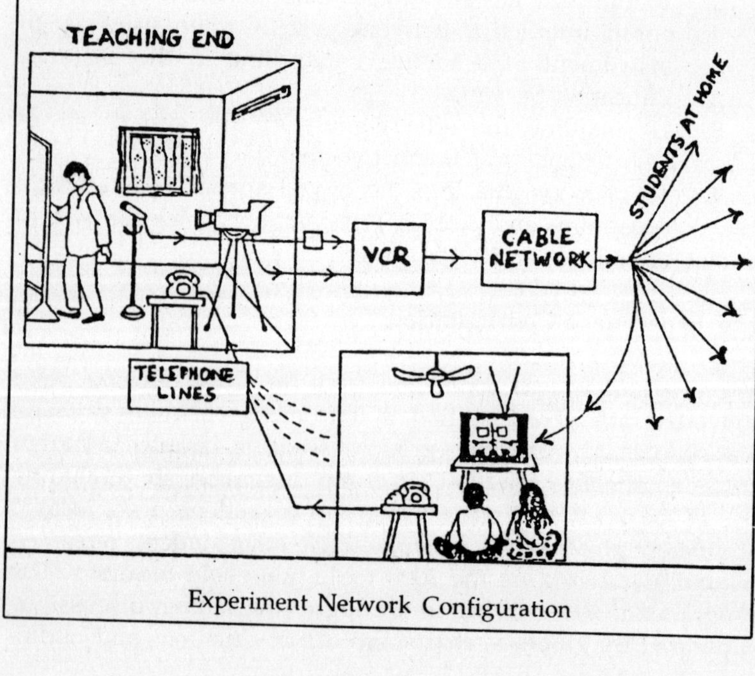

Experiment Network Configuration

Programme Structure

The subject areas selected were *(i)* Food and Nutrition, *(ii)* Communication skill development (English) *(iii)* Career counselling. Lack of knowledge, particularly among the women adversely affects the family function—its growth and health. This subject had a general appeal to all and had a special relevance for IGNOU students who were enrolled in its "Certificate Programme on Food and Nutrition." Since a large group of female students enrolled in this programme were local and this group was incidentally located on Modasa CATV network, the area of Food and Nutrition was, therefore, chosen for the experiment. Moreover the young students would be looking for guidance on career opportunities after their examinations in April, and as such they would like to improve their communications skills which would help them in preparing for various competitions and facing interviews. The programmes of the second session were oriented towards this practical aspect of life. In addition to an academic course, an application-oriented programme, therefore, had also been selected for this experiment. Each session was of forty minutes duration excluding the revision session of fifteen minutes.

The approach adopted in handling these topics, was like in counselling sessions, as well as technique-oriented with a problem solving/functional approach. This way of counselling unlike teaching is expected to generate a learning atmosphere demanding a greater involvement of students and crating a climate which helps the learners in better understanding of the course content and brings a definite improvement in their skills.

The experts at the studio-cum-teaching end consisted of Resource Persons from IGNOU Study Centre and Arts College, Modasa. Guest faculty from outside was also invited.

Some Observations

— "Necessity is the mother of invention"—the CATV interactive network configuration system has developed out of absolute field compulsions. Team-mode of efforts made it possible to develop it in record time.

- The Experiment configuration used locally available, easily affordable and simple studio systems, which required no additional manpower for its operations.
- The local resource person with the help of the usual blackboard could conduct the telecounselling/teaching sessions in their own dialect.
- The conduct of this seven days experiment has developed self-confidence in the cable operator. Realising that even if the network system is used for education, it can still become a viable commercial proposition by hiring teachers for running tutorials. The cable operator, therefore, seems to have considered this a strong reason to make it operational.
- It has been realised that an effective counselling programme needs time for publicity; identification of relevant subject areas and; such resource persons who communicate well. *Inter alia*, convincing the effectiveness of the new technology to the cable TV households in general, student population, who is currently enjoying post-examination vacation in particular, is a crucial factor. Taking into consideration all these factors including its utility a wise decision of telecasting the educational programmes after vacations once a week, therefore, has been taken by the cable operator.
- The tele-teacher unlike a normal classroom has to come well prepared. In case his answer to a question is wrong, an intelligent and knowledgeable student takes no time to ring up the teacher and to tell his mistake which is heard by everyone on the network.
- One direct telephone for Talk-back with the tele-teacher was found to be quite sufficient. With initial difficulties, the teachers could also easily adapt to the new technology and understand the question received in the Studio Centre.
- The teaching was conducted for students' groups, organised at six distant locations. However, one group of students located at the Teaching End provided a great confidence to the teacher for conduct of teaching/discussion.

— The farthest group of students was located at a distance of 2.5 km and yet the audio-video quality constantly remained good at all the locations. Though a simple video home movie system VHS camera was used in an ordinary fluorescent tube light studio, sentences written on blackboard were easily read by students.
— The programme timings were considered inconvenient by the participants. Question-answer session of 20 minutes made the programme very lively and many students wanted to even increase its duration.
— Field organisation is a real challenge which requires continuous and constant efforts. If properly managed, the network system has great potential for educational communication and possibly can become operational soon in the country.

However, on the whole the Modasa Experiment has taught us new lessons on how community resources with little additional investment and careful planning can be utilised for imparting education by private entrepreneur even without any government support.

India's Communication Challenge

There can be no meaningful communication planning in a developing country like India without consciously relating it to India's vision of a New Society evolved in major way under the leadership of Mahatma Gandhi and Jawaharlal Nehru. Also, there can be no purposeful communication-building without adapting communication to the changing socio-political imperatives and techno-economic compulsions of the contemporary world.

It is noteworthy that in recent years, modern communication technology has been introduced without evolving a communication philosophy, approach and policy relevant to Indian conditions and needs. This exercise must be done by involving practitioners of all relevant disciplines as well as a cross-section of Indian citizens. Communication is much too serious a matter to be left to the technocratic, bureaucratic and political elites alone. There exists today a wide gulf between communication experts, bureaucrats, and politicians in power who have been left free to design the communication revolution on the one hand and scientists and social scientists, specialists in the area of art and culture, social and political workers at the grass-roots, and people's representatives who constitute the social, cultural and political 'think-tank' and conscience of the Indian nation outside the state sector on the other. No effective forums have been created for necessary interaction and collaboration between the decision-makers in the field of communication and agents of development and change.

In recent years there has been no significant initiative either by state or by non-state social agencies to evolve a national-consensus on a communication policy through public discussion and dialogue. Consensus-building by latecomer nations requires taking account of nation-building and development experiences of developed capitalist as well as socialist countries. It also requires taking account of cultural traditions and communication modes as derived from India's long history—specially from its cultural renaissance and the freedom struggle. During the freedom struggle, India evolved and developed a communication philosophy and communication modes the significance of which was not restricted to the pre-independence period. These must be consciously explored and exploited for the post-independence period of nation-building, development and social change. We must also take note of the great and recent leaps in the field of communication technology and tap them for evolving a communication system suited to India's subcontinental size and diversity. In evolving this New Communication Order we must keep in view the complex and compelling needs of national integration, economic development and social emancipation in a multi-regional, multi-lingual and multi-religious society.

Cultural Past

A communication planner must always remember that India is the inheritor of a culturally rich, unified as well as diverse, civilisation having a history of thousands of years. A communication tradition, rich and refined both in theory and practice, has been an inseparable part of Indian culture and civilisation (D.P. Mukerji 1958:228-241). Yet India was one of the first among the developing countries to realise that India's requirements in today's scientific and industrial age cannot be met entirely by the traditional communication approach and modes; tradition had to be re-adapted and renovated. It was necessary to reappraise the inherited communication modes and styles in the light of contemporary challenges. Such a re-appraisal did not imply rejection but critique of tradition; it involved both assimilation and supersession. Re-appraising meant learning to synthesise the old with the new, and blending traditional communication with modern communication based on the latest scientific advances in communication theory and technology. India was much ahead of all developing countries in creating an awareness of the role of communication in nation-building and development. It was also much ahead of other developing countries in mobilising talented scientists and experts for evolving a broad perspective and strategy for communication planning suited to the goals of national development and social transformation in a country of subcontinental size and diversity and long historical tradition.

The first initiative was taken much before India won its political independence. The National Planning Committee set up by the Indian National Congress under the chairmanship of Pandit Jawaharlal Nehru recognised communication planning as an essential part of national planning. It accepted the role of communication as a powerful agent of rapid and planned development, especially in a backward country. Consequently, the National Planning Committee set up a special panel to study the communication question, to evolve a basic approach relevant to Indian conditions and to formulate guidelines for a communication plan for independent India. The panel's report on communication (1948) was a path-breaking policy document in the history of communication planning in India. Specially noteworthy were the recommendations of this panel on promoting the role of radio as a development agent. These recommendations contributed significantly towards pulling All India Radio out of the colonial communication mould and rebuilding it as a tool of social and economic development in a newly independent country.

The second major initiative was undertaken during the Indira era when the national leadership sought the guidance of eminent scientists like Homi Bhabha and Vikram Sarabhai to provide a technical blueprint for tapping the great advances in modern communication technology as an aid for planned economic and social development. The paper entitled "Television for Development" prepared by Vikram Sarabhai constituted a major conceptual advance in the field of communication planning for poor countries (Vikram Sarabhai and Kamla Chaudhury, 1974). Dr. Sarabhai's paper effectively countered the argument that countries like India were too poor to afford investment in advanced space research or in introducing modern communication technology which only the rich countries could afford. Dr. Sarabhai put forward the view that modern communication technology had a tremendous potential to contribute to the war against underdevelopment and poverty in India. Moreover, according to him, modern communication had a time-saving and distance-reducing role and this was enormously significant for latecomers in the race for development for whom *time was the scarcest resource and distance between the knowledge generating and policy-making centres and the productive classes and masses in a country of India's size constituted one of the most formidable constraints on development planning.*

Vision-Reality Gap

That modern communication should be introduced in the most backward and poor regions of the country through public investment in hardware and software with a view to promoting information transfer and to providing motivated stimulus to enable people in these regions to get out of the poverty-illiteracy trap is an innovative and revolutionary concept marking a tremendous advance both in growth theory as well as in communication theory. This new approach of "developmental communication" put India much ahead among all developing countries. It made India a pioneer in evolving new concepts and approaches to development and nation-building. This approach was concretised in the SITE experiment in rural development and mass education. It was a major landmark in communication history, which revealed how communication potential could be used as a resource for development, as a force for poverty eradication and social transformation in a predominantly agrarian country like India. The concept of community television and to community-oriented software for the village helped to blend the Gandhian vision of village reconstruction and mass uplift with the use of most advanced technology.

Following the SITE experiment, India has in recent years made phenomenal progress in extending and expanding its communication capacity and communication can now potentially cover a large part of the country and a large part of the population. Success has been achieved in bringing in large part of the rural and urban areas of the country potentially within the reach of policy and decision-making centres through modern communication. And yet this success is only partial so far as there exists a vast gap between communication *potential* and its actual exploitation. On the one hand, there exists the *potential* of modern communication to cover every region, remote or close to the centre, and to encompass every section of society, rural or urban, rich or poor. On the other, it is only the privileged classes and regions which have actual access to the benefits of modern communication technology. This is borne out by the fact that most of the five million or so television sets are concentrated in metropolitan centres and urbanised villages. The *potential-actual* lag is also confirmed by the fact that the television programmes on the whole are not development-and-social-change-promoting, that they are largely elite-oriented and not mass-oriented; that they are entertainment-oriented and not information and education-oriented.

Further, equally disquieting is the *vision-reality gap*. Social resources and public funds are provided for modern communication in a poor and underdeveloped country on the basis of professed objectives of utilising the vast potential of communication for development of the majority and their cultural enrichment. In practice, however, there is a sharp departure from the professed social goals; communication far from reducing the gap between: rich and poor, elite and masses, urban and rural areas and the centre and the periphery is in fact widening it. These trends have emerged on account of sharp deviation from the Bhabha-Sarabhai approach to communication planning and to the earlier approach of the Communication Panel set up by the National Planning Committee.

What is disquieting today is that in the communication sector the clarification of *ends* has lagged behind the sophistication of *means*. Further, the concept of planning has been relegated to the background, and communication development has been equated with accelerated transfer of communication technology from developed to underdeveloped countries. Here is a situation of lop-sided emphasis on *means* without any concept of integrating *means* and social *ends*. Technology without a social framework is bound to have unintended consequences. Let us remember that technology is not culture-neutral. Thus the hiatus between *ends* and *means* has the unintended consequence of converting the *means* (i.e., technology) into an autonomous carrier of culture values and life-styles from the affluent to the poor countries; uncritical borrowing of technology exposes the borrower to cultural invasion by the richer countries. The communication revolution is thus acting as a powerful promoter of international demonstration effect; the logical consequence of this process is the explosion of "elite of consumerism" in the borrower country. The transfer of communication technology in its present form is thus sharply accentuating "structural dualism" within the country.

Relevant Models

India's recent communication revolution is most conspicuously an engineers' revolution and not yet truly a national communication revolution. It is predominantly an exercise in *physical engineering* which is still to be transformed into innovative *social engineering*. We must recognise that we do not have a readymade model of communication revolution suited to a developing country like India. There is on the one hand the untapped potential of modern communication technology for poor countries and on the other its inability to realise this potential and adapt it to the needs of agrarian societies fighting poverty, illiteracy and social inequality. *This untapped potential has yet to be transformed into a Development Communication Model suited to India*. Since the communication revolution belongs to the post-industrial stage of economic evolution, in its present form it suits the affluent rather than the poor countries. A mechanical transfer of the communication models of affluent countries benefits the affluent sections of the Indian society and not the vast masses in the rural and urban areas (P.C. Joshi

1985: 1-27). The National Planning Committee Panel on Communication and the Bhabha-Sarabhai approach to communication treated communication planning not as mindless imitation of Western countries but as a creative exercise in terms of evolving communication models suited to poor countries. The SITE experiment was the first exercise in this direction on a pilot basis to be later extended to all parts of the country. However, instead of such extension what followed was the abandonment of even the limited experiment in favour of an entertainment-cum-propaganda-oriented communication approach through the national network.

The earlier tradition of innovative thinking in communication matters needs, however, to be reviewed, thus replacing the value-neutral, technocratic planning by social goal-oriented, value-oriented, planning. There is an urgent need to bridge the widening gap between *physical* and *social* engineering, between *hardware* and *software*, between *means* and *ends*. This can only be done after a national debate and dialogue involving engineers and social scientists, hardware producers and software producers, message-makers and recipients of the message, communicators and development and change agents. India has a large intellectual community encompassing both natural and social sciences. It has also high quality expertise in classical, folk and traditional arts and culture. We have development specialists and change agents combining competence with dedication both within the state structure and outside. Despite this great wealth of human resources which India possesses, there has been no significant attempt in recent times to involve the large community of gifted professionals and enlightened citizens in creative thinking on vital issues, thrown up by the communication revolution.

An Indian communicator has to derive the value premises and perspective for communication from the vision of a New India inherited from the Indian renaissance and from an understanding and insight into nation-building and development challenges of the present age. *Clarity about the concepts of nation-building, development and social transformation are, therefore, essential for clarity in the approach to communication.* And clarity about communication approach is necessary for clarity about social mobilisation strategies of development and social change. In recent years, the broader question of the perspective and path of India's nation-building, development and change have been largely evaded by the Indian intellectual and political elite.

The Nehru Vision

Jawaharlal Nehru was perhaps the last in the chain of national thinkers on perspectives and paths of development and social change in India. He can be called the last of the philosophers of nation-building in India, who consciously tried to evolve a broader view by placing India in the world context and to formulate a synthetic view by taking all the important national viewpoints and approaches into account. Nehru viewed the problems of India with a sense of history; he viewed them as problems of a latecomer to the scientific and industrial age, trying desperately to skip several stages and epochs of the normal transition to the modern age as exemplified in the case of the Western countries. Nehru also evolved the concept of avoiding the social costs and political pitfalls associated with Western path of industrialisation.

Nehru internalised in this approach the fundamental Gandhian concerns for integrating the moral issue with the economic issue and of preserving harmony between man and nature in the development process. More importantly, Nehru was perhaps the only national leader who clearly traced the roots of India's loss of political independence under colonialism to the fact that a modern scientific and industrial revolution had eluded India. He also clearly identified the roots of India's inner crises to the fact that the Indian society failed to resolve the issue of economic and social inequality. In Nehru's view, the persistence of the worst forms of inequality had incapacitated the Indian people to such an extent that they could not make the desired transition towards a unified nationhood. Nehru grasped and appreciated the vast dimensions and tasks of nation-building arising from the historical context of India's arrested growth for several centuries and her belated entry into the arena of modern development based on acceptance of scientific temper on the one hand and social justice and equality on the other.

In this context, Nehru interpreted the perspective of nation-building for development countries of Asia not in terms of an evolutionary sequence of stage-by-stage development. In his view,

Asia could no longer afford a gradualist path covering several centuries. In the Western case, social changes created the conditions for the economic take-off and the economic breakthrough created the conditions for political democracy and the welfare state. In the Asian case, this West-European, sequential pattern was rendered topsy-turvy. Take the case of India where vast political changes like the introduction of adult franchise and the concept of social justice and a welfare state preceded economic and social development. As a result, India had no option but to "leap-frog," thus skipping several intermediate stages. India had to work for an almost simultaneous consummation of four historical transitions (P.N. Haksar 1979: 20-21) which have taken several centuries in the Western context. These transitions were as follows:

(a) The transition from a pre-industrial agricultural economy based predominantly on primitive technology and on subsistence to an agro-industrial economy based on modern science and advanced technology and on commodity production;

(b) The transition from a hierarchical, and closed social system based on social inequality and lack of individual freedom to an open and just society based on individual freedom, mobility and equality of opportunity;

(c) The transition from a traditional orientation based on fear of the supernatural and on blind religiosity to a modern secular and scientific outlook;

(d) And, the transition from an authoritarian, upper class and monarchical political regime to a democratic, popular and welfare-oriented nation-state.

Nehru carried forward Gandhi's heroic endeavour to re-interpret the meaning of anti-colonial movements sweeping Asian countries. The ideologues of the pre-Gandhi era were inclined to interpret India's anti-colonial struggle in narrow terms of the overthrow of the colonial regime oppressing the Indian people and its replacement by a native regime. Gandhi imparted new content to the anti-colonial movement in terms of rejection of Westernisation in favour of alternative paths of modernisation and in terms of emancipation of the vast masses from the economic and social burdens imposed by colonial rulers and their native allies. Nehru carried forward this Gandhian heritage of exploring non-Western model of development and of bridge-building between national liberation and socio-economic emancipation.

Nehru's major contribution lay in perceiving and exploring the complementary and mutually reinforcing role of the freedom struggle and the struggle for socio-economic emancipation. This was of historical significance because previously the freedom fighters were indifferent to social and economic objectives and fighters for the social and economic causes were not sufficiently sensitive to the economic and social implication of the freedom struggle. Nehru made a historical contribution by promoting an integrated view of the national and the socio-economic tasks.

Nehru regarded the national revolution as a vehicle for socio-economic transformation, and he saw in socio-economic development and transformation the continuation of the national revolution under the sponsorship of the nation-state. In his view, nation-building must be interpreted in the broadest sense of the term and must encompass social and economic transformation. Then alone can it provide a unifying frame to all the productive and patriotic classes of India in the new era following the achievement of political independence. From this perspective, nation-building could no longer be interpreted in the nineteenth-century terms of economic and social development unrelated to social justice and democratic rights for the masses. The search, therefore, was for a new model of nation-building and development which harmonised growth with social justice within the framework of political democracy and which transformed development into a means of national integration in a multi-regional, multi-lingual and multi-ethnic society.

New Approach

What theorists of economic and social development wrote about the complexity of nation-building and development processes in developing countries like India in the period following the Second World War was anticipated by Gandhi and Nehru by a few decades. Commenting on the dissimilarities between European and Asian nationalism, Gunnar Myrdal, for instance, remarks how in Asia "the historical process that in Europe spanned centuries is telescoped within a few decades and the order of happenings is deranged." Further, "there is no practical possibility in any of the South Asian countries of chaining the forces of nationalism and inaugurating a sequence of events like that in Europe where first the feudal order was overcome by the strong stages and the church gradually weakened. In these states, nationalism could thereafter grow while the time ripened for political democracy founded on general literacy and for egalitarian reforms. Even if it were possible, which it is not, to stamp out nationalism, the events that unfolded in this sequence in Europe could not occur, in any case not so rapidly as South Asia required because of the population explosion and for many other reasons. The difficulties in this syncopation of policies, the historical necessity of which is seen by all enlightened elements, intellectuals and political leaders in the region are immense." (Gunnar Myrdal, 1968: 2109-2119).

India was perhaps unique among developing countries in evolving and upholding the vision of building a just society based on the application of modern science and technology within the framework of a political democracy and an open policy based on pursuit of world peace and international co-operation. The fundamental premises of a new approach to nation-building and development implicit in this approach were as follows:

(a) An endeavour to harmonise growth based on modern science and technology with social justice i.e., with the widest access to the fruits of growth, wide popular participation in growth processes and sharing of power;

(b) An endeavour to achieve basic changes in socio-economic structures required both for growth and social justice without larger-scale restriction of liberty, coercion and violence, that is an endeavour to achieve a comprehensive and deep-going social transformation with "the consent of the people," by narrowing the scope of conflict and tension and by preserving the fundamental freedoms of a free society;

(c) An endeavour to push a people rooted in the habits and outlook of a pre-industrial, ancient civilisation and

culture on the path of modernisation, that is, acceptance of scientific temper and a secular outlook, pursuit of material progress and prosperity along with social equality, individual freedom and women's emancipation within the framework of a political democracy;

(d) An endeavour to combine *(e)* with rootedness in the national tradition and in moral values and ideals nourished and upheld by a succession of saints and sages thrown up by India in its long history which found expression in the concept of a good life seeking harmony between individual fulfilment and collective good, between the self and non-self all through the ages;

(e) An endeavour to harmonise the pursuit of national interest with that of international brotherhood, co-operation and peace and to correct India's over-exposure to the Anglo-American blocs and to promote scientific, cultural and economic exchange, contact and co-operation with all parts of the world, specially with countries of the Socialist and Third worlds;

(f) And, the endeavour to promote unity in diversity within the country taking adequate cognizance of the multi-religious, multi-ethnic, multi-lingual nature of the society and civilisation of country like India having sub-continental size and diversity.

While reaffirming this vision and the path of development inherent in the pursuit of this vision, Nehru recognised the inner strains and stresses, tensions and conflicts which were a source of acute anxiety and concern to him during the closing years of his life. We reproduce below some of Nehru's observations which embody both re-affirmation of his commitment to this vision and a concern and anxiety at the new social and economic trends thwarting the realisation of this vision. To quote:

"We are far from being averse to change; we have embarked upon far-reaching changes and we propose to preserve with our plans and programmes; but we are convinced that the methods by which changes are brought about are at least as important as the changes themselves. We believe that any change should come through our own volition, as a result of our own experience and that it should not be foisted on us through any kind of force or pressure. In the pursuit of change, we should seek to carry the mass of the people with us and win their support. This way of dealing with our problems may not result in as swift or spectacular transformation as we might wish, but at least the progress achieved will have a solid basis in the nation's consent and avoid a degree of dislocation and disorganisation that we can ill afford.

"It is in this spirit that we have set our hand to the task of developing in this ancient land, a system combining political democracy and economic justice.

"Can this enterprise survive the new strains and stresses? The question goes to the heart of the issues involved in the present conflict, and the answer lies only in part, though perhaps in large part, with us in India, I am confident in my own mind that we cannot let ourselves be panicked into abandoning either the goal or the methods of our policy as I have stated it" (Jawaharlal Nehru, 1965: 541-542).

Creative Minority

In the post-Nehru era, the issue of the relationship between the Gandhi-Nehru vision of a new India and the actual course of Indian evolution has been raised again and again from political platforms as well as academic forums. Do processes of Indian economic, social and political development broadly correspond to the vision articulated and cherished by Nehru to the last? Or does one witness a widening gap between vision and reality, and increasing departure from both the goals and the methods underlying the vision? There are some who believe that a deviation from the vision has occurred not because of a conscious break from the goals, path and the methods but because of the weakness of instruments available to Nehru and his successors or forged by Nehru and his successors to realise the vision (P.N. Haksar, 1979: 18-30). There are others who hold the view that the vision itself was progressively diluted, specially the hard core of the vision's relation to radical changes in the internal economic and social structure, with a view to ensuring national unity by soft-pedalling class issues. As a result, the mass mobilisation for class issues was relegated to the background. And yet a third view focusses attention on the progressive dilution of the revolutionary content of this vision but finds the source of dilution in the formidable pressure from vested interests and the endeavour of the ruling political elite to explore the possibilities of development without attacking the dominant interest groups (Gunnar Myrdal, 1968). According to this view the weakness of instruments was not inherent in the objective situation but arose from political compromise by the political elite under the pressure of vested interests and as a sequel to the absence of organised pressure from the masses. In this background, patriotic and radical social forces perceive new possibilities of overcoming the ignorance and passivity of the masses and of transforming them into a political force with the aid of Communication Revolution.

It is important to note that a certain communication approach and philosophy was also implicitly in Nehru's social philosophy and vision. Generalising from the history of India from ancient to the modern times, Nehru observed that no country or civilisation could progress without the existence of a creative minority; but the existence of a creative minority was a necessary and not a sufficient condition (Jawaharlal Nehru, 1956: 82-83). A creative minority can act as a force for progress only when it can communicate with the vast majority and is able to capture their imagination with the new concepts. Nehru was of the view that the communication between the creative minority and the majority had acquired a much greater role and significance in the context of India's commitment to build a just society within a democratic framework and to ensure higher levels of living to her vast and growing population. In Nehru's own words, "democratic planning requires widespread understanding in order to link millions and millions of people in a common task." Further: "We can hardly have a political democracy without mass education. In other countries, full-blooded political democracy came after education had spread a good deal as a result of the economic revolution which had prepared the ground for it. But in most Asian countries, certainly in India, we have taken a high jump to hundred per cent political democracy without the wherewithal to supply the demands which a politically conscious electorate makes. That is the essence of the problem in all Asian countries. All our political life is really concerned with how rapidly we can bridge this hiatus between the desires and fulfilment" (Jawaharlal Nehru, 1964).

Leadership implied, in Nehru's view, combining the role of a "prophet" with that of a "politician": the prophetic element implied the capacity to look ahead beyond the immediate concerns and to lead the people even against their natural inclinations. The role of a politician implies taking full account of the inclinations, interests and even weaknesses and prejudices of the people at a given moment and not to get cut off from them while trying to take them forward. A leader in other words has to be not only forward-looking and innovative in thought and action; he has also to be a good communicator in the sense that he should be able to translate progressive ideas into concepts, images and messages which are understood by the people and which can influence their action and behaviour (Jawaharlal Nehru, 1956: 457-458).

A vision of nation-building and development which remains confined to an elite and which is not shared by the vast majority loses its importance as a propelling force for change. In the context of the vision-reality gap mentioned earlier, a view has been expressed that this gap has been growing not merely because of the increasing influence of the vested interests; it has also been growing because of the widening communication gap between the elite and the masses on the other. The failure of the elite to communicate with the masses and the constraints experienced by the masses in communicating with the elite have significantly contributed towards creating and accentuating the vision-reality gap.

Aims of Research

Gandhi had once remarked that the realisation of a noble idea was dependent on dedicated "human agents." The freedom struggle had thrown up political activists who were also excellent communicators of the message of freedom at the grass-roots. *For a single Gandhi at the top, there were lakhs of smaller Gandhis at the grass-roots working among the people and carrying to them the message of freedom and social change.* During the era of development and social change following the achievement of independence, the principal reliance was placed on the state agencies and not on creating human agents as capable communicators to vast millions still dependent on the oral mode of communication. The *communication barrier* between the elite and the masses was no less formidable than the *class* barrier in restricting the scope of mass participation in development and in denying the masses the benefits of a series of legislative enactments of which they were often uninformed and ignorant. The important point to note is that the more advanced the communication technology, the greater the scope for the class barrier to be reinforced by the communication barrier and the greater was also the dominance of the communication and information system by the privileged classes and social strata. Nation-building and development process in conformity with the social vision thus require social activists in vast numbers who can serve as communicators of the message of social change and development. *Communication technology is no substitute for the sensitive communicator who uses the technology for desired purpose and ends.*

The purpose of the proposed research programme on communication for India is to explore both the *constraints* and *possibilities* of the communication revolution in relation to and in the context of the background provided above. The programme should try to bring together a representative group from different social science disciplines like economics, sociology, political science, history, social psychology, etc., and from different fields of traditional and modern culture along with communication and media experts. The programme should explore the trends of change in the social and economic structure and the processes and dynamics of development from the point of view of achieving the goals of economic *Swarajya* and national integration on the one hand and equality and social justice on the other. It should also discuss and evaluate the concept of secularism on the basis of experience and reformulate this concept in response to new challenges and problems in the context of growing communal, ethnic and religious tensions and conflicts. It should focus specially on the growing threats to the goals of national integration and just society from the emergence of a 'dual society' in recent years (V.K.R.V. Rao, 1980).

The discussion on communication planning should be focussed on identifying the constraints on growth with social justice from the growing linkages between communication and elite consumerism and on exploring an alternative strategy of communication as part of an alternative strategy of development which aims at enabling the vast masses in rural and urban areas to cross the barrier of poverty and illiteracy and at setting them on the path of socio-economic emancipation. It should also study the socio-economic implications of an over-centralised communication structure and should explore the possibilities of an alternative communication model which is conducive to promoting unity in diversity, continuity and change suited to an ancient civilisation with rich cultural traditions and to a multi-regional, multi-lingual, multi-religious country.

Finally, it should explore the concept of meaningful life-styles and the new dimensions of national cultural identity in the context of the vastly enlarged scope for erosion of this identity and of distortion of life styles with the modern communication technology opening up developing countries including India to the "cultural invasion" from the West. The programme should focus specially on processes of "pseudo-modernisation" on the one hand and cultural revivalism and fundamentalism on the other getting vastly accentuated through the introduction of modern technology in general and communication technology in particular unrelated to a nationally relevant social philosophy and value-system.

The specific questions for the research programme can be spelled out as follows:

Major question for the Research Programme on "Communication in the context of Nation-Building, development and social change".

Question I

(i) What concepts of nation-building and development are relevant for latecomer societies like India? To what extent the Gandhi-Nehru approach served this purpose in the past and what is its relevance?

(ii) What problems were posed for Indian nationalists by the colonial ideology and by the colonial strategy of modernisation and what were the divergent responses in India to the colonial challenge?

(iii) Did the Indian response to the challenge of modernisation correspond to a Western liberal-democratic approach? What new elements and features characterised the Indian response under Gandhi's leadership? What

was the socialist impact on the Indian response?

(iv) Did the Indian response belong to the species of a "bourgeois approach"? Or did it emerge as "a New Third World Approach" under the Gandhi-Nehru leadership?

Question II

Communication as a force in evolution of human societies in general and evolution of modern societies in particular:

(a) What were the communication concepts and modes relevant for human progress and emancipation through the ages?

(b) What are the communication concepts and modes relevant for class and colonial oppression and exploitation?

(c) What were the communication concepts and modes which are being harnessed in the service of democracy, human rights and socialism in developed and developing countries?

(d) What has been the role of media and communication in the freedom struggle and the national cultural renaissance and what are its lessons for today?

Question III

What alternatives can be envisaged in terms of planning media and communication systems for India:

(a) Alternatives in approach and philosophy

(b) Alternatives in the planning of hardware

(c) Alternatives in the planning of software

(d) Alternatives in the management and administrative structures with a view to harmonising autonomy with accountability.

Question IV Specific Issues

The following specific issues can be posed and identified for specialised studies:

(i) Communication model or national integration.
(ii) Communication strategy for poverty eradication in a predominantly agrarian society with illiterate population.
(iii) Communication support for children, emancipation of women and uplift of weaker sections.
(iv) Communication support for eradication of illiteracy and for primary education and educational development.
(v) Communication support for cultural planning:
   (a) Communication and people's culture;
   (b) Communication and classical performing arts.

Question V

Country studies for communication planning in Third World countries with special reference to communication support for rural transformation.

Role of Computers

While the focus of public consumer attention has quite naturally been put on reception systems, very major changes—of great importance to broadcasting—have taken place in the origination of TV signals. Transportable satellite uplink stations working with outdoor recording units have made it feasible to originate a TV programme from any place within the coverage zone of a satellite. Thus, events of importance and interest—news, sports, etc.—can be broadcast in real-time from the actual locale, however remote it may be. Further, the transportable stations have, with technological advances in both earth station and satellite technologies, been getting smaller and thus more mobile.

In India, an indigenous truck-mounted transportable terminal was designed, developed and demonstrated by ISRO over a decade ago (in 1976, with the ATS-6 satellite). This terminal has since been used for a large number of demonstrations, and is today being operationally used on a routine basis to provide the uplink to INSAT from Hyderabad for the Andhra Pradesh regional TV network. While this terminal uses a 6.1 m diameter antenna, it is now possible to provide a satellite-based news-gathering (SNG) service with even a 2.5 m diameter terminal and an amplifier of about 20 watts output. Terminals of this type are now beginning to proliferate in the advanced countries, and an indigenous one may soon be demonstrated by ISRO.

Use of satellites for radio broadcasting is, of course, a far simpler proposition since it involves transmission/reception of only a voice channel. INSAT is already providing the means for networking of all the radio stations in the country, leading to a far superior technical quality of such networked programmes (e.g., news). Apart from the fixed uplinking (origination) capability from the four major cities, there are also transportable terminals for originating programmes from any location in the country.

The technical feasibility of direct broadcasting of radio programmes via satellite to simple receivers has been established by various studies. The satellite configuration and cost would depend upon whether such broadcasts are to be received at fixed sites or by mobile units (car radios, for example). While both are technically feasible and within the range of present-day technology, the costs of such a service do not make it attractive—especially where an extensive ground network of radio stations already exists. No such direct radio-broadcast satellite is operational now, anywhere in the world, and neither do firm plans exist to set up such a system.

Satellite radio-broadcasting has been used for many years for educational purposes (e.g., by the University of the South Pacific). However, the mode is basically one of teleconferencing, rather than broadcasting as normally understood. USAID, through its Rural Programme, has also initiated experiments in the use of audio-teleconferencing in a number of countries. These experiments have used existing satellites, and have focussed on their use for such purposes rather than on developing new technologies/systems.

Future trends in satellite broadcasting technology are in the direction of using higher frequencies (12 GHz and above), higher power, spot beams, smaller and lower-cost DRS, and superior quality (high-definition TV, stereophonic sound). In the advanced countries, direct broadcasting has not been used as extensively as its protagonist had expected a decade ago. In the United States, in particular, it has made little headway—mainly because the networking mode combined with the rapid expansion of cable TV systems has provided viewers with a vast choice of channel. In the more remote areas, TVRO terminals (cheap, mini receive-only earth terminals, rather than DRS) have sprouted widely and advancing technology (and lower costs) have really blurred the dividing line between the TVRO and DRS.

Europe and Japan, on the other hand, are proceeding with direct broadcast systems, and the last few years have—if anything—seen a revival in interest in them in these countries. Australia and China too seem to be proceeding in the same direction. However, the only systems using the 2.5 GHz band for direct (or, given the power levels, quasi-direct) broadcasting via satellite are INSAT and ARABSAT (a consortium of Arab countries).

Computers and Broadcasting

The widespread use of computers for any function connected directly with broadcasting is of recent origin, and is even now limited to a few countries. The use of computers in broadcasting is for different aspects: in programme production, transmission, planning and scheduling, and house-keeping.

The major and growing use of computers in programme production has made possible vast improvements in technical quality, provided greater flexibility and given rise to innovative approaches to production. Microprocessors are now an integral part of all major studio equipment—cameras, VCR's, time-base correctors, vision mixers, etc. However, the impact is greater in terms of post-production and for such purposes as sub-titling and animation. Computer animation, in particular, has tremendous potential utility, especially for educational/ instructional programmes.

Computers are also used in some networks for transmission; for on-line programmed cueing of programmes and operation of VCRs as per the schedule.

On an off-line basis, computers are very useful in optimal scheduling of facilities and for planning purposes. An important use is for retrieval of programme information, enabling appropriate scheduling of programmes. It also enables the selection of appropriate "filler," on the basis of pre-determined criteria (e.g., a 150-second filler, that has not been transmitted in the last four months and on a health topic). Computerisation of the tape library can be done at the overall programme level, or it can also include brief descriptions of shots, enabling full use—through immediate access—of stock shots. Other off-line uses are for transmission content analysis, how many times a particular tape has been played, how many times it has been erased, etc.

Computers are also used for house-keeping and management functions. This includes a stores inventory of spares, facilitating immediate access to information and providing appropriate inventory control. It can also be used to monitor the output per day, the output of each producer, number of appearances of an artiste, programme budgets, etc.

However, most of these—except for computer animation—probably reflect only incremental improvements to present systems. A really new application is the use of computers for teletext and videotex. This provides access to a massive amount and wide variety of information—sometimes on an interactive basis—stored in a central computer. The potential uses of such a system seem exciting, but somehow (like satellite direct broadcasting) the early promise has not been fulfilled. Only in France does there seem to be large-scale use and, being an interactive system, it is provided through the telecommunication network. In India, while a teletext service has been started in Delhi, it is limited in scope, and expensive. A widening in the scope of services, its extension via satellite to the whole country and a lowering of equipment costs could serve to reinforce such other, and make full use of the great potential to teletext.

Though not strictly a "broadcasting" service, computer-to-computer communication, or computer networking on a wide scale has many promising applications, if used in the broadcast (i.e., one to very many) mode. For example, it is possible to prepare a text-graphic "lesson" on a computer and then transmit this via satellite to all the computers in a network, for use locally. Now, technology has led to the development of low cost terminals for such computer networking. Already, the National Informatics Centre is setting up such a network (NICNET) for inter-connecting its computer centres in all district headquarters to Delhi. The rapid fall in the price of micro-computers ("Personal Computers") along with the low cost of a satellite networking terminal makes it feasible to think of a range of applications involving computer networking.

Satellites and Computers in Broadcasting

India was among the pioneers in the use of satellites for broadcasting. SITE in 1975-76 was the first large-scale use of direct-from-satellite TV broadcasting. Even now, India, through INSAT, continues to be among the few countries that use direct broadcasting.

A major use of INSAT has been the networking of TV transmitters. Almost all the approximately 250 transmitters in the network are connected to INSAT is the only source for programmes. Through INSAT, any transmitter can be linked to a central originating point. As noted earlier, it is this that made possible the very rapid expansion of the TV network, without awaiting the setting up of programme-origination facilities at each location.

Apart from networking the transmitters for the national programme, and providing a programme-feed to all the low and very low power TV transmitters (LPTs and VLPTs), INSAT has also made it possible to have two separate regional TV networks: in Maharashtra and Andhra Pradesh. While the direct broadcasting and national/general networking is done using the two S-band transponders on INSAT, the regional networks use a single C-band transponder in a two-channels-per transponder mode.

INSAT is also used to originate programme from various locations in the country. Thus, major sports events, in particular, have been seen "live" all over the country irrespective of the site of the event. Occasionally, news-feed has also been done from some locations via satellite, for incorporation in the national news bulletins. Such origination has so far depended upon fairly large transportable terminals, and true SNG terminals are not yet in use.

INSAT use for radio has been primarily for networking all the radio stations, providing thereby a reliable and high-quality means of relaying national programmes. Limited use has also been made of the capability to originate programmes from various locations.

On an experimental basis, video tele-conferencing has been done in India, using India's first experimental communication satellite, APPLE was also used for an interactive educational experiment, when a video course on satellite communication was relayed via APPLE to four locations, and students at these locations could ask questions (relayed via satellite) to the instructor for an immediate, on-screen reply.

The use of computers in broadcasting has so far been very limited. The facilities for computer animation are extremely few, and computer-aided post-production is yet to really begin. Use of computers for planning, library purposes and house-keeping is fairly new yet, and both the expertise and "culture" for this are yet to spread. As mentioned, teletext is operational in Delhi, but its scope is yet limited. However, in all these fields, the interest and need are high, and the expertise is now building up to the critical mass necessary for really widespread use.

Future Possibilities and Implications

From even the very cursory assessment made here, it is obvious that the technologies of satellites and computers have had a very considerable effect on broadcasting in India. Certainly satellites have been responsible for very dramatic developments in the area of television. Computers have not yet had the same magnitude of direct impact, but do promise to substantially affect not only the hardware systems, but also the software. Further advances in not only satellite and computer technology but also in broadcasting, are bound to be rapid. The coming together of these in a synergistic manner is, therefore, certain to have major implications.

Larger satellites—already being fabricated in India (INSAT-II)—will enable the setting up of many more regional networks. Advances in related ground systems should lead to a reduction in the cost of DRS, enabling TV to reach those areas not covered by VHF TV transmitters. It would also make possible comparatively low-cost "talk-back" terminals for interactive learning. Advanced SNG terminals would enable "live" coverage of events from even remote locations.

Large computers with constantly updated data-bases on a wide variety of topic and low-cost decoders would be available, leading to the widespread use of teletext, which would be available country-wide via satellite. Low-cost computer-networking satellite-terminals will enable interactive access to data and computing power, between small and large computers. It will also make possible the distribution via satellite of graphics-cum-text learning/training material from a central location to thousands of PCs.

Use of computer graphics and computer animation will become routine, especially in educational TV programmes. Producers will be able to locate and stock-shots almost instantly by checking through a computerised library-search programme. Programme editing will become sophisticated and the producer can see what the edited version will look like before doing the actual editing. All this can lead to an improvement in programme quality. This would, however, be meaningful only if such techniques are used for producing socially relevant programmes. If it only results in more polished packaging of commercials, the advances would be of little value.

Many persons have—quite rightly—been concerned with the centralising tendencies that seem to be inherent in many advanced technologies. Satellites, for example, make it feasible to blanket a country with a single programme, originating from a single point. Similarly, good communication networks and large computers can lead to centralised decision-making. However, actual experience shows that appropriate system design backed by enlightened policy can, in fact, promote a different approach. Thus, access to large data bases can facilitate decentralised decision-making. Similarly, a satellite can be used to develop regional networks, rather than only a national network. More important, SNG systems can be used to bring in programme inputs from various locations, including especially rural and remote areas. Not only will this enrich the programming, it will also serve to "educate" urban viewers and bring about genuine integration. So far, only the reach of the satellite system has received great emphasis; equally important is this aspect of "from anywhere."

Availability of more channels (through direct broadcasting) could provide adequate time for educational and developmental broadcasts; it would also provide diversity and choice, and thus move away from the narrowness and single-mindedness that a single channel sometimes engenders.

While new technologies will make possible low cost DRS, this will have real meaning and relevance only if it is used for providing access to the disadvantaged through community sets. Any system design that does not provide for such access through community VHF set and DRS (which are required for the 40 per cent population—all rural and largely in backward areas—not within the coverage range of VHF transmitters) can only accentuate the elitist and hedonistic tendencies that are already evident, and will inevitably lead to a social upheaval.

It would seem that advances in satellite and computer technologies offer us an opportunity to redesign our system configurations to take advantage of their emerging possibilities. We could use them to further education, to provide choice and promote diversity, to reflect and nourish the richness of different languages and cultures and to strongly support "integrated decentralisation" or diversity-within-unity. Such possibilities exist, but can be realised only by conscious choice and political will. It not, it is entirely possible that the technological vector will push us into the direction of a homogenised, mechanistic, consumerist elite, living parasitically on a mass of deprived, disadvantaged people.

References

Braid, R., 1979, Cited in: *Development Communication*, Asian Mass Communication Research and Information Centre, Singapore.

Habermann, P. and De Fontgalland, G., 1978, *Development Communication—Rhetoric and Reality*, Asian Mass Communication Research and Information Centre, Singapore.

Johnston, M., 1982, Can Mass Media Change Behaviour, *J. Ext. 20:* 10-14.

Quebral, N., 1975, Cited in: *Development Communication*, Asian Mass Communication Research and Information Centre, Singapore.

Samanta, R.K., 1990, *Development Communication for Agriculture* (Ed.), New Delhi, B.R. Pub. Corporation.

Sondhi, K., 1981, *Problems of Communication in Developing Countries*, Vision Books, New Delhi.

Venkatappiah, B., 1984, Communication for Development, *Social Change*, 14(1): 3-8.

Yadava, J.S., 1986, Mass Media and Social Change in India, *Social Change*, 16 (243).

4

Communications and Society: Affirmations and Contradictions

When prehistoric man sat before his campfire describing to his son the most efficient way of stalking a prey, one of his concerns was the effect his lesson would have on the child. When the medieval court jester practiced a new trick or learned a new joke, he was concerned with how his communications would be received by members of the court. When a Presidential candidate rewrites a speech for the second or third time, carefully stages the speaker's platform, and hires a make-up man, he is obviously concerned with the effect his message will have on the voting public. In short, the assumption that communications can and do have effects underlies almost all communication behaviour. Indeed, most communications are produced with the intent of structuring a situation for someone else, of influencing him to act, or believe, or feel in a certain way.

On the other hand, millions have been spent on advertising campaigns which have led to no discernible change in the behaviour of consumers; thousands of words have been exchanged by diplomats around peace tables, yet wars go on and on; and in spite of all the conversation implied in courtship, marriage, and years of living together, practically every husband or wife on earth has at one time or another "failed to communicate" with his or her spouse. Are we then to assume that only some communications have effects, or that communications are effective only some of the time? Is there any way to predict which communications will lead to the desired results, or when a message will be effective?

Perhaps even more to the point, we might ask what we mean by the "effects" of communication. If we speak to a friend, or send a business letter, or write a newspaper story, what is it that we expect to happen? Indeed, what are the consequences of the very fact that we are capable of speaking to a friend, sending a letter, or writing a newspaper story?

In the pages that follow we attempt to examine what is meant by the effects of *communication*—the process—and by the effects of *communications*—specific messages produced with some intent on the part of the communicator. For the most part, we will look at one half of the communication dyad, concentrating on how a person interprets and responds to communications, assuming that the message has gotten through, that it has not been ignored, or avoided, or overlooked.

We will look first at the consequences of man's unique ability to engage in social communication. Next we will turn to more specific results of particular communications. Finally, we shall briefly examine the nature of mass communication effects.

Consequences of the Communication Process

Information and the Environment. In the opening chapter of this book, Wilbur Schramm defines information as any content which reduces uncertainty or the number of possible alternatives in a situation. Another way of saying this is that information is any content that helps one *structure* or *organise* those aspects of the environment which are relevant to a situation in which he must act. For example, suppose you are at point *A* and wish to go to some distant point *B*, but that you have no idea where point *B* is located. This is a highly unstructured situation. There could be a vast number of alternative roads you might take, roads leading to all points of the compass, no one of which seems any more certain than any other to lead you to your destination. To the extent that information which will structure this situation is available, you can reduce your uncertainty by reducing the number of alternative roads likely to lead to point *B*. Simply the information that *B* is in a southerly direction from

A would enable you to eliminate many of the roads you might have chosen to follow. As you add other pieces of information--say that point *B* is near some mountains—you can probably further reduce the number of likely alternative roads. In other words, each new piece of information enables you to formulate a clearer picture of the best way to get from point *A* to point *B*, to build a kind of map. Indeed, the most useful information you could get would be that contained in a map showing the various routes leading from *A* to *B*. Such a map would completely structure the spatial aspects of this situation, reducing uncertainty about alternative routes to almost zero. (However, some uncertainty could still exist if you were also interested in taking the most scenic route, or the best-paved road, or the highway with the most gasoline stations. Depending on the road map, other information might be needed to structure the environment on dimensions such as these.)

Our example of how information provides structure to the environment need not be limited to humans or map-making. As Kenneth Boulding has pointed out, in order to function successfully all living systems, whether one-celled organisms or human beings, structure or form an "image" of aspects of their environment which are relevant to whatever goals they might pursue, regardless of how we define goal (e.g., survival, freedom from tension, money, happiness).[1] Were it not for the ability to use information to organise the environment, it would be difficult to conceive of anything but random behaviour on the part of organisms. Thus, for example, bacteria in a Petri dish must organise their environment, the culture medium, at least into nutrient and nonnutrient; plants must structure their environment in order to "decide" where to send out roots in search of water and which way to orient to take best advantage of light sources; wild animals must organise their environment so that more probable sources of water or locations of food are discriminable from those which are less probable; the businessman must form some idea or image of which activities are likely to lead to profit and which to loss in order to pursue his goals successfully. Clearly there are differences among these organisms in the nature of the environments which are relevant to each (e.g., the bacteria's culture medium vs. the wild animal's forest), in the nature of the informational signs each interprets (e.g., the plant interprets radiation from the sun while the businessman reads the *Wall Street Journal*), and in the nature of the specific goals each pursues (nutrients to assimilate, energy for photosynthesis, a prey to be stalked, a product that will sell). Nevertheless, it is also clear that the general result of such information processing is common to all. Interpretation of information enables living systems to structure, or organise, or form an image of, or "know" their environments so that some alternatives (e.g., routes, behaviours, choices) seem more likely than others to facilitate the pursuit of goals within those environments.[2]

We have noted examples of how living systems organise particular aspects of their environment. Clearly, however, organisms structure of the environment on numerous dimensions. For example, a college student may have an image of the layout of his campus, of the best way to get good grades, of how to interact with friends, of how to drive a car, of his parents' expectations of him, of which political party he favours, and so forth. For that student, all the images of all the various dimensions of his environment comprise a general picture of the world in which he operates—his subjective reality, so to speak. Here we are ignoring the metaphysical question of the nature of an absolute reality in favour of a more practicable approach. That is, for any given organism, reality is conceived as consisting of the world it "knows." What Schramm calls the frame of reference, that fund of stored, usable experience which the organism has processed and organised, is the reality to which it responds. It follows that an organism's *potential* reality is circumscribed by those aspects of the environment about which it may process information which, in turn, are a function of the availability of information to process and the kinds of information the organism is capable of processing.

Insofar as there is any compelling evidence, it appears that most living systems interpret information about the environment primarily from what George Herbert Mead called "natural signs."[3] Briefly, such signs are simply indicators of a referent which are "naturally" related to that referent. For example, smoke is a sign of fire, the growl of a dog over a bone a sign of danger, the dance of the bees studied by von Frisch a sign of the location of pollen-bearing flowers.[4] In each case the sign is directly related to its referent; the sign and the referent usually, if not always, occur together so that either through learning or through innate sets to respond the sign comes to stand for or "means" the referent. Hence, for any given organism a sign usually carries one meaning which is specific to the situation in which it occurs.

Several scholars have defined the meaning of an informational sign as the response it elicits in an organism, regardless of whether the response is overt or covert, cognitive or emotional, connotative or denotative, or any combination of these.[5] For example, having experienced fire, possibly having been burned by it, seeing its destructive power, noting its colour, heat, odour, that it gives off smoke, and so forth, at some later time simply seeing smoke (or smelling something burning, or experiencing intense heat) will call up stored memories of the earlier experience, memories of the earlier responses. Although responses to any of these signs will not be identical to responses to fire itself, the sign acts as a code capable of calling up memories and responses highly similar to those elicited by the original referent—thus giving the sign meaning.

Given the preceding definitions of natural signs and of meaning, most organisms are limited in their communicative capabilities. Earlier Schramm noted that while a dog may growl to indicate his willingness to defend a particular bone in a particular situation, he cannot write a history of bones, nor can he discourse upon the principles of gnawing. He can only produce a sign which carries information in the context in which it was emitted. Moreover, even with two animals within the same context, there is no reason to assume that the growl carries the same meaning for the dog emitting it as for the dog interpreting it. They do not *share* the meaning of the sign. For the dog protecting the bone, the growl may raise feelings of fighting and winning; whereas in the interpreting animal the growl may arouse feelings of fighting and losing, or of fleeing, or of winning. Although the two animals' responses to the sign may be co-ordinated (e.g., one dog growls and the other flees), there need be no assumption that the meaning of the sign is similar for each, that one animal has an image or expectation of what the sign means to the other.[6]

The implication of all this is that the reality structured by most organisms is closely tied to direct experience with what humans would call the objective or physical environment. Most sign-referent relationships are established because the two naturally co-occur in that environment (e.g., smoke and fire). In addition, unless its response to a sign is innate (as may be the case with von Frisch's bees), an organism must *experience* the co-occurrence of sign and referent in order for a significatory relationship to be established. One organism cannot *share* the meaning of either a sign or a referent with another. Hence, reality for most organisms is structured out of direct interaction with tangible, physical aspects of their environment.

Communication and Human "Reality." Man is like other living systems in that he, too, structures reality out of information about the environment in which he functions. Like the one-celled organism and the four-legged animal, man interprets natural signs which carry such information as food or not-food, danger or safety—information which enables him to organise those dimensions of the world that a physical scientist might measure. However, human reality includes much more than just aspects of the immediate, physical environment. For example, Franklin Fearing wrote of man's "geographic stimulus field," which refers to direct, physical reality, and of his "behavioural stimulus field," which includes such factors as human needs, meanings, values, beliefs, and so forth; W. Phillips Davison describes the environment men experience as containing not only physical features, but also social, expected, and imagined features; Kenneth Boulding lists ten dimensions comprising man's image of the world, only some of which pertain to the "objective" environment.[7]

Regardless of how we subdivide and label its various aspects, it is clear that man creates a reality which extends well beyond the objective environment. His world contains abstract concepts such as justice, morality, and love. It spans continents, oceans, cultures; it recognises roles, norms, and expectations; it extends backward into history and forward into the future; it touches on gods and angels, devils and furies. In short, human reality contains many features which an individual never directly experiences, many dimensions for which no tangible referents exist. Such a reality cannot possibly be structured completely out of the information contained in natural signs. Indeed, one of the more remarkable characteristics of human reality is the large proportion of information concerning it that can be passed on *only* by other persons, whether in a face-to-face exchange or through the pages of a book or the channels of a television set. In other words, much of human reality is structured not from interpretation of informational signs which occur naturally in the environment, but from interpretation of informational signs which men create and through which they exchange information—from human communication.

Basic to man's reality, then, is his ability to produce and use signs which are not limited to a specific situation, which are capable of conveying meaning across time and space, which do not depend for significance on direct experience of the co-occurrence of sign and referent, and which have meaning that is shared among men. These are the signs which Mead called *significant symbols*. DeFleur cities two fundamental characteristics of such symbols: the association between the symbol and its referent is arbitrary; the meaning of the symbol is based on convention, on agreement among its users that a given sign will stand for a given referent. It makes no difference what set of letters, or marks, or sound elements we attach to a referent as long as those using the symbol *agree* that whatever we choose will stand for the referent. If all English-speaking persons agreed, we could label the referent house with the symbol "house," or "car," or "apple," or anything else. We need only think of the development and spread of the Morse Code or recall the role of "Newspeak" in George Orwell's *1984* for examples of symbol sets which are manifestly both arbitrary and based on convention.[8]

Such agreement, of course, is usually implicit. When we learn to speak a language or become a member of some cultural or subcultural group, we implicitly accept and share the conventions on which that language or culture is based, conventions which give meaning to the symbols we use. This is not to say that every user of a symbol set such as the English language will have precisely the same meaning for the same symbol. Schramm's earlier discussion of the "shared frame of reference" indicates that a symbol's meaning is shared to the extent that the experiences of the users of the symbol are similar. The word (symbol) "dog" may very well call up different responses in the Park Avenue matron who thinks of dogs in terms of French poodles than in the hunter who has experienced primarily retrievers or the veterinarian who encounters many dogs. Nevertheless, for most purposes enough of the meaning of "dog" is shared to enable an information exchange about dogs. Of course, as the need for precision increases, explicit agreement on the meaning of a symbol becomes more important. Thus philosophers, scientists, and occasionally even politicians often "define their terms" before engaging in a discussion or debate.

Because significant symbols are arbitrary and derive their communicative significance from shared conventions, they enable man to create and structure a reality far more subtle and complex than would be possible were he limited to the information contained in natural signs. Moreover, they enable man to communicate about that reality with others. Symbolic communication allows one to place objects in contexts, to draw the attention of others to what concerns him, to convey information across time and space, to express emotionally toned attitudes toward objects, actions, or situations, to enable participation in each other's attitudes and motives, to understand each other's intents and meanings, to generalise referents by placing them in broad categories. The symbol enables us not only to communicate about relationships among objects, but about relationships among abstractions, and about relationships among relationships themselves, and about relationships that *might* exist in the future. And perhaps most important, symbols enable men to share experiences, whether the experience is an event in someone's life, a feeling, or an idea, and through such sharing to manipulate the meaning of experience—to manipulate reality itself.

Discussing human communication. Melvin DeFleur writes:

> It is no exaggeration to say that the human communicative act, proceeding on the basis of the significant symbol, is a prerequisite ability without which it would not be possible for man to have developed his societies and cultures to the elaborate degree that he has. In fact, it is not possible to imagine any form of human society that could exist without this facility. The communicative act is the means by which a group's norms are expressed, by means of which social control

> is exerted, roles are allocated, co-ordination of effort is achieved, expectations are made manifest, and the entire social process is carried on. Without such exchanges of influence human society would simply collapse.
>
> It is equally true that the involvement of the individual in the community of language is the key to his psychological nature. Without learning to use symbols and their associated internal meanings, he would be unable to manipulate meanings, form beliefs about himself, ponder a problem, have human emotions, grasp a principle, plan ahead, learn in retrospect from the lessons of the past, and perform other human acts.[9]

In short, communication via the significant symbol provides men with the information necessary to define both their world and themselves within that world. The most basic and all-encompassing consequence of human communication, then, is the creation of the human condition itself.

Effects of Specific Communications

The preceding pages discuss the general consequences of the *process* of human communication, looking at how man's ability to share information with others of his kind results in the creation of a uniquely human reality. Most questions about communication effects, however, inquire about the specific results of specific communications or kinds of communications. We ask whether a professor's lecture facilitates learning, whether a sales message encourages buying, whether a warning sign engenders caution, a comedian's joke laughter, a candidate's speech a vote, a news programme a better informed public.

The Cause and Effect Model. In a loose sense, some kind of stimulus-response or cause-effect model underlies most such questions about communication effects. That is, whether we give a lecture, "pitch" a product, tell a joke, or report the news, we expect the message to act as a stimulus which incurs some kind of response in the receiver. This does not mean that a person's response to a communication can be predicted from the message itself, however. As Schramm notes, the past several decades have witnessed a great deal of modification and elaboration of the simple S-R model of communication. A variety of different variables—personality, social relationships, social and cultural background, past experience, needs, motives, and so forth—have been postulated to intervene between the message and a person's response to it. Any of these variables may influence how a receiver interprets a message, and effects derive not from the message itself but from how that message is interpreted. Nevertheless, to the extent that a communication activates the interpretation process, some form of the stimulus-response assumption—that a communication serves to stimulate, or cue, or activate, or in some way cause a response, or behaviour, or effect—is implicit in most of the various approaches to communication effects.

Usually, then, a communication is judged to have an effect to the extent that it is followed by an observable response on the part of the receiver which appears to derive from the message. We study the effects of communications by looking for changes in the behaviour of people after they have been exposed to messages or at differences in the behaviour of people, some of whom have been exposed to a message and some of whom have not. We observe whether the audience begins to laugh after the comedian tells his joke, whether students who attended the professor's lecture do better on an examination than students who were absent, whether the fund-raising speech results in an increase or a decrease in the number of contributions, whether when we ask for the salt our tablemate passes it to us or continues to read the paper. Indeed, most of us are probably aware of instances where people go so far as to reverse the process, observing some behaviour and inferring that a certain kind of communication must have taken place ("Stop that, John! You've been watching French movies again!"). Regardless of what behaviour we choose to observe, if it follows the message, and if it seems conceptually related to what we perceive to be the content and/or intent of the message, then we are likely to infer that the communication has been effective. This has been the basic paradigm of most studies of communication effects.

There are, however, several difficulties with this approach to communication effects. First, we are limited to inferring that a message has had an influence only when we are able to observe a *change* or *difference* in the response chosen as the indicator of effect.[10] Thus, if a person who has always voted for Democratic candidates is by some means limited to reading and hearing only Republican campaign literature and is then observed to vote a GOP ticket, we are relatively safe in assuming that the pro-Republican messages have had an effect. On the other hand, if a perennial Democrat is exposed to Democratic campaign literature and continues to vote for Democratic candidates, we cannot determine whether he was influenced by the messages he received or whether he would have voted Democratic anyway. The absence of an *observed* change in his vote provides no basis on which to decide whether the communications did or did not have an effect.

It is possible, however, had we chosen some other measure of communication effect, that we might have found our captive Democrat was wavering in his party loyalty and that the messages served to bring him back into the fold. Our second point, then, is that we are at the mercy of the indicators of effect we choose to observe. If we decide to judge the effectiveness of campaign messages only on the basis of voting behaviour, we may fail to note a variety of other effects (e.g., campaign messages may increase contributions to the party, encourage people to engage in precinct work, strengthen party loyalties, etc.) which could follow from the message even though voting behaviour remained constant. Obviously one way of overcoming this difficulty is to use multiple indicators of effect. However, there is a limit to the number of different responses we can observe.

In addition, we may fail to consider possibly significant responses which might follow from a communication simply because we don't expect them. Since we generally produce messages with a specific goal in mind, there is a tendency to look for effects which relate to the communicator's intent. For example, there is evidence that the pro-social, justified violence manifested in many television programmes in order to demonstrate that "crime doesn't pay" (e.g., the sheriff shoots the villain, the "good guy" beats up the "bad guy") may actually serve to increase the probability of violent behaviour on the part of young children.[11] The unexpected result of such communications may be to show children how to justify their own violent behaviour, just the opposite of the message's intent.

Similarly, Upton Sinclair wrote *The Jungle* as an expose of the horrendous working conditions existing in the meat-packing industry, intending to arouse public sentiment which would lead to legislation protecting the workers. The response engendered by the book, however, was an outcry against food packing standards and, eventually, pure food legislation. Had Sinclair attempted to evaluate the effectiveness of his work solely on the basis of indicators related to its intent, he might well have concluded the book was a failure. Of course, from his point of view it may well have been a failure; but history tells us that on at least one dimension *The Jungle* was a very effective communication. In other words, while observation of any set of indicators may enable us to evaluate the effects of a communication *on those indicators,* to the extent that we are bound to overlook a variety of other possible effects they do not enable us to make statements about how a communication affects a receiver in any total sense.

Messages and the Image. The preceding points indicate a third major problem with communication effects as we generally measure them. Regardless of which responses or behaviours we choose to measure, most *observable* indicators of communication effects are, at minimum, one step removed from the fundamental locus of effect. Communications do not *directly* mediate overt behaviour. Rather, they tend to affect the way a receiver organises his image of the environment, and this organisation influences the way he bahaves. We have already seen that individuals interpret information in order to organise or structure their world, thereby facilitating interaction with the environment. Hence we assume that the way a person behaves, the attitudes and values he expresses, and the knowledge he manifests are all mediated by, and thus reflections of, the image of the environment he has structured. If, for example, a person has organised his environment such that he associates the Democratic party with people and policies he favours, and if he associates casting a ballot with being a good citizen, and if he values good citizenship, then we would generally expect this image to mediate his overt behaviour—a vote for the Democrats. To change that behaviour, then, we must somehow affect the way he organises his world by providing him with new or different information. In order to do this we confront him with communications aimed at causing a restructuring or redefinition of his image. We can produce messages which attempt to dissociate favoured people and policies from the Democratic Party, or to devalue those people and policies, or to denigrate the value of voting, or to demonstrate that the Republicans are sure to win and that there is greater value in voting for a winner than for a policy, and so on. If the receiver accepts these new associations and incorporates them into his organisation of reality, we might expect him to change his vote to the Republican Party. Most communicators at least implicitly recognise that the way to encourage a desired response is to influence such redefinition of the receiver's image through messages.

We can conceive of messages as providing *prestructured* information—information organised such that certain relationships and associations are salient (and often such that others are not) in the hope that a receiver's interpretation of those prestructurings will influence his image of the environment, hence his behaviour. Professors attempt to facilitate understanding by relating complex theoretical concepts to concrete examples familiar to their students; a husband seeks an expression of love, or a hot meal, or a night out with the boys, by tying his request to a compliment on his wife's new dress; a reporter tries to inform his audience by relating the latest piece of legislation to its supporters and opponents, its costs and benefits, its place in the larger scheme of things; advertisements show bikini-clad beauties caressing the latest in deodorants with the hope that men will recall this association the next time they stroll through a drugstore. In each instance, communications may be seen as attempts by communicators to structure aspects of the environment *for* receivers by creating certain associations. Boulding writes that "messages consist of information in the sense that they are structured experiences." And he goes on to say that "the meaning of a message is the change which it produces in the image."[12] Hence we can view the production of messages as attempts to influence the way a receiver structures his world.

To summarise, the *primary* effects of communications are not directly observable. Primary effects occur at the level of the image a receiver has organised—inside the "black box," so to speak. While we can make inferences about communication effects based on the receiver's behaviour, the true effect of a message may be more or less subtle, far-reaching and complex than an observable measures can indicate.

Types of Effects on the Image. Even though we cannot directly observe the effects of a particular communication on a receiver's image of his world, we can nevertheless consider the types of effect which may take place. Assuming that a message is not ignored or avoided, various dimensions of a receiver's image of the environment may be affected in one of two fundamental ways: they may be *redefined*, or they may be *maintained*. In other words, a message can be interpreted such that it either results in a change in some part of the image or such that it does not. This is not to say, however, that maintenance of the image is synonymous with "no effect." Quite the contrary. For purposes of interacting with the environment, information indicating that our structuring needs no redefinition is just as valuable as information indicating a need for change. We are continually checking to see whether or not the way we have organised reality is still valid.

To the extent that a receiver interprets a message as repeating information he has already organised, then, the effect is one of *maintenance* of that orgnisation. If, for example, a teacher has organised an image of a student as one of the best pupils in his class, each time the teacher interprets a message from that student (exam, term paper, response to a question) as worth a high grade, his image is maintained. Such messages indicate that there is no need for restructuring, that his image of this aspect of the environment is still valid. A large proportion of the communications we interpret daily serve this function. The smile and "hello" from our neighbour, a mother's instructions to "eat all your vegetables," the newspaper headline indicating the world is in a state of crisis—messages like these usually tell us that things are still the same. They tell us that we can plan our behaviour according to the image we have previously structured.

Redefinition effects, on the other hand, occur whenever information is interpreted as being different from that which makes up the existing image, as incongruent with the organisation a receiver has previously imposed upon his world. If a receiver interprets a message as indicating that some aspect of his view of reality is incomplete, or invalid, or ill-defined, then we assume that a redefinition of his image will take place. For example, should the above-mentioned teacher begin to interpret his "best" student's papers or examination answers as inadequate—as worth, say, only a D grade—he should somehow change or redefine his existing image. The nature of such redefinition will vary with the interpretation given to the message. Different kinds of messages and/or messages about different parts of the environment may give rise to different types and amounts of incongruity between dimensions of the receiver's image and the new information. Differences in incongruity should lead to different modes of change.

Kenneth Boulding lists three ways in which a message might engender redefinition of a receiver's image: through addition, through reorganisation, and through clarification.[13]

First, the image may be added to. This occurs when a receiver interprets information about some aspect of the environment which he has not previously organised, or new information about a previously organised aspect of the environment which does not conflict with the existing organisation. When we learn a new skill, or read about some part of the world with which we have never previously concerned ourselves, or obtain additional information about a subject which interests us, our image of reality may simply be expanded. No fundamental change within existing structures need occur; the image is simply redefined through addition of new information.

Second, the structure of existing aspects of the image may be reorganised. This kind of redefinition can be expected when a message is interpreted as indicating either that some part of the environment has changed (e.g., we hear that a President has been assassinated; we receive a wedding announcement from our supposed fiancee) or that we have incorrectly organised some part of the environment (e.g., campaign literature convinces us that it is the Republicans, not the Democrats, who more frequently support organised labour). In either case, the effect on a receiver's image is one of reorganisation, of creating new relationships, new meanings. Of course, depending on the aspect of the environment with which the message deals and the importance of that part of the environment to the receiver, the ensuing reorganisation may be more or less radical. Messages may engender restructuring of the image as minor as a change in preference for one brand of toothpaste over another, or as major as a religious conversion.

Third, a message may act to clarify some dimension of the image. That is, we may have structured certain aspects of the environment with more or less certainty, more or less clarity. Given lack of clarity about some part of the environment, we can conceive of communications which neither add anything new to the image nor result in reorganisation of it, but which nevertheless engender a change in that they reduce our uncertainty by giving some aspect of the image higher definition. For example, when we read over a set of directions which refresh our memory of how to perform some task, the effect is often one of clarification. In a sense, clarification is similar to the maintenance effect discussed above. Both result from messages interpreted as repeating information which has already been organised. The difference lies in the amount of certainty which characterizes relevant dimensions of the image at the time the message is received, a difference more of degree than of kind.

Determinants of Effects. As Schramm points out in his discussion of the communication process, whether a given message is interpreted such that it maintains the image or results in one of the types of redefinition depends on what the receiver brings to the communication situation—on his previous organisation of the environment. We have already noted that new information, whether from direct experience on from socially mediated messages, is interpreted in terms of the image of reality one has already organised. In a sense, the "image," which is simply a metaphor representing the totality of all the information about the world any individual has processed, organised, and stored, may be conceived as a kind of template or standard against which new information is compared in order to give it meaning. This template includes the frame of reference and the needs, values, beliefs, and expectations which influence what a receiver takes from a communication situation. And it is a dynamic template in that each new piece of information processed has the potential to change the image and because, depending on the situation, various parts of the image may exert more or less impact on an interpretation at different times.

Illustrations of how differences in the way people have structured their world lead to differing interpretations of and responses to a communication are plentiful. Cooper and Jahoda found that a series of cartoons, which were viewed by unprejudiced people as ridiculing bigotry and anti-minority feelings (as the creator of the cartoons intended), were given entirely different interpretations by prejudiced receivers. Those who came to the experiment with an image of the world in which minority groups were stereotyped and denigrated tended to interpret the cartoons as making points entirely unrelated to prejudice, or to find the messages too difficult to understand ("I don't get the point"), or even to view them as supporting their existing prejudices.[14] Similar differences are exemplified in the following responses to a *Time* story describing a violent confrontation between construction workers and peace demonstrators, letters which reveal not only differing interpretations of the story, but also different experiential bases underlying each correspondent's organisation of his world. One reader wrote:

> The recent display by New York hardhats with their Gestapo-type invasion of a peace rally was disgusting! As a 28-year-old college student, ex-paratrooper and active participant in peace demonstrations, I was enraged at their actions.
>
> It is actions like theirs that will lead to a violent revolution in this country.

But another reader responded with:

> Congratulations to the New York construction workers, the best thing that's happened in this country for a long time. I would advise some of the academic community and some other persons of less than mediocre common sense to help maintain order and to encourage political action instead of demonstrations, mobs, arson and destruction. A lot of us working people, military people and law enforcement people are waiting for enough excuse to join the construction workers.[15]

Finally, most of us are probably aware that we ourselves are open to information dealing with some aspects of the environment but will tend to ignore or avoid or "misinterpret" messages dealing with other aspects. In each instance, such differences in interpretation of messages are heavily influenced by how the receiver has structured his world prior to receiving the message. In short, the nature of the information inherent in people's history of experience with the environment, regardless of whether that experience is direct or socially mediated, forms the basis on which each organises his own image of reality—of the way things are and should be, of what is good and bad, of what is important and unimportant, of what will serve their needs and what will not, indeed, of what many of those needs are. To the extent that no two people ever encounter precisely the same experiences or process exactly the same communications, we can expect them to structure different images of reality, thus to interpret the same messages differently.

Let us look more closely at how the nature of an individual's image mediates the effects of communications. Generally, by the time we reach adulthood we have organised a relatively stable image of reality, and we tend to process information such that it remains stable. That is, we are more open to messages maintaining the image than to those indicating a need for redefinition. Similarly, we are more apt to add to our organisation of reality than to restructure it. In other words, the effects of communications on individuals seem to follow a kind of principle of least effort. Messages which repeat information we have already organised demand little effort of interpretation. We simply relate such information to existing parts of the image. Messages which deal with aspects of the environment we have not previously organised demand a bit more effort. To give them meaning we must establish new categories, new relationships. Messages which call the existing structure into question demand the most effort. In this case dimensions of the existing image must be reorganised; old associations and meanings must be done away with and new ones established in their place.

For example, if we tell a person who believes the world is flat that the world is flat, he should have little difficulty accepting our message. It agrees with the way he has already organised reality. If we tell him that, flat world or not, a new continent has been discovered to lie between where he stands and what he perceives as the edge of the world, he might experience more difficulty dealing with our message, but to the extent that he has never considered the possibility of there being another continent he can probably add this information to his image without too much effort. If, however, we attempt to convince him that the world is around, our message will probably meet with a great deal of resistance. For him to accept this information implies a need for reorganisation of much of his view of reality. Indeed, depending on how closely related this aspect of his image is to other aspects, it could demand not only changes in the way he perceives the shape of the earth, but also changes in his image of religion, of science, of other people who believed the earth to be flat, and so forth. Clearly such reorganisation demands a great deal of effort.

Given this tendency for people's interpretations of communications to follow the path of least resistance, we can make several generalisations about how and when communications will affect receivers.

First, we tend to be more open to messages which are consonant with our existing image, messages which appear to maintain or reinforce our beliefs and values. Communications which are not consonant tend to be resisted by avoiding or ignoring them, by counterarguing against and discrediting them, by attacking the credentials of their source, by "misinterpreting" or distorting them, and so on. Further, the more important to the receiver the aspect of the image to which the incongruent message pertains, the more resistant he will be. Thus Sherif and Hovland found the people tended to distort toward their own positions messages advocating positions slightly different from their own. Conversely, people interpreted messages advocating beliefs very dissimilar from their own as being even more incongruent than they actually were. Moreover, these assimilation and contrast effects became more marked as the importance of the issue to the receiver increased.[16]

Second, messages which are incongruent with the value dimensions of a receiver's image usually tend to engender more resistance than messages incongruent with cognitive dimensions. For example, a bigoted person will experience less difficulty with a message attacking one of his cognitions about a minority group (e.g., "They are not dirty; they bathe daily") than with a message attacking his general evaluation of that group (i.e., "They are not bad; they are good"). He can accept the former message by changing only a small part of his image while other cognitions about the group and his general evaluation of the group remain unaffected. To accept a message advocating reevaluation, however, implies change throughout this part of his image. If the communication convinces him that the group he had previously evaluated as "bad" is, in fact, "good," then he must somehow change many, if not all, other relevant aspects of the image. Obviously members of the group cannot be "good" and remain "dirty," "rude," and "lazy." In other words, the value dimension tends to rank among the more important aspects of a person's image in that it relates to almost all cognitions. Davison's discussion of communication effects is based on the proposition that a person's attitudinal structure is fundamental to how he responds to any communication, and Boulding writes that "the value scales of any individual or organisation are perhaps the most important single element determining the effect of the messages it receives on its image of the world."[17]

Our third generalisation is that to the extent we positively value fulfilment of our needs, messages which contain information which is useful, which indicates a way to get more benefit for less cost, which in some way facilitates the pursuit of goals, will be more easily accepted than messages which do not. We tend to be relatively open to information relevant to our needs. People who hate mice, people whose careers are devoted to the elimination of mice, and small cafe owners who face being closed by the board of health unless they get rid of the mice in the storeroom all are very likely to listen carefully to the man who builds a better mousetrap.

Fourth, since we process information in order to structure the social and physical environment, as changes in the environment are perceived we are concomitantly more open to incoming messages. Perception of changes in the environment implies some degree of uncertainty about the accuracy of our existing image of the world, hus uncertainty about how to behave in that world. Hence we seek new information in order to either validate or reorganise that image. When President John F. Kennedy was assassinated, almost the entire nation turned to the communication media, processing every available bit of information in an attempt to reorganise an environment which had been so tragically changed.[18] Of course, communications about the event were interpreted in a variety of ways, depending on each receiver's pre-existing image. Nevertheless, messages were interpreted and images of reality were redefined. Similarly, when Orson Welles presented a Halloween programme in the form of a radio newscast describing an invasion by ranks of horrifying monsters from Mars, at a time when many people were unsure about the state of the world, it had a tremendous effect on those whose image of reality seemed most marked by uncertainty.[19]

Finally, each of the preceding points is mediated by the nature of the social communication situation. A message which is interpreted as congruent with our organisation of reality and which leads to maintenance effects in one situation may be seen as highly incongruent and lead to redefinition effects in another. As Schramm has already detailed, the source of a message, the channel and medium chosen to convey the message, elements such as others in the audience, the type of room, what we were doing before receiving a message and what we expect to do afterward, factors like these contain information which is processed along with information in the message per se. To the extent that such factors tend to cause different aspects of an individual's image to be more or less salient, to activate different needs, emphasise different values, recall different reference groups, roles, and expectations, they can exert a strong influence on how a message is interpreted and what effect it will have.

Several experiments serve to illustrate how various aspects of the total communication situation may affect interpretation of a message. Solomon Asch presented people with identical statements attributed to different authors and asked them to write a paragraph indicating what the statements meant. Different authors led to very different interpretations. For example, consider the following statement: "I hold it that a little rebellion, now and then, is a good thing, and is as necessary in the political world as storms are in the physical." When attributed to Thomas Jefferson, this statement was interpreted as implying a need for peaceful political agitation; when attributed to Lenin, it was taken to be a justification of the Russian Revolution. In addition, Lorge, whose experiment Asch was replicating, found that people were likely to agree with the statement when it was attributed to Jefferson and disagree with it when attributed to Lenin. It appears that simply differences in the perceived source of the message served to make different aspects of the image more salient in the interpretation process, leading to differences both in interpretation and in effect.[20] In a similar vein, Wilson and Shaffer found that when third-graders were offered a choice of learning about how fish swim by reading either a comic book, a textbook, or a typewritten page, the children overwhelmingly chose to read the textbook. When questioned about their choices, they explained that although they liked comics for entertainment, they associated them with fantasy, distortion of reality, and caprice. For authentic information, they placed their confidence in textbooks. Here, differing expectations about the proper functions of various communication channels affected responses to the message.[21]

The Image, Information, and Observable Behaviour. Just as all the information inherent in a communication situation may potentially influence the effect of a message on a receiver's image of the world, so too may the information in any behavioural situation influence more observable responses to messages. While the largest proportion of our behaviour appears to reflect the way we have structured the world, and while many of our observable responses to a message are, in fact, indicative of how a message has affected our image, instances when behaviour appears to belie the image are not infrequent. We are probably all familiar with situations in which we have behaved in a manner very different from how certain dimensions of our image of the world indicated we should have behaved. Most of us have responded to a greeting from a friend with a smile and a "Just fine! How are you?" on occasions when we couldn't have felt worse and perceived the world to be the bleakest of places. And it is not unheard of for a registered Democrat, who believes in all of the principles of his party, to vote for a Republican; for a lover of desserts to refuse a second piece of pie; for a sincerely religious person apparently to ignore the tenets of his faith.

Acutally, given the complexity of the world a human must structure, and thus of his image of the world, such behaviour is not too surprising. We continually process and respond to information from all parts of the environment, and the nature of this information influences which aspects of the image are more salient and exert more influence on our behaviour at any given time. For example, the greeting from our friend provides us not only with an opportunity to obtain company for our misery, but, depending on other elements in the situation, may also bring to mind a certain set of social responsibilities which dictate that one does not burden a friend with woes, or a need to maintain the impression of being an eternal optimist, or the feeling from his tone of voice that his greeting was simply an observance of convention, hence the response need be nothing more. Thus messages which we agree with and incorporate into our image at one time may have no observable effect on our behaviour at a specific later moment. This is not to say, however, that the message had no effect, for at some third time, in a still different situation, the structure it provided our environment may again function to influence our overt acts.

One of the more dramatic instances of this apparent incongruence between the way people have structured their world and the way they behave is reported by R.T. LaPiere, LaPiere travelled throughout the United States with a young Chinese couple, stopping at 66 hotels, auto camps, and tourist homes, and dining in 184 restaurants and cafes. During this trip, they were refused service only once. Six months later, LaPiere sent questionnaires to all of the establishments visited, asking if they would accept Chinese as guests. Of the 50 per cent who replied, over 90 per cent said "No."[22]

Now, unless we are willing to believe that a fantastic proportion of people changed their image of the Chinese during the time between the trip and the questionnaire, it seems that information inherent in the situation at time one (e.g., I am face-to-face with the Chinese couple) caused one part of the proprietors' image to exert more influence (e.g., to refuse service in a face-to-face situation could cause an ugly scene, which is something I want to avoid), while information inherent in the situation at time two (e.g., this questionnaire is anonymous, and to be filled out in private; etc.) caused or allowed other parts of the image to exert more influence (e.g., I can maintain the white, Anglo-Saxon "purity" of my establishment at little risk). In other words, elements inherent in the face-to-face encounter appear to have influenced behaviour in accord with those parts of the image which indicate that avoidance of ugly scenes is important, while elements of the private situation made expression of their prejudices more satisfying. Given the nature of our society and culture we are reasonably justified in assuming that, at some point prior to the time LaPiere and the Chinese couple made their tour, most of these proprietors had received and accepted some messages indicating that people should avoid scenes, and others indicating that minority-group members were to be shunned. To the extent that this assumption is valid, we can say that *both* sets of messages were effective. That is, such messages did influence how the proprietors organised their world and, depending on the nature of the information inherent in each situation, they did influence overt responses.

The important point is that no message, no piece of information, ever exerts influence in a vacuum. When we conceive of communication effects at some observable, behavioural level, we must keep in mind that any given communication *contributes* to effects depending on how it interacts with other information in the situation and with what the receiver brings to the message. It is seldom, if ever, the sole cause of any effect.

Mass Communication Effects

One of the more striking features of contemporary society is the ubiquitous presence of the mass communication media. Thousands of people and billions of dollars are devoted to collecting, structuring, reproducing, and transmitting a seemingly endless barrage of messages at those millions of individuals who comprise the mass audience. In the United States, for example, circulation of daily newspapers exceeds one per household; there are over four radios for every household in the country; ownership of the newest mass medium, television, passed one per household in 1960, and the figure is still rising.[23] Indeed, one of the more obvious and indisputable effects of mass communications is simply that they take a great deal of our time. Various studies of media use patterns in the United States have shown, for example, that by the end of the grade-school years children average over three hours per day of television viewing, a figure which, with minor increases and decreases at various age levels, represents a good estimate of the amount of time adults spend with the television set; that use of all mass media combined accounts for over 50 per cent of the leisure time of adults; that by the time he graduates from high school a typical teenager has spent more time watching television than in the classroom.[24]

But what about other possible effects? Given that the simple fact of the mass media's existence results in our devoting a great deal of time (and money) to them, are we in any way influenced by what they say or how they say it? Is there anything in the nature of mass communications which might lead us to expect a person to be affected differently by them than he would be by interpersonal communications? Does the fact that the media are capable of quickly transmitting vast amounts of information across large distances to millions of people have implications for how society is organised? Does it have implications for how any given individual structures his image of reality? Does simply the awareness that the mass media are capable of bringing any act, event, or idea into the public eye affect the behaviour of individuals, groups, or nations?

As the preceding questions indicate, the effects of mass communication may be approached from many perspectives. We can ask about effects on individuals, on societies, on cultures. We can look for short-term effects or long-term effects. We may be concerned about the influence of the mass *media* or of mass *communication*. Or we may continue the distinction made in the opening pages of this chapter and think in terms of the effect of mass *communication* or of the effects of mass *communications*.

Many of the early fears that the broad reach of the mass media would place entire populations at the mercy of a small set of propagandists have proven to be largely unfounded, at least in terms of *immediate* effects. Schramm's early description of the process of communication as an act of "sharing," Raymond Bauer's concept of the "obstinate audience," Carl Hovland's classic explanation of why persuasive techniques so successful in the laboratory appeared to fail when applied to mass communications in the field—all these helped us to realise that mass communications were not omnipotent in terms of controlling the minds and behaviour of members of the mass audience.[25] In 1960 Joseph Klapper reviewed much of the existing research on the effects of mass communication and concluded that rather than radical reorganisation of the way an individual organises his image of the world, the most likely effect of mass communication is maintenance of the status quo.[26]

That mass communications are not the most effective means for influencing immediate change of *established* beliefs, opinions, attitudes, or values is not too surprising. Because of the nature of the media and the heterogeneity of the mass audience, the mass media cannot tailor their messages to meet the needs and beliefs of individual receivers. They do not have available to them the necessary, immediate feedback which might indicate when to repeat or clarify a point, when to reinforce a response, when to concentrate on an apparent weakening of resolve. The mass communication situation usually does not activate the social norms inherent in interpersonal situations, norms which constrain one to attend, to manifest interest, to consider politely the other's point of view, any or all of which can increase the impact of a persuasive message. Moreover, mass communications often reach an audience that is on its guard, that expects the sponsor, or the politician, or the commentator to attempt to change its mind. It is an audience which is ready to resist. And finally, in societies where the media are free of any sort of central control, many of the messages which attempt to persuade receivers of one specific point of view must compete with messages advocating just the opposite. The Democratic candidate is usually rebutted by the Republican, who, in turn, is attacked by the Democrat. The commercial claiming that Brand X is the best widget in the world is usually countered by Brand Y's contention that *it* is the best widget in the world. In short, the nature of the mass media, the mass audience, and the mass communication situation tends to minimise the probability that mass-mediated messages will cause a receiver to reorganise radically *established* beliefs, opinions, or values.

On the other hand, mass communications may have a great deal to do with how we structure the world over the long-term, and with how we organise *new* aspects of the image, form new opinions and beliefs. Early in this chapter we noted that human reality is unique in the large proportion of information concerning it that can be passed on only by other persons. We can go a step further and say that twentieth-century man is unique in that he derives so much of his image of reality from mass-mediated information. Although most of us will never set foot on the moon, participate in a Middle Eastern war, or experience a heart transplant, because of information the mass media have made available, each of these events probably contributes to aspects of our image of the environment to which we respond.

Clearly there is a good deal of truth in Marshall McLuhan's conception of the mass media as "extensions" of man's senses.[27] Because of the media, the small-town grocer can respond not only to his customer's expressed desires or his immediate competitors' prices, but he can also plan his behaviour on the basis of knowledge about a drought in Kansas or a shipping strike on the East coast. The Midwestern coed's image of fashion is based not only on what she actually sees her classmates wearing or what she finds in the local stores, but also on what the media tell her about high-fashion salons in Paris, boutiques in London, and California casual wear. Alberta Siegel cites an excellent example of how a newspaper reporter covering the 1968 Presidential elections in rural Iowa found farmers to be less preoccupied with political issues immediately affecting their local communities and livelihoods than with the issues filling the mass media:

> Other issues have become so overriding as to obscure the farmer's problems, even in his own mind. Through some miracle of modern communication and repetition, the farmer lives in rural solitude and dwells upon crime-filled city streets, fiery demonstrations, bloody riots, bearded campus protestors, the frustrating war in Vietnam. And all indications are that those are the images that will fill the farmer's mind when he walks into the voting booth on November 5.[28]

In other words, because the media can and to make available large amounts of information about the world which we can never directly experience, mass communications are well suited to affect additions to our image of reality and to influence strongly how we structure parts of the environment about which we have little opportunity to acquire firsthand knowledge.

One of the major consequences of the mass media's ability to transmit messages quickly across great distances and to supply us with otherwise unobtainable information is that we have come to *expect* them to maintain a constant surveillance of distant parts of the environment and to provide us with information about the broader world. And we rely on such information—a reliance which has several important implications both for individuals and for society.

First, the *news* media have tremendous potential for directing our attention. We tend to assume that the events they cover are important, if only because they are reported in the media. That is, our awareness that mass-mediated messages reach millions of people and that they are produced by large organisations whose avowed purpose is to ferret out and report significant events in the environment influences us to view much of what is reported as important—as worthy of our attention. Lazarsfeld and Merton write of the mass media's status-conferral function, contending that simply recognition by the media of some person or group singles them out from the "large, anonymous masses" and bestows prestige and authority upon them. They write: "The audiences of mass media apparently subscribe to the circular belief: 'If you really matter, you will be at the focus of mass attention and, if you *are* at the focus of mass attention, then surely you must really matter'."[29] It is also worth noting here that the media's ability to confer status often tends to affect the behaviour of people who seek status. Stories of how the young movie starlet or the aspiring politician attempt to manoeuvre themselves within range of the camera or onto the front page of the newspaper are legion, and Joe McGinnis has provided us with an excellent description of how, during the 1968 Presidential campaign, Richard Nixon's advisers went to great lengths to map the Republican candidate's every move with an eye to the television camera.[30]

Nor do we need to limit this attention-directing, status-conferring effect of the media to individuals, groups, or institutions. Issues and events also assume importance to the extent that they receive, media coverage. If a Senate bill, or a social action programme, or the publication of a new book receives attention from the media, we are likely to ascribe importance to the event. Even though the Iowa farmer described earlier is not *directly* affected by distant campus demonstrations or crime-filled city streets, the mass communication media, simply because they devote to a great deal of time and space to such events, encourage their incorporation as important parts of his image of the environment. And, as with attention-seeking individuals, we also find attention-seeking events. Daniel Boorstin provides us with a detailed description of the birth and growth of pseudo-events—Press conferences, publicity stunts, manufactured issues—created to make some idea, policy, or act seem important.[31] Indeed, several times in the past few years at least one radio and one television station in the San Francisco area have received calls from individuals planning demonstrations and protests. The expressed purpose of the calls was to determine at what time to hold the demonstration in order to be assured of maximum Press coverage!

A second implication of our reliance on the media for much of our information is that to the extent that mass communications present a distorted, stereotyped or biased picture of some part of the environment, and to the extent that a receiver is *unable to test the accuracy of that picture against some nonmedia standard,* then the image he structures on the basis of that information is apt to be distorted, stereotyped, or biased. For example, just a few years ago it was not difficult to find Europeans who conceived of the United States as a land given over entirely to cowboys and Indians in the West and gangsters and gun molls in the East, an image structured mainly on the basis of Hollywood movies. Even today, if the hypothetical "man from Mars" about whom we often hear were to construct an image of this country *solely* on the basis of current television fare, he might well conceive of a nation populated by widows and widowers, engaged in only white-collar occupations, and resorting to violence to resolve a large proportion of their problems.[32]

Third, and closely related to the second point, what the media *do not report* may be as significant as what they do report. That is, the way we organise our image of reality can be an easily distorted because we receive incomplete or no information about parts of the environment as because we receive stereotyped or biased information. William Rivers contends that had the media covered urban ghettos *before* they erupted in the late

1960's, public awareness and concern might have been mobilised in order to correct intolerable conditions and head off the riots. As it was, a large part of the population was taken by surprise; they had received little previous information about conditions in the inner city.[33]

The potential importance of the effects of what the media do not report becomes particularly clear when we consider that the men who run the cameras and presses *must select* some information to be passed along while condemning other information to the cutting-room floor or the copy editor's wastebasket. There simply is not enough time or space to report everything. David Manning White's classic "gatekeeper" studies found that of the approximately 12,400 column inches of wire copy received during one week by the wire editor of a Midwestern newspaper, 1,297 column inches (about 10 per cent) were finally used! When we consider that each story passed through several additional "gates" (e.g., wire-service reporters and editors) before reaching the local wire copyeditor, the loss becomes even greater. Moreover, when questioned about why he rejected many of the stories which never made it into print, the editor's comments included such reasons as "Not interesting . . . Goes on all the time . . . Propaganda . . . Too far away . . . Too regional . . . He's too Red . . . B.S."![34]

The consequences of such a selection process may well be one of the major reasons that Klapper found mass communications more likely to contribute to the *status quo* than to create change.[35] Several factors seem to combine to encourage the selecting out of information and material which is too contrary to the established order of things and the inclusion of materials congruent with the *status quo*. First, the individual reporter or editor views and interprets the world in terms of his own image of reality—his own beliefs, values, and norms. Thus, to the extent that his image reflects existing norms and values, he is likely to overlook or ignore new ways of perceiving the world or approaching problems. Second, Warren Breed has shown that newsmen respond to a number of subtle pressures which influence them to "slant" their reporting of events so as to conform with the publisher's implicit policy.[36] For example, an editorial policy which tends to be pro-Republican, cool toward organised labour, against a newly proposed highway route, and so forth, is likely to make itself felt not only in terms of stories favouring this policy, but also in the omission of information which counters it. Thus, to the extent that media policy reflects the norms of a given culture or subculture, so too will the information they transmit. Third, the fact that the media, particularly the entertainment media, must compete for a large share of the mass audience in order to maintain advertising revenue tends to influence them to shy away from the novel, the controversial, or anything which does not appear to be guaranteed to gain them a large audience. For example, it has become almost a truism among television critics that any particular dramatic formula which attracts viewers on one network is relatively certain to be copied by competing networks. A brief glance at television programme lastings over the years will indicate that a successful "medical" show (e.g., Dr. Kildare) soon engenders a number of competing hospitals, doctors, and nurses; that a hit Western seems to ensure a spate of prime-time showdowns at sundown; and that a widow (never a divorcee) with children who attracts an audience is soon to be joined by other single-parent families. One clear result of such programming is to impede effectively, if not eliminate, new, different, and/or controversial types of programmes. In addition, Fred Friendly has described situations in which, when it came to a choice between broadcasting entertainment programmes which attract large audiences and advertising revenues or something like a Senate committee hearing which tends to reduce audience size, the entertainment programmes usually won out.[37] The point is that any or all of these factors encourage mass communication of information congruent with the *status quo* and discourage contrary or different messages.

Finally, mass communication's ability to influence how receivers organise new, previously unstructured aspects of the environment becomes particularly compelling when we consider that a large share of the mass audience, particularly the television audience, is composed of children. Fundamentally, childhood is a period of information-seeking during which the child learns what to expect from his environment and what his environment expects from him. It is a period during which much of the information the child encounters pertains, by definition, to new, previously unstructured aspects of his world. It is a period during which he is particularly dependent on others for information.

Thus young children are particularly susceptible to the influence of communications. While it is obvious that children may obtain much of their conception of the world from parents and from other nonmedia sources (e.g., direct experience, friends, school), it is also clear that children need and obtain much information which these sources do not, cannot, or will not pass on. Albert Bandura points out that "under conditions of rapid social and technological change, many parental interests, attitudes, and role behaviours that were serviceable at an earlier period may have little functional value for members of the younger generation." He goes on to point out that the demonstrated efficacy of learning through symbolic modelling and the large amount of time young children spend watching television, which is a continuous source of symbolic models, provide ample reason to expect children to construct a significant part of their image of the world on the basis of mass-mediated information.[38]

Indeed, there is a good deal of evidence that children (and adults) learn behaviours, norms, attitudes, and so forth, from film and television-mediated presentations. For example, Flanders lists an extensive range of behaviours which have been demonstrated to follow from observation of symbolic models, including such things as problem-solving, delay of gratification, self-rewarding behaviour, moral judgment, altruism, aggression, and resistance to temptation. Moreover, Bandura and his associates have shown that children are equally likely to learn such behaviours whether they observe a live or a film-mediated model, and a number of additional studies which have not made live-model vs. film-model comparisons have nevertheless demonstrated learning of film-mediated behaviour. Similarly, early research on "Motion Pictures and Youth," conducted under the auspices of the Payne Fund, found that a single showing, to relatively naive children ranging from the fourth grade to senior high school, of movies such as "All Quiet on the Western Front" or "Birth of a Nation" significantly influenced attitudes on issues as varied as capital punishment, war, the Chinese, the Negro—influences which in some cases persisted as long as nineteen months after viewing of the films. More recently, Albert Siegel found that a dramatic radio presentation affected the role expectations of naive second-graders. Numerous other studies could be cited.[39] Suffice it to say that there is convincing experimental evidence that the mass media and their messages, particularly television to which the child has very early access,[40] can influence the way children organise their image of the world, at least over the short-term.

There are still, however, a great many unanswered questions about the long-term effects of the mass media on children, about how television's repetitive themes might affect the child's developing image of reality. Such questions become particularly pressing when we consider that television drama, to which children are most likely to attend, presents a world dominated by white-collar occupations, bumbling fathers, and three-bedroom homes. It's a world in which, during 1968, conflict situations resulted in violence in almost 80 per cent of all dramatic presentations. And it's a world of quarter-hourly messages that "to consume is to be happy." Well we might ask whether the norms and values inherent in such programming influence the norms and values of the child viewer, and to what extent the world of the picture tube shapes the child's expectations about the environment in which he must function. Recently there appeared in *The New Yorker* a cartoon showing an automobile with a flat tire pulled to the side of the road in a rainstorm, and two small children peering from within the car at their father as he knelt in the puddles and tried to change the tire. The caption represented the words of the father as he replied to an implied request from the two children: "Don't you understand? This is *life,* this is what is happening. We *can't* switch to another channel." One senses that the cartoon may strike alarmingly close to the truth.[41]

The foregoing by no means exhausts the catalog of possible mass media affects. McLuhan, for example, contends that simply the nature of the medium—the way each structures and presents information—influences the way we perceive the world. Lazarsfeld and Merton point out that another social effect of the media's constant surveillance of the environment is the enforcement of social norms, almost the reverse of status conferral. That is, simply the threat of public exposure through the media may exert strong pressures against "deviant" behaviour. Given the flood of information the media provide us, we may also ask about the effect of an information glut. Lazarsfeld and Merton speculated about a possible "narcotising dysfunction," a substitution of knowledge and concern about the problems of the day for *doing* something about them. Some twenty years later we can go further and ask whether the sheer number of communications with which the media barrage us might not result in our overlooking important messages—or even in a kind of avoidance of communications.[42]

Space precludes any comprehensive examination of all of the various effects that have been hypothesised or demonstrated to follow from the mass media and mass communication.[43] It should be clear, however, that mass communications can and do affect our lives—just as interpersonal communications do. The media have given us a much wider window on the world than was available to individuals and societies which preceded ours. We attend to mass communications, we learn from them, and for certain things we rely on them.

Nevertheless, with the media as with all other sources of information we must remember that each individual receiver is in control. He decides what to attend to, what to select from the array of messages available to him, what any communication means, and how to respond to it.

References

1. Kenneth E. Boulding, *The Image: Knowledge in Life and Society* (Ann Arbor, University of Michigan Press, 1961). This chapter owes a good deal to ideas stimulated by Boulding's book.
2. For convenience, we will adopt Kenneth Boulding's use of the term "image." We do not use the term in any exclusively pictorial sense. "Image" here refers to all those dimensions which contribute to the way an organism "knows" its environment—the facts, beliefs, values, expectations, emotions, and so forth, which both stem from and contribute to the processing of information.
3. George Herbert Mead, *Mind, Self, and Society* (Chicago: University of Chicago Press, 1934).
4. Karl von Frisch, "Dialectics in the Language of Bees," *Scientific American* 207, no. 2, (1962), 78-87.
5. See, for example, Melvin L. DeFleur, *Theories of Mass Communication*, 2nd ed. (New York, David McKay, 1970); Boulding, *The Image;* Wilbur Schramm, "The Nature of Communication between Humans," in this volume.

6. A clear, concise discussion of shared meaning versus co-ordinated responses is provided by DeFleur, *Theories of Mass Communication,* pp. 78-86.
7. Franklin Fearing, "Human Communication," *Audio-Visual Communication Review* 10 (1962): 78-108; W. Phillips Davison, "On the Effects of Communication," *Public Opinion Quarterly* 23(1959): 343-60; Boulding, *The Image.*
8. Mead, *Mind, Self, and Society;* DeFleur, *Theories of Mass Communication.*
9. DeFleur, *Theories of Mass Communication,* p. 90.
10. We include here not only observable motor behaviours, but also responses on a variety of paper-and-pencil measures (e.g., learning tests, attitude scales, and so forth).
11. See, for example, various sections of Robert K. Baker and Sandra J. Ball, eds., *Violence and the Media,* a staff report to the National Commission on the Causes and Prevention of Violence (Washington, U.S. Government Printing Office, 1969); Leonard Berkowitz and E. Rawlings, "Effects of Film Violence on Inhibitions against Subsequent Aggression," *Journal of Abnormal and Social Psychology 66* (1963): 405-12; R.S. Albert, "The Role of the Mass Media and the Effects of Aggressive Film Content upon Children's Aggressive Responses and Identification Choices," *Genetic Psychology Monographs 55* (1957): 221-85.
12. Boulding, *The Image,* p. 7.
13. *Ibid.*
14. E. Cooper and M. Jahoda, "The Evasion of Propaganda," *Journal of Psychology 23* (1947): 15-25, and in this volume.
15. "Letters to the Editor," *Time,* June 15, 1970.
16. Muzafer Sherif and Carl I. Hovland, *Social Judgment: Assimilation and Contrast Effects in Communication and Attitude Change* (New Haven, Yale University Press, 1961); see also C. Sherif, M. Sherif, and R. Nebergall, *Attitude and Attitude Change* (Philadelphia, Saunders, 1965).
17. Davison, "On the Effects of Communication"; Boulding, *The Image.*
18. See various papers in B.S. Greenberg and E.B. Parker, eds., *The Kennedy Assassination and the American Public: Social Communication in Crisis* (Stanford, Stanford University Press, 1965).
19. Hadley Cantril, *The Invasion from Mars* (Princeton, Princeton University Press, 1947), and in this volume.
20. S. Asch, "The Doctrine of Suggestion, Prestige, and Imitation in Social Psychology," *Psychological Review 55* (1948): 250-76; I. Lorge, "Prestige, Suggestion and Attitude," *Journal of Social Psychology* 7 (1936), 386-402.

21. R.C. Wilson and E.J. Shaffer, "Reading Comics to Learn," *Elementary School Journal 66* (1965): 81-82.
22. R.T. LaPiere, "Attitudes vs. Actions," *Social Forces 14* (1934); 230-37.
23. DeFleur, *Theories of Mass Communication;* also see Jack Lyle, "Contemporary Functions of the Mass Media," in Baker and Ball, *Violence and the Media,* pp. 187-216.
24. See for example, Wilbur Schramm, "Mass Communication in the Human Life Cycle," in *Melanges Roger Clausse* (Brussels: Editions de l'Institut de Sociologie, 1971). For a detailed review of the media use patterns of children, see Donald F. Roberts, "Communication and Children: A Developmental Approach," in Wilbur Schramm, Ithiel de Sola Pool, *et al.*, eds., *Handbook of Communication* (Chicago, Rand McNally, in press).
25. Wilbur Schramm, "How Communication Works," in Wilbur Schramm, ed., *The Process and Effects of Mass Communication* (Urbana, University of Illinois Press, 1954), pp. 3-26; Raymond A. Bauer, "The Obstinate Audience," *American Psychologist 19* (1964): 319-28; Carl I. Hovland, "Reconciling Conflicting Results Derived from Experimental and Survey Studies of Attitude Change," *American Psychologist 14* (1959): 8-17.
26. Joseph T. Klapper, *The Effects of Mass Communication* (Glencoe, Illinois, The Free Press, 1960).
27. Marshall McLuhan, *Understanding Media: The Extensions of Man* (New York, McGraw-Hill, 1964).
28. Douglas E. Kneeland, "Pocketbook Issues Secondary in Rural Iowa," *New York Times,* Oct. 18, 1968, p. 34, cited in Alberta Siegel, "The Effects of Media Violence on Social Learning," in Baker and Ball, *Violence and the Media,* p. 268.
29. Paul F. Lazarsfeld and Robert K. Merton, "Mass Communication, Popular Taste and Organised Social Action," in Lyman Bryson, ed., *The Communication of Ideas* (New York, Institute for Religious and Social Studies, 1948), pp. 95-118.
30. Joe McGinnis, *The Selling of the President, 1968* (New York, Trident Press, 1969).
31. Daniel J. Boorstin, *The Image: A Guide to Pseudo-Events in America* (New York, Harper and Row, 1964).
32. For a number of interesting discussions of how films and television present various characters, situations, and themes, see various papers in Bernard Rosenberg and David Manning White, eds., *Mass Culture: The Popular Arts in America* (New York, The Free Press, 1957).

33. William L. Rivers and Wilbur Schramm, *Responsibility in Mass Communications*, rev. ed. (New York, Harper and Row, 1969), pp. 175-89.
34. David Manning White, "The 'Gate Keeper': A Case Study in the Selection of News," *Journalism Quarterly* 27 (1950): 383-90.
35. Klapper, *The Effects of Mass Communication*.
36. Warren Breed, "Social Control in the Newsroom: A Descriptive Study," *Social Forces* 33 (1955): 326-35.
37. Fred W. Friendly, *Due to Circumstances Beyond Our Control . . .* (New York, Vintage Books, 1967).
38. Albert Bandura, "Social Learning Theory of Identificatory Processes," in D.A. Goslin, ed., *Handbook of Socialisation Theory and Research* (Chicago, Rand McNally, 1969), p. 248.
39. J.P. Flanders, "A Review of Research on Imitative Behaviour," *Psychological Bulletin* 69 (1968): 316-37; Albert Bandura, Dorothea Ross, and Sheila A. Ross, "Imitation of Film-Mediated Aggression," *Journal of Abnormal and Social Psychology* 67 (1963): 601-7; Ruth C. Peterson and L.L. Thurston, *Motion Pictures and the Social Attitudes of Children* (New York, Macmillan, 1933); Alberta Siegel, "The Influence of Violence in the Mass Media upon Children's Role Expectations," *Child Development* 29 (1958): 35-56.
40. As Eleanor Maccoby reports in her review of the effects of mass communication on children, instances of playpens being placed in front of a television set so that infants can watch the screen are not uncommon.
41. For more extensive and detailed reviews of the effects of mass communications on children, see Eleanor E. Maccoby, "Effects of the Mass Media," in M.L. Hoffman and Lois W. Hoffman, eds., *Review of Child Development Research*, vol. 1 (New York, Russell Sage Foundation, 1964), pp. 239-52; Roberts, "Communication and Children."
42. McLuhan, *Understanding Media;* Lazarsfeld and Merton, "Mass Communication, Popular Taste and Organised Social Action."
43. For example, Klapper, *The Effects of Mass Communication;* Walter Weiss "Effects of the Mass Media of Communication," in Gardner Lindzey and Elliot Aronson, eds., *Handbook of Social Psychology*, 2nd ed., vol. 5 (Reading, Mass., Addison-Wesley, 1969), pp. 77-195; Walter Weiss, "Mass Communication," in *Annual Review of Psychology*, 1971 (Palo Alto, Annual Reviews, Inc., 1969).

5

Transnational Corporations and Transborder Data Flows: Their Role and Impact

Ever since the United Nations Centre on Transnational Corporations (UNCTC) was founded, the Commission on Transnational Corporations has expressed an interest in studying "Measures adopted by Governments nationally and regionally to strengthen their negotiating capacity in their relations with transnational corporations, and lessons to be learned therefrom" [E/C 20/16, para 29 (g)]. Under this mandate, UNCTC is submitting to the Commission at its seventh session a report summarising the main characteristics of the role and impact of transnational corporations in transborder data flows (E/C. 10/87). The report is accompanied by a technical paper (ST/CTC/23), dealing in detail with the same subject-matter. The purpose of these documents is to draw attention to a new phenomenon that will have profound economic, political, social and legal implications. Without an awareness and appreciation of the costs and benefits of this phenomenon, it may not be possible to harness transborder data flows to the maximum extent possible for a self-reliant development process and to avoid the emergence of a new area of tension between developed and developing countries.

The past decade and a half has witnessed rapid advances in both computer and telecommunication technologies which have resulted in the convergence of these formerly separate technologies into an integrated activity, telematics. Telematics provides instant access to, and utilisation of, sophisticated computer networks from any given remote location for purposes of processing, storage and retrieval of machine-readable data, and overcomes distance and time as barriers to communication. The transnationalisation of this process, in turn, has given rise to transborder data flows: international data transmissions over transnational computer communication networks.

Transnational corporations play a key role in the expansion and utilisation of transborder data flows. They are both the principal suppliers of the necessary infrastructure (hardware, software, peripheral equipment, communication links) and the principal users of this infrastructure, be it for corporate management purposes or the provision of international data-processing and information-retrieval services.

Commercial and Corporate Transborder Data Flows

As a result of latest developments in the field of information technology, an international market has been created for transborder data flow equipment, software and technology as well as the production, processing, transport and distribution of a wide variety of data of economic, political and social interest. The main components of this market are value-added networks, data processing, storage and retrieval-service companies, and remote-sensing operations.

Value-added networks are enhanced communication systems specifically dedicated to data transmission for processing, storage and retrieval services. They are operated on a leased-line basis. Such networks operate in a regional context—such as EURONET—and an international framework—such as TELENET and TYMNET: the last two are so far the only publicly accessible intercontinental networks that exist. These networks are growing rapidly, and, since the beginning of 1991, also extend to some socialist countries and offer an expanding transnational telecommunications infrastructure for transborder data flows.

Data processing, storage and retrieval services are offered commercially by computer service bureaux, the largest of which include COMSHARE, CYBERNET, INFONET, MARK III and

TYMSHARE (the parent corporation of TYMNET). These bureaux offer their powerful and highly sophisticated hardware for two major types of services: time shared data processing and data-base information retrieval. In addition, and this is of increasing importance, service bureaux provide complex software packages which are often directed to highly sophisticated needs, and frequently also allow access to large data bases. Since these services are offered on a cost-shared basis and with all the necessary in-house expertise and support capabilities, many organisations find it cheaper to rely on service bureaux than to build up and maintain their own computer and telecommunication capabilities. The data-processing market has expanded rapidly over the past decade. Measured in terms of total revenues, for instance, the computer-services industry in the United States increased from $ 2 billion in 1970 to $ 8 billion in 1978 (to which revenues of about $ 800 million from non-United States customers have to be added). The number of publicly accessible machine-readable data bases is also expanding at a very high rate (see Table 5.1). These data bases contain up-to-date information for decision-making in a wide range of subject areas, especially concerning scientific and technological and economic matters.

Table 5.1
Reference Data Bases and Data-base Records: Geographical Distribution (Numbers)

Area	*1978*	*1987*	*1992*
United States of America			
Number of data bases	177	208	259
Number of records (millions)	46	58	94
Other developed market economies			
Number of data bases	124	154	269
Number of records (millions)	6	13	55
Total			
Number of data bases	301	362	528
Number of records (millions)	52	71	148

Remote sensing data, finally, are data pertaining to the resources and the environment of a specific area monitored by earth-resource satellites. They are commercially available through the Landsat programme of the United States National Aeronautics and Space Administration.

If commercial transborder data flows involve transactions that occur in the international data market, corporate transborder data flows take place either through intra-corporate channels or among corporations in closed user-group networks. Intra-corporate networks—frequently linking remote terminals to a main-frame computer located at the corporate headquarters—are used by transnational corporations to monitor and co-ordinate more closely their foreign affiliates, to introduce greater efficiency into their operations, and to pursue a more integrated global strategy. Areas of application range across most corporate functions which include production planning, standardisation and co-ordination; financial control; research and development; customer and purchasing information; legal reporting; and employee relations.

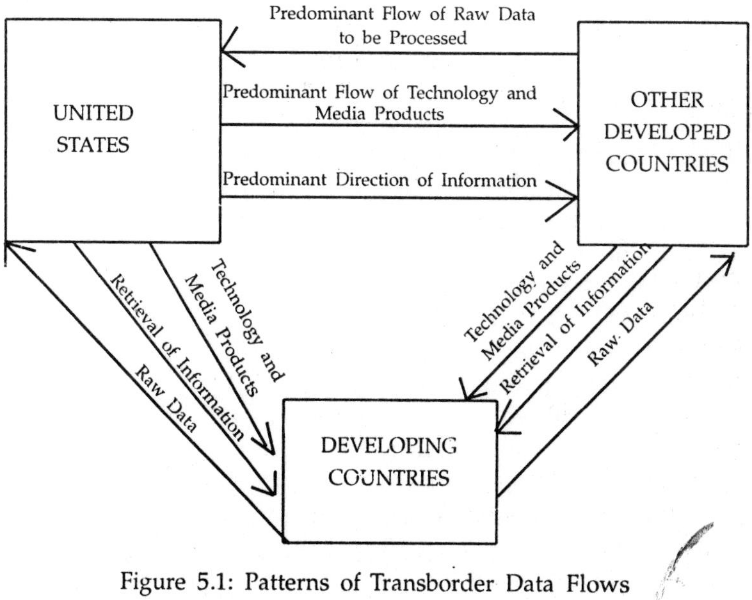

Figure 5.1: Patterns of Transborder Data Flows

Closed user-group networks provide service to information-intensive industries for which access to and exchange of data on an international scale have become an essential requirement for effective and competitive performance. The banking and airline communities, in particular, have established such networks, with, respectively, the Society or Worldwide Interbank Financial Communications (SWIFT) and the Societe internationale de telecommunications aeronautiques (SITA) (see Fig. 5.1).

Why Does it Matter?

Information is a resource. It makes alternatives known, reduces uncertainty about their implications, and facilitates their implementation. Hence, information, appropriately applied in the pursuit of a well-defined objective, is central to decision-making. And, increasingly, decision-making depends on access to a great variety of data, which have to be stored and processed on computers to make them manageable. As a result, the uncertainties involved in any given decision-making process are no longer a mere function of information available per se but are increasingly becoming a function of access to and participation in the international data market.

To date, however, access to this market and the application of the underlying technology and equipment have remained almost exclusively confined to institutions (especially transnational corporations) of the developed market economies. The experience of developing countries has been mainly one of the supplying data, buying the processed data—information—and acquiring the capital goods needed for their mostly rudimentary telematics sectors. The resulting over-all patterns of transborder data flows—which, however, may change in the future—is schematically summarised in figure 5.1. It is this situation that has led to the observation that "A system to which only financially powerful users have access must be avoided or international information networks, instead of contributing to the transparency of the world economic system, will make it more opaque and will increase existing disparities between the 'information rich' and the 'information poor'." (Hans Peter Gassmann in *OECD Observer,* November 1978.)

This pattern of transborder data flows reflects, of course, the global patterns of technological development. In light of the importance of information, the present structure of the international data market and the uneven distribution of the capabilities of applying transborder data flows raise a number of concerns. For the developing countries, in particular, they include the impact of transborder data flows on the international division of labour: the capacity of the developing countries to establish their own telematics and transborder data flow facilities: the competitiveness of domestic corporations of host countries: the bargaining position of host countries vis-a-vis developed countries and, more specifically, transnational corporations (whose foreign affiliates may lose decision-making power and, hence, a part of their capacity to react favourably to host country needs): and even issues relating to national sovereignty. Some of these concerns are summarised in the following quotation: "Data export for processing abroad comes to be regarded in an information age in the way the export of raw materials for manufacturing abroad is regarded in an industrial age—as the best way to fall behind: as a mark of underdevelopment." (Charles M. Dalfen, of the Canadian Radio-Television and Telecommunications Organisation).

The implications of such concerns reach beyond the economic sphere and may affect the relations between developed and developing countries in general. For, to the extent that information is a basis of power, the ability to collect and store it, have access to it, process and work with it can give countries (as well as groups and institutions within them) political, economic and social advantages over other countries (and their groups and institutions). Transborder data flows may thus lead to an accentuation of existing imbalances—and in fact, to the emergence of a new set of imbalances—between the developed and the developing countries. But, on the other hand, if the developing countries' capabilities to utilise transborder data flows and their access to the international data market can be improved sufficiently, these flows may well play a positive role in furthering the development objectives of the developing countries and, in the final analysis, in contributing to the redressing of the present imbalances. In fact, if the necessary networks can be established, transborder data flows may facilitate the establishment of an information infrastructure for a more self-reliant development. A key issue is, therefore, how it can be ensured either through the provision of adequate access to the international data market or through the strengthening of appropriate national industrial and regulatory capacities—that the entire international community can participate in the opportunities created by transborder data flows.

This is all the more important since transborder data flows harbour many opportunities. If they can be harnessed, they have the potential of providing an unlimited number of users at any given remote location with access to an exponentially expanding and diversifying pool of knowledge. This, in turn, can fuel scientific and technological progress, facilitate the transfer of data relevant for accelerating the development process, and improve the bargaining position of developing countries, in particular vis-a-vis transnational corporations.

What to Do?

The increasing awareness of the importance of information and the growing realisation of the possible political, economic, social and cultural impacts of transborder data flows have led national governments to search for adequate responses to this new phenomenon. Reflecting the longer and more intense experience of the developed market economies with telematics and transborder data flows, these countries have taken the lead in the process. So far, however, the search for suitable regulatory frameworks on a domestic or international level has only commenced—with the notable exception of questions pertaining to transborder data flows of personal data. Concerns about safeguarding the privacy of these flows, in fact, have served to focus attention on transborder data flows in general, triggering national and, eventually, international actions.

In fact, these actions have resulted in the first international frameworks placed specifically on transborder data flows. At the end of last year, the Council of Europe adopted the Convention for the Protection of Individuals with Regard to Automatic Processing of Personal Data (which explicitly also dealt with transborder data flows) and OECD approved Guidelines Governing the Protection of Privacy and Transborder Flows of Personal Data. With agreement having been reached on the treatment of transborder flows of personal data, OECD is now beginning to investigate the legal and economic problems related to the transborder data flows of non-personal data (i.e., primarily economic and technological data), with a view towards developing guidelines in this area as well as filling the existent legal void: a programme of research on these issues is already under way.

On the other hand, the developing countries and the socialist countries as groups have so far not adopted a common stand specifically designed to deal with the impact of transborder data flows and the role of transnational corporations in them. They may thus be leaving to one group of countries alone the formulation of what may conceivably be naissant international law for an area of increasing importance for economic development.

Even if at present no legal infrastructure exists that could sustain a transition to a world economy in which transborder data flows play a growing role, it is not advisable that actions in this area be taken before the implications associated with this phenomenon are better known. Yet since transborder data flows are a new phenomenon, their impact—particularly in the developing countries—has neither manifested itself clearly nor been subject to much empirical research. A full appreciation of the possible benefits and costs associated with transborder data flows is particularly important since many developing countries might, on the one hand, want to speed up the introduction of transborder data flow technology in order to reap its potential benefits, while, on the other hand, they will want to avoid the potential problems associated with it.

What is needed most, therefore, is research on the impact of transborder data flows and, since transnational corporations are of key importance in practically all aspects of transborder data flows, research would automatically focus on their role and contribution.

Probably the most important item to examine empirically and in detail would be the impact of transborder data flows on developing countries. In the same manner in which a number of developed countries—most notable Canada and France—have found it necessary to prepare indepth evaluations of the effect of transborder data flows on their societies and economies, it may be necessary for individual developing countries to study the impact of this new phenomenon on their societies and economies as well, particularly in light of their development objectives.

Information Revolution and Global Economics

Information and the conduits for its transmission are playing an ever increasing role in the economic and social development of countries around the world. The potential dynamic change in the ASEAN region will hinge to a major extent, upon each country's information handling and telecommunication ability.

Trade, tourism, manufacturing, marketing and public services are becoming more and more information dependent. Singapore, realising this fact has positioned itself to be a major information node as an adjunct to its role as a shipping hub. As an example of how the two go together, the paperwork needed to clear a cargo vessel took an average of eight hours. Now with Electronic Document Interchange it takes about fifteen minutes.

Current levels of telecommunications infrastructure vary considerably within the region. So, too, do the approaches to the role of government and the role of competition in providing telecommunication services.

Moves are headway in all ASEAN countries to upgrade and expand their facilities. In most countries there is also an ongoing discussion of governments' role and most importantly a discussion of the importance of the information technology infrastructure.

Several long-term scenarios are possible. A major factor is likely to be the extent to which the ASEAN countries are able to join in co-operative ventures, building on the strengths of each other. Major shifts in this direction, however, could well be seen as a threat to national identity.

Some regional co-operation is underway. Underseas fibre optic networks are being put in place. Co-operation in the use of satellites is evidenced by continued use of Palapa. A real test may be the ability to focus the ASEAN planning process to foresee a truly regional satellite sometime in the future.

Political stability in the region and global economic stability are needed ingredients for the successful transition to more information based economies.

The role of the Information Revolution in changing the pattern of economic and social values is just beginning to be understood. Changes in economic demand that stem from technological innovations in telecommunications are undoubtedly linked with socio cultural issues and value conflicts for legitimising such changes. As microelectronic technology invades the home, the factory, and the market, nations find that their concepts of power and equity are really dimensions of information power and information equity.

Two world wars radically altered the economic base of the products of the Industrial Revolution, but the model of the economic base remained. This model was determined by the causal links which bind social variables with new forms of energy, communications, and information. The post-Industrial society is marked by another set of changes that are altering the basic equations, leading to just as fundamental a change in our lives as when the Industrial Revolution transformed society. It has dramatically altered the political and economic landscape and limited our ability to predict future changes (Rex 1986).

In social equations concerning technological innovation, supply is generally an assumed variable. Demand for the diffusion of information technology is the determining variable. However, it is difficult to categorically establish the relationship between an information sector within an economy and the operation of economic forces. If demand has become the engine of growth, it may be moving entrepreneurs into a search for new modes of innovation. The dilemma of demandpull diffusion of communication technology becomes more complex as the service sector expands more rapidly than the traditional sectors of the industrial society. In the 1950s and 1960s, capital equipment was considered the *sine qua non* of economic development. In the decades ahead, the hardware and software of telecommunications will contribute to the growth of national incomes for both developed and developing countries.

As the interface between satellites and computers grow and telematics becomes more widespread, countries find their economic health and viability determined by their investments in innovative telecommunications technology. With the proliferation of global information systems and the rapid transmission of data flows across national boundaries, the nation state begins to lose its meanings. National boundaries get blurred and claims of national sovereignty over the geosynchronous orbit and the magnetic frequency spectrum being to grow weak as technology moves towards integrated services digital networks (ISDN) and intersatellite links.

It is difficult to predict the future outcome of the catalytic changes sweeping the telecommunications industry as deregulation spreads and natural monopolies decline. Whether they will widen the gulf between rich and poor nations or help to create a global "republic of technology" remains to be seen. Equitable access to information will be a key dimension for policy makers in the future even as distribution of income now is. Perhaps the ubiqutous application of the new technology will help to forge between different regions within a country and help to unify the aspirations of people across national boundaries.

This chapter examines the impact of information technologies on industrial structures, the resulting risks and opportunities for the developed and developing worlds, the changes wrought in the system of international trade, the issues of transborder data flows, the tensions created by the technology gap between the developed and the developing countries, and the future impact on the global economy.

Information Technologies and Emerging Industrial Structures

Information technologies have developed at a much more rapid rate than the policies designed to deal with the issues they pose. The very nature of information, combined with electronic gathering, storing and disseminating techniques, makes it difficult to contain and control within national boundaries (Strong 1985). Existing regulatory mechanisms are becoming obsolete as nations find that former supply systems are unable to cope effectively with new and enhanced services flooding the domestic and international markets. In order to ensure the benefits of the new technology for their citizens, countries find it expeditious to co-operate with other governments and take advantage of interdependent systems.

The Information Revolution is proving to be a major driving force behind economic development for two reasons. First, the information sector is a highly dynamic and expanding one, creating wealth and employment. Second, its potential impact on existing economic activities is revitalising, leading to higher productivity and improved allocation of resources. A range of studies over the past ten years, including a recent study of ten countries in the Pacific region by the East-West Center had led to the conclusion that information-related economic activities are contributing to a growing share of the national income (Jussawalla 1986a).

As the telecommunications industry reshapes its structure and organisation, benefits of increased productivity can be measured in sectors that are becoming more information-intensive through the use of microelectronic and optoelectronic technology. Such productivity increases are being generated by three classes of emerging corporations:

(a) those supplying information processing and storage services;
(b) those that distribute information; and
(c) those that manufacture the hardware.

During the 1970s, U.S. productivity grew by 20 per cent while Japan's output per worker soared by 145 per cent and the Federal Republic of Germany's by 75 per cent. According to Terleckyj (1984), gains in overall productivity are likely to grow at only 2.9 per cent annually in the United States for the period through 1990, while growth in the communications sector is estimated at 6.5 per cent average growth. The more rapid productivity gains in communications are occurring because information is not just a commodity but a resource that is catalytic and feeds on itself.

Information technology is rapidly becoming a part of the production function in both the manufacturing and service sectors. The advantage of information technology is that it increases the productivity not only of labour but also that of capital. Innovation generates positive income effects by creating expanded economies of scale with their positive externalities. Information innovation generates increased demand for investment goods, greater competition, higher profit margins, and improved factor allocations.

Deregulation in trucking, civil aviation, and telecommunications has subjected these sectors to strong competitive forces. In telecommunications, the tidy concept of natural monopoly based on economies of scale and scope has been swept away as the industry in the OECD countries heads into a period of painful readjustment (Dodsworth 1986). Not only has technology radically altered the economics of the telecommunications industry, but users are making equally strong demands for more sophisticated networks. Governments have become more supportive of ideas of competitive efficiency. As deregulation puts down roots in several countries like the United States, Japan, and the United Kingdom and as the trend becomes evident in France and West Germany, the question still remains whether customers receive better services from a tightly organised monopoly or from a free-reined competitive system. One thing remains clear: the Information Revolution has caused a dramatic transition in the supply of telecommunication equipment and services such that users have abundant choice, and scarcity of supplies is now a thing of the past.

Information technologies are an integral part of social and economic systems. There exists a symbiotic relationship inasmuch as technological change affects our economic, political, and social structures, and is in turn dependent on the resources our economies produce, on the political framework, and on the capacity of the social system to adjust to new ideas, to generate and absorb them (Michalski 1986). Theoretically speaking, technical progress together with demand are determinants of economic growth. However, the interconnectivity of telecommunication equipment creates problems of vulnerability, confidentiality of information in the distribution of data, that pose challenges to the economy and to society.

The short lifespan of the technology renders investment decisions difficult. It becomes imperative to invest in the next generation information technology before competitors do so, and this has to be done within the framework of a shortening product cycle (Snow & Jussawalla 1986). Capital as well as labour can be adversely affected by technology-induced changes. Declining industries and their employees can best be compensated by farsighted planning and forecasting. Propping up declining industries with subsidies, tax incentives, or tariff protectionism is usually counter-productive in the long run. Policies have to be geared to achieve the correct balance between declining and emerging industries that results from the macroeconomic transition from manufacturing to information industries.

Globalisation and Integration

The sector most affected by the Information Revolution is that of finance and banking. The money float is being replaced by the information float as a consequence of telecommunication services, thereby diversifying and reducing risks. Two hitherto separate networks, namely banking and telecommunications, are now interlinked via computers inducing powerful changes in the global velocity or circulation of money or its reciprocal, money demand, and rapid changes in currency exchange rates, interest rates, and international capital flows. The upper limit to the use of telecommunications technology by the banking networks will be determined by the volume of transactions it can carry in a cost-effective manner.

Bank profits today are less sensitive to interest rates inasmuch as banks are no longer recovering cost of services from interest margins, but from providing new customised services to meet changing requirements of consumers (Jussawalla 1985). Financial intermediation also is essentially an information industry and changes with the newer systems of processing, storing and changing information. In modern market economies, financial intermediaries stand at the intersection of production and consumption and provide the conduit through which information valuable to investors and borrowers is exchanged both intra- and internationally.

The importance of telematics to financial services is indicated by the large amounts invested by the industry in telecommunication equipment. Salomon Brothers estimated that between 1980 and 1985 the big U.S. banks spent US$ 7 billion on electronic banking technology. European banks are estimated to spend one billion dollars annually on terminals and automating equipment. Automatic teller machines (ATMs) are being added in OECD markets at a rate of 10,000 per year.

Japan currently has more ATMs per capita than any other country (320/million) and has invested in an all-bank data and funds transfer system called Zengin.

It has been found through empirical studies that scale economies are substantial in automated clearing houses which use computerised networks for same-day transfer of interbank accounts. Systems like CHIPs (Clearinghouse Interbank Payments System) in New York, CHAPs (Clearinghouse Automated Payments System) in London, and CHATs (Clearinghouse Automated Transfer System) in Hong Kong carry an enormous volume of funds settlement. Whereas in 1981 the U.S. banking system completed US$ 15 trillion worth of check transactions for one year, CHIPS does this same volume in three months. The banking industry also uses the computerised system called SWIFT (Society for Worldwide Interbank Financial Telecommunications), which is wholly owned by member banks in 50 countries and is organised under Belgian law and eliminates the reliance of banks on PTTs.

Telecommunications are now a major part of the fixed costs of banking, determined by the network vendor who in many instances may be a regulated monopolist. The major problem for the banking industry, and also for the telecommunications industry, is that the product is not a single one distributed through a single network (Revell 1983). Financial services have diverse products that can be delivered through paper transactions as well as electronic ones. The former are subject to rising costs and the latter to falling costs. Therefore, the theory of public utility pricing is not applicable to electronic banking. Economies of scale are constantly changing with changes in technology. Oligopoly conditions in the banking industry make the markets contestable vulnerable to hit-and-miss entry (Baumol *et al*, 1982), which in turn is a deterrent to incumbent suppliers of electronic funds transfer and reduces the need for regulation.

An important outcome of the impact of the Information Revolution on the banking industry is that central bank control has become difficult to enforce due to the instantaneous movement of diverse forms of purchasing power across continents. Monetary policies have to become more flexible and integrated with international flows of funds since the lines of demarcation between domestic and international vendors have been blurred due to the growth of global transmission networks. It is now possible to clear funds outside the control of the central bank. The degree and penetration of electronic funds transfer in a country will depend on the availability and costs of the telecommunications infrastructure.

Electronic funds transfers have defied the theoretical constructs underlying monetary policy by rendering currencies highly substitutable within constraints from exchange rate movements. McKinnon (1982) has argued that global demand for funds is a better indicator of inflation than any single country's supply of money. In other words, national monetary policy gets neutralised by the actions of other nations monetary policies in view of the telematic integration of money markets. Regulators and policy makers find that their *de jure* enactments are not keeping abreast of *de facto* developments in technology.

There have emerged some negative externalities as a consequence of these developments because regulations can be bypassed with comparative ease. Not only has the power and influence of insider information in brokerage transactions grown, but institutional investors have become major players almost eliminating individual investors. While arbitragers are important in greasing the wheels of corporate mergers that are sweeping the U.S. and the other OECD countries, the negative consequences challenge regulators to respond to these changes.

Developing countries are still not fully integrated into global financial markets with the exception of Newly Industrialised countries like Singapore and Hong Kong. Most developing countries are still subject to technological dualism with sophisticated networks in their metropolitan centres and the lack of any organised financial services in the remote regions. The Maitland Commission's report, "The Missing Link," (1984) pointed out the disparities between developed market and developing economies and led to setting up of the Center of Development of Telecommunications under the auspices of the International Telecommunications Union.

Impact on Trade and Trans-border Data Flows

Information services emerging from telecommunication innovations are a major component of the service economy, which is rapidly overtaking the manufacturing sector in growth and value. Services are not sufficiently homogeneous to lend themselves to simple generalisations, but according to Baumol (1985) few activities can match the productivity record of telecommunication and computation.

Information trade is considered as a part of services trade and is, therefore, vulnerable to taxation, tariffs, and subsidy, not to mention non-tariff barriers. The phenomenon of trade in information, or transborder data flows (TDF), occurs in a complex mixture of mechanical and electronic processes where in the information transmitted is not openly visible in physical form. Since these flows rely on telecommunications conduits, the demand for them grows with every decline in the cost of telecommunications network. The value of these flows depends in part on their scarcity in the market. Broadcasting, by contrast, derives its value from maximum dispersion of information.

The International Telecommunication Union (ITU) in the past was responsible for making the world's telecommunication system work like a single machine when changes in technology were incremental rather than revolutionary (Reed 1985). With innovative and constantly changing technology, telecommunication services can no longer be shared. They have to be traded. In the absence of legal restrictions on interconnection or entry, the market for TDF is contestable in the sense that potential firms can avail themselves of the same set of production techniques and market demand as those facing incumbent firms. The mere threat of market entry is sufficient to ensure efficiency as long as market entry and exit costs are sufficiently low (Baumol & Panzar 1982).

The line of demarcation between providing networks and providing services over them has become invisible, which makes TDF fall outside the purview of the perceived theory of comparative advantage. Another reason for dealing with TDF separately is the concept of splintered tradables in which services are splintered from goods and goods from services, and in which the former are considered the dynamic component and the latter as the static one (Bhagwati 1984). A similar concept is defined by Sampson and Snape (1985) in which services are separated from those relating to the production of goods. In this process there is also a disembodiment effect, inasmuch as the service is available across distances without the presence of the provider as is the case with TDF. Conventional theory made no room for variables such as technical change emerging from inputs of knowledge. Comparative cost ratios are only an indirect response to price change and should not be treated as the basis for trade in information (Jussawalla & Cheah 1985).

The major players in the market for TDF are transnational corporations (TNCs) that have their own private networks and internalise their information flows. In international markets, TNCs make low-cost transfers of technological inputs to their subsidiaries in host countries. Terms of trade are effected by the transfer of information technology to the host country as subsidiaries become members of a closed user network. In theory, information trade is dependent on the joint supply of three resources, namely computer systems, telecommunication networks, and data. A set of complementary products is generating economies of scale and scope which may entitle the operations to fall under the rubric of natural monopoly. The natural barrier to entry would then be the huge sunk costs of providing information systems.

Global Networking

Generally, services are traded in response to an intermediate rather than a final demand. Information services provide an essential link among economic agents. Such a link facilitates the interdependent functioning of international markets. Protectionist policies are prevalent widely for TDF in both developed and developing countries. Because of a strong link between trade in information services and foreign direct investment, LDC governments were wary of negotiating multilateral rules in GATT without first introducing controls on direct external investments. However, electronic transmission of information makes such restrictions difficult to implement. It is difficult to locate the point of entry for information flowing through computers that talk to each other via terrestrial, undersea, and satellite linkages. Furthermore, TNCs operating in an imperfectly competitive market are prepared to pay the extra costs of internalised networks in order to protect the efficiency of operations of geographically dispersed units. When this advantage is threatened by covert barriers to trade, there is a demand for transparency of trade regulations and reciprocity.

The world is no longer tied to monetary standards as telecommunications technology transforms the services sector. The U.S. service economy in 1986 contributed two-thirds of the GNP, and 60 per cent of new jobs were in the services sector (Dougabn 1987). The manufacturing sector jobs increased by only five per cent. Institutional services play a major role in these changes. An OECD study on invisible transactions (1986) shows that service exports are growing faster than goods exports and that developing countries have as much stake in the global service economy as developed countries do. The ITU Center for Communication Development is looking for pragmatic ways of helping LDCs.

When trade protection enters the area of telecommunications and data services, it has a significant impact on the service economy. Free market forces need to be supported, but the rhetoric has changed from free trade to "fair trade" because of the growing service economy and the global interdependence caused by information technology. The realities of free and fair access to TDF are becoming a cause of concern to policy makers.

The balance of payments effect of information trade on developing countries of the Asia-Pacific region remains a major issue of concern but is extremely difficult to quantify or to evaluate. In the past, international financial credits and other financial services were calculated on the basis of residuals which were not directly related to trade. The conditions of such transfers are now changed and can no longer be treated as residuals. The globalisation of banking and the multinational spread of non financial business increased the international fungibility of financial resources by reducing market segmentation. The focus has shifted from authorised flows of data and financial services to flows of direct investments overseas and unauthorised flows of data.

The concerns of LDCs grow because of the impact of data and financial flows on their balance of payments. They find themselves in the old colonial role of exporters of raw data and the importers of processed information akin to their exports of raw materials and imports of capital goods. The burden of these flows is not only on their trade balances but also on their cultural mores. This induces them to take prior action to protect their nascent information-intensive industries and to prevent a resurgence of colonial trade patterns. In fact, Krommenaker (1984) opines that the social sensitivity argument is seldom invoked with regard to goods but is frequently invoked against satellite-based mass media.

Bilateral agreements between the leading trading nations have been termed "black protection" because they are symptomatic of managed trade and not of free trade. An example of such managed trade is the agreement between the United States and Japan on market-sharing and supervision of the cost and price of semiconductors. It is called "black protection" because the agreements are outside the rules of the game. These official rules are written down in 38 articles of the GATT which are binding on its 92 member countries.

While trends towards deregulation exist in most OECD countries, there is a simultaneous trend to protectionist pressures. The low import propensity of the trade-surplus countries stands in the way of smoother trade negotiations at GATT. The developing countries have come to regard GATT as a rich man's club which allows discrimination against LDC exports, despite the privileges developing countries enjoy under the generalised system of preferences.

It is difficult to measure the impact of non-tariff barriers to information trade, but the World Bank calculates that for 1985, 27 per cent of imports of 16 industrial countries are subjected to invisible control. Such control becomes all the more difficult to locate when nations impose invisible barriers to invisible trade like data flows. Black protection is applied in many ingenious ways such as local content requirements, pollution and safely tests, and standards compliances. The World Bank has counted an increase of 2,500 non-tariff barriers in two years. Consequently this eighth round of trade talks of GATT members will attempt to halt the proliferation of barriers to trade in services, from banking to air travel to consultancies. The link between goods, services, and overseas investment has to be recognised for GATT talks to achieve any measure of success.

Developing countries are aware of the economic impact of the movement of information resources and the social impact of information technology. The first LDC to take action in this regard was Brazil, which in 1978 strengthened its domestic information processing industry. It planned to increase information resources within the country by setting up its own information processing system, data bases and telecommunication networks for integrating these services. It categorised data flows into corporate data and commercial data on the basis of which permission is granted for integrating with foreign data bases. Links with Societe Internationale des Telecommunications Aeronautique (SITA) and SWIFT are examined the government on a case-by-case basis. Data generated in Brazil cannot be stored abroad, and retrieval services are to be located within the country. Despite these restrictions, Brazil is aware that in an interdependent world economy it is impossible to isolate networks or to prevent the use of external data bases.

In 1985, Brazil had the support of India, South Korea, Argentina, and Yugoslavia in its demand for a separate institution to deal with trade in services. But with the lapse of time this support has waned because of the protectionist trends that are beginning to appear in the developed countries. Brazil rationalises its own protectionist policies against foreign direct investment and against information technology imports on the grounds that trade rules should be different between the North and the South. Developing countries generally are paying 40 per cent of their export earnings on debt servicing in addition to trade deficits in services.

Developing countries in Asia find that almost 50 per cent of their data can be generated from within the country itself, but scientific and technological data has to be imported. How much data they should opt in from abroad will depend on the development stage of their telecommunications infrastructure. They need to obtain data on science and technology applications, on market information, and on the learning curves of the developing countries. What is significant for the Pacific region countries is that South-South trade in information is as important to the development of the emerging economies as is data from the industrially advanced nations. In any case, data from the advanced countries filters in through the TNCs and brings negative externalities for domestic corporations pursuing the same lines of business. It is wrong to believe that foreign data remains unutilised in developing countries; one need only consider the use to which Brazil, India, China, and Indonesia have put their imports of technological data in their satellite and computer networks. For example, China has emerged at the forefront of satellite-launching technology, which it is commercially selling to Europe and the U.S.

Information Revolution and Developing Countries

Development planners have underestimated the contribution of telecommunication technologies to economic growth and welfare. The MacBride Commission's Report (1980) declared that communication systems are linked to economic systems, just as communication development is linked to national development.

Technological change and institutional change have been treated in economic theory as exogenous to the economic system. However, technical progress in conjunction with demand is a major determinant of economic growth because it leads to increased demand for investment goods. It renders production activities more competitive, increases profit margins, and enhances institutional responsiveness to changing conditions as a consequence of better factor allocation. Due to the time lag between the introduction of new technology and its positive income effects the benefits are not easily discernible. Development theory has preferred to apply comparative statistics to the examination of speedy growth states. The focus has been on resource utilisation and improved measures for generating savings and investment.

It is only very recently that technology has been treated as endogenous to the development process. Innovation in technology came to be recognised in the 1960s as the engine of growth within the teteological framework of maximising per capita consumption of essential commodities and services. In this wider penumbra of technological innovation and its diffusion through transfer, the relationship between communications technology and economic development came to be debated. The demand for communication services is a function of economic variables such as income, population, price, and infrastructure of a country. Business, industry, and government are dependent upon improved communications which generate higher incomes for these sector, which in turn generate further demand for communication.

It is important to bear in mind that the viability of a given technology will depend on the economic environment into which it is introduced. Technology transfer as it has evolved through economic history requires for its assessment a frame of reference: technology transfer for what? benefits for whom? who bears the economic and social costs of the transfer? These are issues that require assessment both in quantitative and qualitative terms. Conventional GDP indicators are no longer useful in reality.

Determinants

Empirical application of technology transfer has established the facts that knowledge of local conditions and the willingness of the recipients to entertain the flow of technology are crucial to a successful transfer. The concept has undergone considerable change in the acknowledgment that technology transfer should be designed to help developing countries acquire and build their own skills and generate their own innovations from within. While technology for development can be all-pervasive and applicable to all sectors, social control of the transfer is essential if scarce resources are to be effectively utilised. When technology transfer is resorted to as an unlimited and unregulated strategy of modernisation, the consequences may worsen the skewed distribution of income that prevails in developing countries (Jussawalla 1980).

The small, elite enclaves in developing countries create a polarisation in decision-making and an equity crisis generated by subsidiaries of TNCs. The urban elite find it in their self-interest to encourage such islands of technology in backward societies and to permit profits to flow out of the country. Such a short-sighted policy helps to perpetuate dependence on technology imports rather than to generate indigenous skill-formation and research and development from within.

In developing countries, expressed demand for telecommunications does not reflect the needs of users; therefore, government policy should be to keep prices for services at artificially low levels. Sufficient profits, then, will not be generated to finance expansion or to attract greater investment. Therefore, telecommunication investment for rural and urban development cannot be related to the advantages of direct users, except in terms of societal progress. Access to the telephone network and benefits in terms of improved health, market information leading to improved productivity, and banking and business information are all gains that accrue to more people than the direct users alone. Resource costs of telecommunications have to be judged in the wider context of a public good. Economists, use the utility concept to show that a subscriber derives added benefits from the service as more people join the system. Therefore, if telephony is to be extended to rural areas as development support communication, pricing policies cannot be formulated for recovering costs. The service has to be priced as a public good. Investment priorities cannot be equated to anticipated returns on capital. The World Bank, in recent years, has been shifting away from the rate-of-return in its lending policies for rural telephone networks in developing countries. The basic hypothesis is that savings in training costs of paraprofessionals, labour costs, organisation, and transportation costs make it worthwhile.

There are three fundamental reasons why the use of financial indicators is not sufficient to support the hypothesis that transfer of telecommunication technology is more effective for developing countries than other forms of technology. First, there is a wide divergence between the market value of telecommunications and its socially appropriate value. Second, the effects of investment in telecommunication technology and income distribution in terms of real goods and services are far greater than what financial indicators would show. Third, the relationship between financial criteria and national strategy for rural development is not adequate in terms of social welfare or economic changes envisaged for rural areas. As argued by Rada (1981) the control of technology often means the control of development, the definition of its aims and even its pace.

Communication technology has so revolutionised global interdependence that it is now possible for developing countries to weigh the options offered by off-the-self technology, calculate its opportunity cost, weigh these against tangible and intangible benefits and then budget for investment in the selected technology or mix of technologies. The rate of obsolescence in telecommunication technology is so rapid that it is relatively easier for LDCs to invest in the latest and most sophisticated networks without having to scrap substantial prior investment. At the same time decision-makers in developing countries have to exercise caution when dealing with technology suppliers who push purchases for equipment which is no longer in demand by industrialised country users. There is always the danger of being landed with equipment that becomes dysfunctional and cannot be cost-effectively maintained or operated.

The heterogeneity of developing countries makes it difficult to devise uniform packages whereby the technology and equipment for telecommunication infrastructure can be transferred to them. These LDCs are, in fact, in a situation in which their domestic development is conditioned not only by the technology transferred but equally by the logic and dynamism of technological advances in the industrialised countries. The microelectronics revolution promises to make international division of labour even more skewed than it is at present because of the concentration of information intensive industries in the advanced countries generating high levels of productivity in all forms of economic activity.

The geosynchronous orbit (GSO) has opened up a whole new resource which is finite and subject to congestion but not to depletion. This means that the economic value of the resource increases with use. However, in accordance with the Outer Space Treaty of 1967, the GSO is a common property resource. In economic terms countries can either over-invest in it because of its universal availability or let it go to waste. In economic theory, monopoly control over a common property resource should not be possible, but the abundance of capital and technological skills have enabled the advanced countries of the globe to exploit this resource and exercise oligopolistic control over it (Jussawalla 1984).

With every advance in technology, there is a greater demand to position the satellites closer together (between two and three degrees apart) and to use higher frequencies in orbit. This involves greater investment in the space segment of the satellite giving it more onboard power and making the earth segment or receiving stations smaller and cheaper.

Since this resource has been declared by the United Nations as a common property resource, proprietary rights are indeterminate. Countries endowed with funds and technology have already exploited the orbit and established "squatters, rights" on a first-come, first-served basis. This has lead to a growing demand from the developing countries to preplan reservations and to charge user fees for the current occupation of the arc. This has become an economic and political issue for international for a like the International Telecommunications Union (ITU) to deal with. It is linked to territorial sovereignty over the orbit similar to the economic zone within territorial waters (Jussawalla 1979). At present the industrially advanced countries have established the use of the preferred slots in the orbit along with other locations.

First World countries claim that their pre-emption of the orbital slots helps to induce efficiency in resource allocation and any contest of this occupation will render their investments in space technology vulnerable. The main problem is that the orbital spectrum is currently not priced, and as much no stakeholder rights have been established. In other words, no country has paid to purchase any segment in space, but many countries are using it to station their satellites for which they have made huge investments in construction costs and launch costs as well as station-keeping costs. The multiproduct nature of satellite services makes it possible for the developed countries to exercise oligopoly control over the GSO. The problem of ownership becomes complicated by the fact that the market price of the spectrum is, at present, zero and as such it can be assumed that there are neither transaction costs nor income effects.

Several alternative suggestions have emerged to overcome this nebulous situation. The adoption of some of these may bring about equitable access to the resource without destroying efficiency. One such proposal is made by Levin (1985) for establishing a lease market under which assignments can be brought and sold through contracts. Negotiations for leases will lead to an efficient outcome in spectrum use regardless of distribution. Transaction costs will emerge such as decision-making, interdependency and enforcement costs. These costs have to be weighted against transaction benefits such as gains in efficiency, scale economies and enlarged communication channels. However, the danger of establishing such a lease market is that if lease rents are bid up too high then LDCs which now own satellites like India, Indonesia, Brazil and Mexico may be required to pay high lease rents to other developing countries, in which case they will be priced out of the lease market. On the other hand, it is possible that if stakeholder rights are established, then developing countries can cartelise and demand very high lease rents, thereby destroying the initiative to invest in space technology.

Resource Duality

Another suggestion for allocation of the spectrum is based on the general principles of efficient markets under which market forces should be allowed to decide the ownership and use of the orbit (Whiborgs Wijkman 1981). The proposal deals with the spectrum as two separate resources: one is the physical orbit and the other is the electromagnetic spectrum without which communication is not possible. It is argued that establishing user rights that are marketable and divisible for the orbit and also a system for enforcing liability rules to guarantee for the efficient use of the space resource. This involves the market behaviour and for distributing rents arising from the use of the orbit. Such free market trading might lead to congestion and interference, and the marginal value to any single user may not equal its opportunity cost or the cost of its next best use. If value dispersion of information pathways is to be optimised, should it be at the cost of economic efficiency or distributional equity? This is the crux of the debate for the ownership of the Clarke orbit and its use.

In the real world it is impossible to create a spectrum market because of the interactive physical characteristics of satellites beaming signals. Centralised control over signal distribution is required to prevent congestion and jamming. The main problem of free market allocation is that to achieve economic efficiency in operations, there must be the option open to users to combine the orbit slot with the frequency spectrum in any combination feasible. This is not possible since the space segment can be obtained only as a package with the frequency allocation. Therefore, there can be no interchange between the two to arrive at an optimal solution and the two resources are complementary. In economic theory to achieve dynamic market efficiency, there must be competition in all relevant markets, and there must be equality to private costs and benefits (Coase 1960). These characteristics do not obtain in the allocation of the orbital spectrum, and much contention has arisen from the present unequal distribution as viewed by the developing countries.

The developing countries have, for many years, claimed that they require planned allocation or *a priori* planning of the GSO. The challenge was first posed in 1976 at a declaration made at Bogota, when eight equatorial countries claimed segments of the orbit directly above them as integral parts of their national territory over which they had sovereign rights, and that all other segments were the common heritage of mankind. They claimed that the orbit was a physical property of the planet which should be regulated under a *sui generis* regime. The use of the term "equitable access" has been frequently used in treaties for the use of outer space as well as in debates in the ITU conferences.

At the 1979 World Administration Radio Conference (WARC) the claim for equitable access was reiterated in Resolution No. 3 and sought to guarantee the principle in practice, meaning that the countries must actually be able to use the spectrum and not just be guaranteed access at a future date. This was changed at the ITU Plenipotentiary conference held at Nairobi in 1982. The change relevant to our discussion is the introduction of the phrase for equitable access "taking account of the special needs of the developing countries and the geographical situation of particular countries." While these changes were made in a climate of increasing demands on the part of the LDCs for technical cooperation and assistance, their effect on existing law must be noted (Gorove 1984). The term "equitable access" presupposes the technical ability to reach the geostationary orbit. It implies admittance but not ownership of any segment of it. On the other hand, the common heritage concept requires equitable sharing of the orbit. The issues involved seem to be sovereignty and appropriation. Spectrum management, therefore, becomes a crucial requirement for any harmonious use of satellite technology that would benefit all users and be extended to existing as well as aspiring users. Even Third World negotiators recognise that exaggerated claims can ensue in an effort to enforce equitable access. But any method that can guarantee access at some point in time, without undue penalty, would reduce the lacuna in the current *a priori* allotment for orbital slots (Srirangan 1981).

Some of these knotty issues were discussed at the Space WARC 1985 held in Geneva in August as part of a two-phase negotiation convened by the ITU to deal with the ownership claims on the orbital resources as well as its uses. Within the framework of the Outer Space Treaty (1967), the discussions at the 1985 Space WARC covered which space services are to be planned, such as the fixed satellite service, and what arrangements are to be made for the guaranteed access. The technical parameters of these issues were provided to the member countries at the 1985 WARC meeting.

Indonesia and India took the lead among LDCs for owning their own domestic satellite systems. The Indonesian Palapa system may become a regional satellite catering to the needs of the ASEAN countries and it is a testimony to the growing demand for satellite services from developing countries.

While the Palapa system has been in operation since 1976, it was used largely for commercial telephony, telex and broadcasting. Since 1984 the system has been used for the development of higher education facilities with assistance from the United States Agency for International Development (USAID) programme (Block 1984). The system uses a highpowered satellite with small, inexpensive earth stations offering the possibility of reaching the remote regions of the archipelago. Instruction is conducted in an interactive mode using a telephone bandwidth. The satellite also provides a link between these eastern universities of Indonesia with the world-renowned agricultural regional research centre in Java. The satellite itself serves as a teleconferencing bridge and is more cost-effective than using a terrestrial bridge. In 1985 Indonesia started experimenting with solar-powered earth stations, giving additional cost advantages for rural communications.

A similar pilot project has been in operation in Peru since 1983 with the assistance of USAID. However, the system uses a beam off the INTELSAT satellite along with 6.2-metre earth stations costing US$ 200,000 each. The project is carried out by the telecommunication authority of Peru called ENTEL to encourage local participation and training in the use of satellite services. Users have accepted community telephones and the system's use in health and agricultural applications is growing. It is one of the few rural development satellite service programmes in the developing world that is trying to establish the link between satellite based telecommunications and economic development of the rural areas.

The University of the West Indies and University of the South Pacific in Suva, Fiji, also bear testimony to the use of satellite communications for furthering education in remote areas and for island nations. NASA had provided the ATS-1 satellite for the use of the PEACESAT system located in Hawaii, for linking the Pacific Islands and the university centre in Suva. Despite the fact that after its use for 18 years when the satellite moved away from orbit, the demand for satellite use for education is persistent. At present, INTELSAT has given the use of Project SHARE (Satellite for Health and Rural Education) to the University.

Satellite Services

India is another country which lacked the infrastructure for point-to-point telecommunications and broadcasting services. Since 1967 India's scientists have been designing and experimenting with various plans for satellite services. But the government has to be convinced of its benefits and had to lay out the investments for such a costly infrastructure. In 1976 India had the advantage of experimenting with the ATS-6 loaned by NASA; this gave Indian scientists and technicians experience in handling satellite service.

Mexico and Brazil have also invested in satellite technology for access to their rural population. At present there are 200 earth stations in Mexico linked to the INTELSAT IV satellite for domestic telecommunications and television services. These earth stations are also used for the new Morelos system which provides data transmission services, rural telephony, and educational television. Brazil is the fifth largest user of the INTELSAT system for international communications and has used the services of INTELSAT since 1969. Since 1974 the telecommunications authority of Brazil, the EMBRATEL, has leased transponders from INTELSAT for domestic communications. Since then, 21 earth stations have been put into operation in the Amazon area in addition to the major urban locations. In 1984 there were 400 earth stations in Brazil providing services for telecommunications, banking networks, and television reception. As the demand for the services continued to grow at an exponential rate, Brazil decided to have its own satellite and its own orbital allocation. In 1982 Brazil entered into a counter-trade agreement with the Spar Corporation of Canada and Hughes Aircraft to build the Brazilsat and with Arianespace to launch it in 1985. Under this countertrade agreement, the two corporations which provided the hardware agreed to purchase US$ 200 million worth of exports from Brazil. The first satellite was launched as scheduled (Albernaz 1985).

The Aussat satellite was launched for Australia by the space shuttle Discovery on August 24, 1985. The second Aussat was deployed on the next shuttle flight in November 1985. The third Aussat which will be launched by Ariane in 1988 will enhance the telecommunications capabilities for the Pacific Islands. This third satellite of the system will be located at 160 East longitude and will reserve three of its transponders for the South Pacific Islands. This will give better telephone service to the thirteen nations who are members of the South Pacific Forum.

Meanwhile Papua New Guinea (PNG) has joined with an American company called TRT based in Washington, D.C., to start the Pacstar satellite system. PNG has applied to ITU for orbital spectrum allocation. Pacstar will offer domestic and regional services using two satellites (and one spare) to be built by Hughes. One of these satellites will cover PNG, Fiji, the Solomon Islands, Japan, and Southeast Asia. The footprint of the other will extend to Hawaii, California, and French Polynesia. Whereas Aussat will operate in the KU band, the Pacstar will have two hybrid satellites using the C band and the KU band.

The major benefit in economic terms of satellite technology for developing countries is the cost savings in point-to-point and point-to-multipoint communications. It is cost effective in the sense that the same equipment used for terrestrial circuits is connected to satellite circuits for long-haul communications. Small, inexpensive and simple earth stations called VAST can be used, as more power is placed on board the satellite. Flexibility in services permits reconfiguration of existing networks at decreasing costs so that voice, data, and facsimile can all be easily added to the same network now used for broadcasting. It becomes possible to set up "invisible colleges" such as those provided by the British.

Equally important is the role of satellites in filling the needs of business. The cost of integrated information services is declining and will continue to do so as the KU band is used. This happens because there is a direct relationship between low-cost information inputs and competitive productivity. The convergence of this transient technology has made the flow of data within corporations and between countries a source of knowledge and its use for production. Global banking relies heavily on such technology for speedy transmittal of funds, and stock exchanges as far apart as Singapore and Chicago are linked in real time.

For developing countries, the crux of the adoption strategy for satellites is the financing of the equipment and the costs of application. First of all, these countries have to find the required foreign exchange to make their full purchase, and in the context of shrinking demand for their exports from developed countries. It is increasingly difficult for them to add to their high debt burdens. While it is true that investment in telecommunications infrastructure brings in higher internal rates of return than industrial investment, the initial costs are the most difficult to obtain both from the national government and from external funding agencies. It is essential for developing countries to prove in accounting terms, the benefits of their investment. Once this is done and low risks established they can borrow both from within their domestic economies and from international lending institutions.

There are many social benefits emerging from satellite communications especially for remote areas of developing countries which cannot be ascertained in terms of a rate of return. While the opportunity costs of such investment may be high in the short-term, the social benefits are permanent and enduring and should not be overlooked by policy-makers.

Future Technologies

In the 1982 *Time* Magazine declared the computer as the "Man of the Year." Information processing technologies had invaded the factory, the bank, the office and even the home. Since then there have been significant advances in blurring of products and markets. Telematics technology is advancing to the teleports which combine use with computers to bypass common carriers and establish networks for computerised purchase and sale even of real estate. This activity is now dubbed "terramatics."

Integrated Services Digital Network (ISDN) will be the single most important technological development of the last quarter of the twentieth century. ISDN promises the complete integration of all computer and telecommunication systems which provide services for information storage, processing and distribution. It is a cost-effective system inasmuch as a single connection serves a wide range of needs. It is an intelligent system which is able to allocate cost effective combinations of information handling.

The initiative for ISDN arose in Japan and Europe in the late 1970s. The United States, by contrast, favours a policy of competition in the marketplace. However, ISDN technology demands uniform standards for integration to take place. Multiple ISDNs will defeat the purpose for which the technology is designed, namely to disperse information globally and speedily through digitalised network.

The anticipated impact is a return to monolithic, monopolist suppliers. It a single ISDN system provides a given combination of service outputs like voice and data and perhaps built-in element of natural monopoly. This cost property suggests a public interest in regulating ISDN against competitive entry or re-regulation of telecommunications (Snow & Jussawalla 1986).

Most industrialised countries have created the infrastructure tor text communications that can optimally utilise person-power and render office work less labour intensive. An efficient use of packet-switched data networks and leased lines requires terminals to be compatible. Teletext renders interworking possible with other communication services. Britain has used the Cefax service since 1975 on a nationwide experimental basis. Viewdata was introduced in Hong Kong in 1980, allowing data to be transmitted through a public-switched telephone network. It also uses a Financial Vision Service which delivers business information on View-data screens. Singapore is studying its national demand for videotex uses. Even so, the market for this technology has not grown commensurately with the innovations which leads to the problem of a technology in search of a market (Thomas 1983). The problems encountered by Prestel in the United Kingdom illustrate the danger of providing consumer-financed services to a mass market. The U.S. market, on the other hand, has the potential for greater exploitation through mass marketing and scale economies. With 100,000 personal computers already in use, 30 per cent penetration of cable television, and 100,000 subscribers to financial news services, the market is already in place for mass videotex systems. Yet market response is poor. It is anticipated that videotex in the United States will have only a seven per cent penetration by 1990. New Zealand and Australia are awaiting decisions on standards before introducing this service to their users. With the introduction of intelligent terminals, the scope for using videotex in various ways is enhanced, and its corporate applications are much greater now than when the service was first introduced. Corporate systems become increasingly cost-effective in processing and distribution of information and in decentralised decision-making with the use of videotex.

Cellular mobile radio is another spectacular innovation in telecommunications technology that promises to change the ways of telephone usage. Each mobile phone is to be linked by microwave to a computerised switch which will transfer a cell to another mobile phone or to any other phone (Dizard 1983). Canada, the United States, Japan, Germany, Saudi Arabia, and Singapore are all either using or planning to use cellular mobile radio and, as costs decline, more aggressive marketing will make this technology used as commonly used as the transistor radio is. It holds tremendous potential for developing countries in bridging the communication gap between the urban elite and the rural population, between the government headquarters and the agencies that operate at the village level. It opens up possibilities for planning interactive communications from the grass-roots upwards, providing a new paradigm of development success.

Interactive cable television is another new media technology that provides the benefits of market information access for consumers while simultaneously creating price barriers which may deprive low-income households of access to this market. Interactive consumer information delivery through cable TV is perhaps best evidenced by the Qube system in the United States. News, financial services, interactive advertising all become possible along with access to educational materials. These subscriber response services not only hold a growing revenue potential for the provider, but many flexible uses for the consumer. However, the increases in entry costs raise the issues of who will benefit most from interactive cable T.V. Will it be primarily professional and managerial workers? Will it exclude households with low incomes and low media literacy from the benefits of market information? Does it create a paradox in offering industrial benefits at the cost of impoverishing culture and raising social barriers between users and nonusers? While the Hunt Enquiry in Britain favoured the use of cable TV, there is the problem of linking entertainment to information access and introducing the artifacts of a post-industrial society (Tracey 1983).

Future trends are clear. New technologies appear on the market at a rate faster than LDCs can afford or absorb. Nevertheless, these nations are waiting to reverse the trends of unequal development and actively participate in the Information Revolution. While these countries vary in levels of economic development and social institutions, their participation in the North-South debate indicates their impatience to enter the information age. They will not permit the microelectronics revolution to pass them by as did the Industrial Revolution. They exhibit an awareness of the leading role of telecommunications in development. They are investing in reinforcing their production and services infrastructures with information technology. Comparative advantage for international trade is no longer dependent on traditional resources. It is manmade advantage stemming from the mastery of science and technology (Rada 1981).

Transnational corporations have become instrumental in demonstrating to LDCs the viability of the microelectronic technology. The transnational corporation becomes a nucleus of a vast network of information flowing from high technology countries. Are there hidden costs in such transfer of information? When telecommunications technology enters the welfare calculus, market distortions have to be assessed. Under conditions of oligopoly in the supply of computers, databases, and launching of satellites, global welfare gets restricted by making LDCs importers of innovative technology.

Despite these constraints, Business Week (February 3, 1983) reports that the main engine of growth for the global economy during 1980-81 was the Third World. Most of the imports are in the form of complete packages of electronic hardware and software. The technological determinism pushed by TNCs will have to be carefully assessed by Third World policy-makers in terms of investment, employment, and opportunity costs. What choices do these countries have and what are the social costs of leapfrogging into sophisticated networks?

Conclusion

Since the future can be predicted only imperfectly, decisions with future consequences must be taken in an environment of considerable uncertainty. Such decisions might involve the timing of research and development; technical choices, such as whether and when to install an ISDN or an optical fibre; financial options regarding the sources of funds for new capital investment; and policy choices affecting matters as diverse as tariff structure and competition in terminal equipment markets. In a free market economy, these decisions will be made primarily by market forces under the influence of economic competition; economies with some measure of central planning will decide with an admixture of direct government intervention. The way members of a society are educated, the jobs available to them, their hobbies and games are all being changed by these new information technologies. Equally important is the impact on businesses. There are new ways of managing inventories, maintaining customer and stock records, and advertising. New means are available to governments at all levels to tax, to subsidise, and to maintain public order (Rubin 1984).

What do these developments mean for the future? New technologies are a mixed blessing. Technology is power and new technology is untrained power. The new information technologies are unbalancing relationships in societies—globally strengthening some societies and rendering others weaker. Businesses need to take steps to preserve their competitive positions in a period of dynamic change. Governments need to operate efficiently to protect individual rights. Society is faced with difficult decisions of laying the ground rules which will govern the use of new technologies to the greatest good of the greatest number. If we fail to anticipate the future, we may make the transition and adjustment more painful.

Many of the dislocations faced by society hold endless promise for the future. There may come a time when small terminal devices will be able to access and explore a plethora of information. It is becoming possible to have automated translations from one language to another with the use of artificial intelligence. People in remote areas will have the same access to consultations and services now available to those who inhabit metropolitan centres. Businesses will be able to operate or service equipment in distant places and make product design changes instantly at manufacturing plants in various geographic locations. Access to the information age will likely be as simple as dialing a telephone today.

Both open architecture and integration will change the way people and nations talk to each other, and this involves more than common standards. It involves the cost-effective use of artificial intelligence. Do nations have a choice or are they driven by new information technology to opt for an information society? Will the cost of opting out of such a society be the new systems, not just from the government policies, but from the users themselves, the members of the information society.

References

Albernaz, J.C.F., 1985, The Brazilian Satellite Communications Programme, In *New Directions in Satellite Communications*, ed. H. Hudson, 221-244, Dedham, MA, Artech House.

Baumol, W.J., 1985, Productivity Policy and the Service Sector, *The Wharton Annual*, 46-54.

Baumol, W., & Panzar, J.C., 1982, *Contestable Markets and the Theory of Industrial Structures*, San Diego, CA, Harcourt Brace Jovanovich.

Bhagwati, J.N., 1984, Splintering and Disembodiment of Services and Developing Nations, *World Economy*, June, 133-143.

Block, C., 1985, Satellite Linkages and Rural Development, In *New Directions in Satellite Communications*, ed. H. Hudson, 135-155, Dedham, MA, Artech House.

Coase, R.M., 1960, The Problem of Social Cost, *Journal of Law and Economics*, 3, 1-44.

Dizard, W., 1983, Reinventing the Telephone, *Intermedia 11, 9-11.*

Dodsworth, T., 1986, World Telecommunications A Whirlwind of Change, *Financial Times*, 1 December, Section III.

Dougan, D., 1987, *User-driven Services, Who Plays, Who Pays, and Who Calls the Tune*, Keynote Address to the Pacific Telecommunications Conference, January.

Gorove, S., 1984, Major Legal Issues Arising from the Use of the Geostationary Orbit, *Regulation of Transnation Communications, Michigan Year Book of International Studies*, 3-12, New York, Clark Boardman Ltd.

Jussawalla, M. & Cheah, 1985, International Trade and Information: Some Welfare Implications, In *Communication and Information Economics*, eds. Jussawalla & Ebenfield, 51-71, Amsterdam, North Holland.

Jussawalla, M., 1979, Policy Outcomes of WARC 79: Their Impact on Developing Countries, *Media Asia* 8(1): 7-12.

—1980, Communication Technology Transfer: Impact on Economic Development, *Telecommunications Policy* 4(4), 249-262.

—1984, The Economic Implications of Satellite Technology and the Industrialisation of Space, *Telecommunications Policy*, September, 237-48.

—1986, The Information Economy and its Importance for the Development of Pacific Region Countries, In *Information, Telecommunications and Development*, ed. W. Richter, 65-86, Geneva, ITU.

Krommenacker, R., 1984, *World Traded Services: The Challenge for the Eighties*, Dedham, MA, Artech House.

Levin, H., 1984, The Political Economy of Orbit Spectrum Leasing, In *Michigan Year Book of International Legal Studies*,41-43, New York, Clark Boardman.

MacBride, S., 1980, *Many Voices One World*, New York, Unipub.

McKinnon, R.I., 1982, Currency Substitution and Instability of the World Dollar Standard, *The American Economic Review*, 72(3), 320-333.

Michalski, W., 1986, *Advanced Information Technologies: Challenges and Opportunities*, Keynote Address to TIDE 2000 Conference, Honolulu, HI, May.

Rada, J., 1981, The Microelectronics Revolution: Implications for the Third World, *Development Dialogue*, 2:41-67.

Reed, A.H., 1985, *Trade in Telecommunication Services, The Current Institutional Framework and the Potential for Changes*,OECD/ICCP2.

Revel, J.R.S., 1983, *Banking and Electronic Funds Transfer*,1-6, Paris, OECD.

Rex, M., 1986, Beyond the Exponential Cascade, *Intermedia*, 14(2):14-31.

Rubin, M., 1983, *Information Economics and Policy in the U.S*, Littleton Co., Libraries Unlimited.

Sampson, G.P. & Snape, R.H., 1985, Identifying the Issues in Trade in Services, *The World Economy*, June.

Snow & Jussawalla, M., 1986, The Impact of Information Technology on the Future of Society in OECD Countries, In *Telecommunications Information Technology for Global Interdependence*, eds. Jussawalla, Araki, & Okuma (forthcoming).

6

Television as a Social Factor

Psychologists are agreed that the effect of television depends on a "true" picture of the event, namely the impression obtained by someone physically present at the scene of the event. The experience of spectators may not be disseminated at all or may be discounted as the biased version of a specially interested participant. Or, again, the spectator's interpretation of his own experience may be reinterpreted when he finds the event in which he participated discussed by friends, newspapermen, and radio commentators. If the significance of the event is magnified, even casual spectatorship assumes importance. The fact of having "been there" is to be remembered—not so much because the event, in itself, has left an impression, but because the event has been recorded by others. At the opposite extreme, privately significant experiences, unless revived in subsequent interpersonal relations, soon recede into the deeper layers of memory.

By taking MacArthur Day in Chicago,[1] as it was experienced by millions of spectators and video viewers, we have attempted to study an event transmitted over video. The basis of this report is the contrast between the actually recorded experience of participant observers on the scene, on the one hand, and the picture which a video viewer received by way of the television screen, and the way in which the event was interpreted, magnified, and took on added significance, on the other. The contrast between these two perspectives from which the larger social environment can be viewed and "known" forms the starting point for the assessment of a particular effect of television in structuring public events.

Research Rationale

The present chapter is the outcome of research undertaken as an exploration in collective behaviour.[2] The design of the communications analysis differs significantly from most studies of content analysis. The usual process of inferring effect from content and validating the effect by means of interviews with an audience and control group is reversed. A generally apparent effect, i.e., the "landslide effect" of national indignation at MacArthur's abrupt dismissal and the impression of enthusiastic support, bordering on "mass hysteria," given to him, was used to make inferences on given aspects of the television content. The concern was with the picture disseminated, especially as it bore on the political atmosphere. To explain how people could have a false imagery (the implication of participant observational data), it was necessary to show how their perspective of the larger political environment was limited and how the occasion of Chicago's welcome to MacArthur, an event mediately known already, was given a particular structure. The concern is how the picture of the events was shaped by selection, emphasis, and suggested inferences which fitted into the already existing pattern of expectations.

The content analysis was, therefore, focused on two aspects—the selections made by the camera and their structuring of the event in terms of foreground and background, and the explanation and interpretations of televised events given by commentators and persons interviewed by them. Moreover, each monitor was instructed to give his impression of what was happening, on the basis of the picture and information received by way of television. The monitors' interpretations and subjective impressions were separately recorded. They served as a check that the structure inferred from the two operations of "objective" analysis of content were, in fact, legitimate inferences.[3] At the same time, utilising the categories of the objective analysis, the devices by which the event was structured could be isolated, and the specific ways in which television reportage differed from the combined observations could be determined.

Thirty-one participant observers took part in the study. They were spatially distributed to allow for the maximum coverage of all the important phases of the day's activities, i.e., no important vantage point of spectatorship was neglected. Since the events were temporally distributed, many observers took more than one station, so that coverage was actually based on more than thirty-one perspectives. Thus the sampling error inherent in individual participant observation or unplanned mass observation was greatly reduced. Observers could witness the arrival at Midway Airport and still arrive in the Loop area long before the scheduled time for the parade. Reports were received from forty-three points of observation.

Volunteers received instruction sheets which drew their attention to principles of observation[4] and details to be carefully recorded. Among these was the directive to take careful note of any activity indicating possible influences of the televising of the event upon the behaviour of spectators, e.g., actions specifically addressed to the cameras, indications that events were staged with an eye toward transmission over television, and the like.

Pattern of Expectations

The mass observation concentrated on discerning the psychological structure of the unfolding event in terms of present and subsequent anticipations. Certainly the crowd which turned out for the MacArthur Day celebration was far from a casual collection of individuals: the members *intended* to be witnesses to this "unusual event." One may call these intentions specific attitudes, emergent acts, expectations, or predispositions. Whatever the label, materials on these patterns of expectations were taken from two sources:

1. all statements of spectators recorded in the observer reports which could be interpreted as indicative of such expectations (coded in terms of the inferences therein);
2. personal expectations of the thirty-one study observers (as stated in the personal questionnaire).

Though not strictly comparable—since the observations on the scene contained purely personal, very short-range, and factually limited expectations—both series of data provide confirmation of a basic pattern of observer expectations. The persons on the scene *anticipated* "mobs" and "wild crowds." They expected some disruption of transportation. Their journey downtown was in search of adventure and excitement. Leaving out such purely personal expectations as "seeing" and "greeting," the second most frequent preconception emphasises the extraordinary nature of the preparations and the entertaining showmanship connected with the spectacle.

As a result of an unfortunate collapsing of several questions regarding personal data into one, the response did not always focus properly on what the observers "expected to see." In some cases no evidence or only an incomplete description of this aspect was obtained. Of those answering, 68 per cent expected excited and wildly enthusiastic crowds. But it is a safe inference from the discussion during the briefing session that this figure tends to underestimate the number who held this type of imagery. The main incentive to volunteer resided, after all, in the opportunity to study crowd behaviour at first hand.

To sum up: most people expected a wild spectacle, in which the large masses of onlookers would take an active part, and which contained an element of threat in view of the absence of ordinary restraints on behaviour and the power of large numbers.

Mass Media and Rising of Expectations

A more detailed examination of the data supports the original assumption that the pattern of expectations was shaped by way of the mass media. For it is in that way that the picture of the larger world comes to sophisticated as well as unsophisticated people. The observers of the study were no exception to this dependence on what newspapers, newsreels, nad television cameras mediated. They were, perhaps, better able than others to describe the origin of these impressions. Thus Observer 14 wrote in evaluating his report and his subjective feelings:

> I had listened to the accounts of MacArthur's arrival in San Francisco, heard radio reports of his progress

> through the United States, and had heard the Washington speech as well as the radio accounts of his New York reception. . . . I had, therefore, expected the crowds to be much more vehement, contagious, and identified with MacArthur. I had expected to hear much political talk, especially anti-Communist and against the Truman administration.
>
> These expectations were completely unfulfilled. I was amazed that not once did I hear Truman criticised, Acheson mentioned, or as much as an allusion to the Communists. . . . I had expected roaring, excited mobs; instead there were quiet, well ordered, dignified people . . . . The air of curiosity and casualness surprised me. Most people seemed to look on the event as simply something that might be interesting to watch.

Other observers made statements of a very similar content.

Conversation in the crowd pointed to a similar awareness. Talk repeatedly turned to television, especially to the comparative merit of "being there" and "seeing it over TV." An effort was consequently made to assess systematically the evidence bearing on the motives for being there in terms of the patterns of expectations previously built up. The procedures of content analysis served as a useful tool, allowing the weighing of all evidence *directly* relevant to this question in terms of confirmatory and contrary evidence. The coding operation involved the selection of two types of indicators:

1. general evaluations and summaries of data; and
2. actual incidents of behaviour which could support or nullify our hypothesis.

Insofar as the observers had been instructed to report concrete behaviour rather than general interpretations, relatively few such generalisations are available for tabulation. Those given were used to formulate the basic headings under which the concrete evidence could be tabulated. The generalisations fall into two types: namely, the crowds had turned out to see a great military figure and a public hero "in the flesh"; and—its logical supplement—they had turned out not so much "to see *him*, as

I noticed, but to see the spectacle" (Observer 5). Six out of eleven concretely stated propositions were of the second type.

An examination of the media content required the introduction of a third heading, which subdivided the interest in MacArthur into two distinct interpretations; that people had come to find vantage points from which to see the man and his family; or, as the official (media and "Chicago official") version held, that they had come to welcome, cheer, and honour him. Not one single observer, in any generalised proposition, confirmed the official generalisation, but there was infrequent mention of isolated incidents which would justify such an interpretation.

The analysis of actual incidents, behaviour, and statements recorded is more revealing. A gross classification of the anticipations which led people to participate is given (according to categories outlined above) in Table 6.1.

Table 6.1
Types of Spectator Interest

Form of Motivation	%
Active hero worship	9.2
Interest in seeing MacArthur	48.1
Passive interest in spectacle	42.7
Total	100.0

A classification of these observations by area in which they were secured gives a clear indication that the Loop throngs thought of the occasion *primarily* as a spectacle. There, the percentage of observations supporting the "spectacle hypothesis" was 59.7. The percentage in other areas was: Negro district, 40.0; Soldiers Field, 22.9; Airport, 17.6; University district, 0.0. Moreover, of the six generalisations advanced on crowd expectations in the Loop, five interpreted the prevalent motivation as the hope of a wild spectacle.

Thus a probe into motivation gives a confirmatory clue regarding the pattern of expectations observed. To this body of data, there should be added the constantly overheard expressions—as the time of waiting increased and excitement failed to materialise—of disillusionment with the particular vantage point. "We should have stayed home and watched it on TV," was the almost universal form that the dissatisfaction took. In relation to the spectatorship experience of extended boredom and sore feet, alleviated only by a brief glimpse of the hero of the day, previous and similar experiences over television had been truly exciting ones which promised even greater "sharing of excitement" *if only one were present*. These expectations were disappointed and favourable allusions to television in this respect were frequent. To present the entire body of evidence bearing on the inadequate release of tension and the widely felt frustration would be to go beyond the scope of this report, in which the primary concern is the study of the television event. But the materials collected present unequivocal proof of the foregoing statements, and this—with one qualified exception—is also the interpretation of each one of the observers.

Moreover, the comparison of the television perspective with that of the participant observers indicates that the video aspects of MacArthur Day in Chicago served to *preserve* rather than disappoint the same pattern of expectations among the viewers. The main difference was that television remained true to form until the very end, interpreting the entire proceedings according to expectations. No hint about the disappointment in the crowd was provided. To cite only one example, taken from what was the high point in the video presentation, the moment when the crowds broke into the parade by surging out into State Street:

> The scene at 2.50 P.M. at State and Jackson was described by the announcer as the "most enthusiastic crowd *ever* in our city. . . . You can feel the tenseness in the air. . . . You can hear that crowd roar." The crowd was described as pushing out into the curb with the police trying to keep it in order, while the camera was still focusing on MacArthur and his party. The final picture was of a bobbing mass of heads as the camera took in the entire view of State Street northward. To the monitor, this mass of people appeared to be pushing and going nowhere. And then, with the remark, "The whole city appears to be marching down State Street behind General MacArthur," holding the picture just long enough for

> the impression to sink in, the picture was suddenly blanked out.

Observer 26, who was monitoring this phase of the television transmission, reported her impression:

> . . . the last buildup on TV concerning the "crowd" (cut off as it was, abruptly at 3.00 P.M.) gave me the impression that the crowd was pressing and straining so hard that it was going to be hard to control. My first thought, "I'm glad I'm not in that" and "I hope nobody gets crushed."

But observers near State and Jackson did not mention the event in an extraordinary context. For example, Observer 24 explained that as MacArthur passed:

> Everybody strained but few could get a really good glimpse of him. A few seconds after he had passed most people merely turned around to shrug and to address their neighbours with such phrases: "That's all," "That was it," "Gee, he looks just as he does in the movies," "What'll we do now?" Mostly teenagers and others with no specific plans flocked into the street after the event.

The references to the friendly and congenial mood of the waiting crowd portended something about the change that was expected to occur.

Moreover, in view of the selectivity of the coverage with its emphasis on close ups,[5] it was possible for each viewer to see himself in a *personal* relationship to the General. As the announcer shouted out: "Look at that chin! Look at those eyes!"—each viewer, regardless of what might have been meant by it, could seek a personal interpretation which best expressed, for him, the real feeling underlying the exterior which appeared on the television screen.[6]

It is against the background of this personal inspection that the significance of the telecast must be interpreted. The cheering crowd, the "seething mass of humanity," was fictionally endowed by the commentators with the same capacity for a direct and personal relationship to MacArthur as the one which television momentarily established for the TV viewer through its close-up shots. The net effect of television thus stems from a convergence of these two phenomena: namely, the seemingly extraordinary scope of the event together with the apparent enthusiasm accompanying it and personalising influence just referred to. In this way the public event was interpreted in a very personal nexus. The total effect of so many people, all shouting, straining, cheering, waving in personal welcome to the General, disseminated the impression of a universal, enthusiastic, overwhelming ovation for the General. The selectivity of the camera and the commentary gave the event a personal dimension, nonexistent for the participants in the crowds, thereby presenting a very specific perspective which contrasted with that of direct observation.

In order to provide a further objective check on the discrepancies between observer impressions and the event as it was interpreted by those who witnessed it over television, a number of spot checks on the reported amount of participation were undertaken. Transportation statistics, counts in offices, and the volume of sales reported by vendors provided such indices.

The results substantiate the above finding. The city and suburban lines showed a very slight increase over their normal loads. To some extent the paltry 50,000 increase in inbound traffic on the street cars and elevated trains might even have been due to rerouting. The suburban lines had their evening rush hour moved up into the early afternoon—before the parade had begun.

Checks at luncheonettes, restaurants, and parking areas indicated no unusual crowding. Samplings in offices disclosed only a minor interest in the parade. Hawkers, perhaps the most sensitive judges of enthusiasm, called the parade a "puzzler" and displayed unsold wares.

Illustration of Contrast

The bridge ceremony provides an illustration of the contrast between the two perspectives. Seven observers witnessed this ceremony from the crowd.

> *TV perspective*: in the words of the announcer, the Bridge ceremony marked "one of the high spots, if not the high spot of the occasion this afternoon. . . . The parade is now reaching its climax at this point."
>
> The announcer, still focusing on MacArthur and the other participating persons, took the opportunity to review the ceremony about to take place. . . . The camera followed and the announcer described the ceremony in detail . . . . The camera focused directly on the General, showing a close-up. . . . There were no shots of the crowd during this period. But the announcer filled in. "A great cheer goes up at the Bataan Bridge, where the General has just placed a wreath in honour of the American boys who died at Bataan and Corregidor. You have heard the speech . . . the General is now walking back . . . the General now enters his car. This is the focal point where all the newsreels . . . frankly, in 25 years of covering the news, we have never seen as many newsreels gathered at one spot. One, two, three, four, five, six. At least eight cars with newsreels rigged on top of them, taking a picture that will be carried over the entire world, over the Chicagoland area by the combined network of these TV stations of Chicago, which have combined for this great occasion and for the solemn occasion which you have just witnessed."

During this scene there were sufficient close-ups for the viewer to gain a definite reaction, positive or negative, to the proceedings. He could see the General's facial expressions and what appeared to be momentary confusion. He could watch the activities of the Gold Star mothers in relation to MacArthur and define this as he wished—as inappropriate for the bereaved moment or as understandable in the light of the occasion. Taking the cue from the announcer, the entire scene could be viewed as rushed. Whether or not, in line with the official interpretation, the TV viewer saw the occasion as *solemn*, it can be assumed that he expected that the participant on the scene was, in fact, experiencing the occasion in the same way as he.

Actually, this is the way what was meant to be a solemn occasion was experienced by those attending, and which constitutes the crowd perspective. The dedication ceremony aroused little of the sentiment it might have elicited under other conditions. According to Observer 31, "People on our corner could not see the dedication ceremony very well, and consequently after he had passed immediately in front of us, there was uncertainty as to what was going on. As soon as word had come down that he had gone down to his car, the crowd dispersed." Observer 8 could not quite see the ceremony from where he was located on Wacker Drive, slightly east of the bridge. Condensed descriptions of two witnesses illustrate the confusion which surrounded the actual wreath-laying ceremony (three other similar descriptions are omitted here).

> It was difficult to see any of them. MacArthur moved swiftly up the steps and immediately shook hands with people on the platform waiting to greet him. There was some cheering when he mounted the platform. He walked north on the platform and did not reappear until some minutes later. In the meantime the crowd was so noisy that it was impossible to understand what was being broadcast from the loudspeakers. Cheering was spotty and intermittent, and there was much talk about Mrs. MacArthur and Arthur . . . (Observer 2).
>
> Those who were not on boxes did not see MacArthur. They did not see Mrs. MacArthur, but only her back. MacArthur went up on the platform, as we were informed by those on boxes, and soon we heard some sound over the loudspeakers. Several cars were standing in the street with their motors running. . . . Some shouted to the cars to shut their motors off, but the people in the cars did not care or did not hear.
>
> . . . The people in our area continued to push forward trying to hear. When people from other areas began to come and walk past us to go toward the train, the people in our area shrugged their shoulders. "Well, I guess it's all over. That noise must have been the speech." One of the three men who had stood there for an hour or more, because it was such a good spot, complained, "This turned out to be a lousy spot. I should have gone home. I bet my wife saw it much better over television" (Observer 30).

Regardless of good intentions on the part of planners and despite any recognition of the solemn purpose of the occasion by individuals in the crowd, the solemnity of the occasion was destroyed, if for no other reason, because officials in the parade were so intent upon the time schedule and cameramen so intent upon recording the solemn dedication for the TV audience and for posterity that the witnesses could not see or hear the ceremony, or feel "solemn" or communicate a mood of solemnity. A crowd of confused spectators, cheated in their hopes of seeing a legendary hero in the flesh, was left unsatisfied.

There is some direct evidence regarding the way in which television imposed its own peculiar perspective on the event. In one case an observer on the scene would watch both what was going and on and what was being televised.

> It was possible for me to view the scene (at Soldiers Field) both naturally and through the lens of the television camera. It was obvious that the camera presented quite a different picture from the one received otherwise. The camera followed the General's car and caught that part of the crowd immediately opposite the car and about 15 rows above it. Thus it caught that part of the crowd that was cheering, giving the impression of a solid mass of wildly cheering people. It did not show the large sections of empty stands, nor did it show that people stopped cheering as soon as the car passed them (Observer 13).

In much the same way, the television viewer received the impression of wildly cheering and enthusiastic crowds before the parade. The camera selected shots of the noisy and waving audience, but in this case, the television camera itself created the incident. The cheering, waving, and shouting was often largely a response to the aiming of the camera. The crowd was thrilled to be on television, and many attempted to make themselves apparent to acquaintances who might be watching. But even beyond that, an event important enough to warrant the most widespread pooling of television facilities in Chicago video history acquired in its own right some magnitude and significance. Casual conversation continually showed that being on television was among the greatest thrills of the day.

Conclusion

It has been claimed for television that it brings the truth directly into the home: the "camera does not lie." Analysis of the above data shows that this assumed reportorial accuracy is far from automatic. Every camera selects, and thereby leaves the unseen part of the subject open to suggestion and inference. The gaps are usually filled in by a commentator. In addition the process directs action and attention to itself.

Examination of a public event by mass observation and by television revealed considerable discrepancy between these two experiences. The contrast in perspectives points to three items whose relevance in structuring a televised event can be inferred from an analysis of the television content:

1. technological bias, *i.e.*, the necessarily arbitrary sequence of telecasting events and their structure in terms of foreground and background, which at the same time contains the choices on the part of the television personnel as to what is important;
2. structuring of an event by an announcer, whose commentary is needed to tie together the shifts from camera to camera, from vista to close-up, helping the spectator to gain the stable orientation from one particular perspective;
3. reciprocal effects, which modify the event itself by staging it in a way to make it more suitable for telecasting and creating among the actors the consciousness of acting for a larger audience.

General attitudes regarding television and viewing habits must also be taken into account. Since the industry is accustomed to thinking in terms of audience ratings—though not to the exclusion of all other considerations—efforts are made to assure steady interest. The telecast was made to conform to what was interpreted as the pattern of viewers' expectations. The drama of MacArthur Day, in line with that pattern, was nonetheless built around unifying symbols, personalities, and general appeals (rahter than issues). But a drama it had to be, even if at the expense of reality.

Unlike other television programmes, news and special events features constitutes part of that basic information about "reality" which we require in order to act in concert with anonymous but like-minded persons in the political process. Action is guided by the possibilities for success, and, as part of this constant assessment, inferences about public opinion as a whole are constantly made. Even though the average citizen does, in fact, see only a small segment of public opinion, few persons refrain from making estimates of the true reading of the public temper. Actions and campaigns are supported by a sense of support from other persons. If not, these others at least constitute an action potential that can be mobilised. The correct evaluation of the public temper is, therefore, of utmost importance; it enters the total political situation as perhaps one of the weightiest factors.

Where no overt expression of public opinion exists, politicians and citizens find it useful to fabricate it. Against such demonstrations as MacArthur Day, poll data lack persuasiveness and, of necessity, must always lag in their publication behind the development of popular attitudes. For the politician who is retroactively able to counter the errors resulting from an undue regard for what at a given time is considered overwhelming public opinion, there may be little significance in this delay. The imagery of momentary opinion may, however, goad him into action which, though justified in the name of public opinion, may objectively be detrimental. It may prevent critics from speaking out when reasoned criticism is desirable, so that action may be deferred until scientific estimates of public opinion can catch up with the prior emergence of new or submerged opinion.

Above all, a more careful formulation of the relations among public opinion, the mass media, and the political process is vital for the understanding of many problems in the field of politics. The reports and telecasts of what purports to be spontaneous homage paid to a political figure assume added meaning within this context. The most important single media effect coming within the scope of the material relevant to the study of

MacArthur Day was the dissemination of an image of overwhelming public sentiment in favour of the General. This effect gathered force as it was incorporated into political strategy, picked up by other media, entered into gossip, and thus came to overshadow immediate reality as it might have been recorded by an observer on the scene. We have labelled this the "landslide effect" because, in view of the widespread dissemination of a particular public welcoming ceremony, the imputed unanimity gathered tremendous force.[7] This "landslide effect" can, in large measure, be attributed to television.

Two characteristics of the video event enhanced this effect (misevaluation of public sentiment). (1) The depiction of the ceremonies in unifying rather than in particularistic symbols (between which a balance was maintained) failed to leave any room for dissent. Because no lines were drawn between the conventional and the partisan aspects of the reception, the traditional welcome assumed political significance in the eyes of the public. (2) A general characteristic of the television presentation was that the field of vision of the viewer was enlarged while, at the same time, the context in which these events could be interpreted was less clear. Whereas a participant was able to make direct inferences about the crowd as a whole, being in constant touch with those around him, the television viewer was in the centre of the entire crowd. Yet, unlike the participant, he was completely at the mercy of the instrument of his perceptions. He could not test his impressions—could not shove back the shover, inspect bystanders' views, or attempt in any way to affect the ongoing activity. To the participant, on the other hand, the direction of the crowd activity as a whole, regardless of its final goal, still appeared as the interplay of certain peculiarly personal and human forces. Political sentiment, wherever encountered, could thus be evaluated and discounted. Antagonistic views could be attributed to insufficient personal powers of persuasion rather than seen as subjugation to the impersonal dynamics of mass hysteria. The television viewer had little opportunity to recognise this personal dimension in the crowd. What was mediated over the screen was, above all, the general trend and the direction of the event, which consequently assumed the proportion of an impersonal force no longer subject to influence.

References

1. "MacArthur Day in Chicago" includes the following occasions which were televised: arrival at Midway Airport, parade through the city including the dedication at the Bataan-Corregidor Bridge, and the evening speech at Soldiers Field.
2. This chapter reports only one aspect of a larger study of MacArthur Day in Chicago. This writeup is limited to drawing together some of the implications concerning the role of television in public events, this particular study being considered as a pilot study for the framing of hypotheses and categories prerequisite for a more complete analysis of other such events in general. The present study could not test these categories, but was limited to an analysis of the television content in terms of the observed "landslide effect" of the telecast. The authors wish to express their indebtedness to Dr. Tamatsu Shibutani (then of the Department of Sociology, University of Chicago) for lending his encouragement and giving us absolute freedom for a study which, due to the short notice of MacArthur's planned arrival in Chicago, had to be prepared and drawn up in three days, and for allowing his classes to be used for soliciting volunteers. No funds of any sort were at our disposal. Dr. Donald Horton was kind enough to supply us with television sets and tape recorders. In discussions of the general problems involved in the analysis of television content, he has indirectly been of invaluable aid. Finally, we are indebted to the other twenty-nine observers, without whose splendid co-operation the data could never have been gathered.
3. That this check together with our observation of the general impression left by MacArthur Day constitutes only a very limited validation is beyond question. Under the conditions of the study—carried on without financial support and as an adjunct to other research commitments—it was the best we could do.
4. Analysis of personal data sheets, filled out by participants prior to MacArthur Day, revealed that "objectivity" in observation was not related to political opinion held, papers and periodicals subscribed to, and previous exposure to radio or TV coverage of MacArthur's homecoming. The significant factor in evaluating the reports for individual or deviant interpretation was found to reside in the degree to which individual observers were committed to scientific and objective procedures. Our observers were all advanced graduate students in the social sciences.

5. In a subsequent interview, a TV producer explained his conception of the MacArthur Day coverage as "being the best in the country." He especially re-called bracketing and then closing in on the General during the motorcade, the assumption being that he was the centre of attraction.
6. During the evening ceremonies, MacArthur's failure to show fatigue in spite of the strenuous experiences of the day received special notice. A report from a public viewing of the evening speech indicates the centering of discussion about this "lack of fatigue" in relation to the General's advanced years (Observer 24).
7. It must be reemphasised that there was no independent check—in the form of a validation—of the specific effect of TV. However, newspaper coverage emphasised the overwhelming enthusiasm. Informal interviews, moreover, even months later, showed that the event was still being interpreted as a display of mass hysteria.

7

Future Perspectives: Beyond Satellites and Space Stations

Perspective

Perhaps you, like me, enjoy thinking back to childhood days when space fantasy was sheer fun, frolic and fiction. Flash Gordon, Superman, Wonder Woman and, my own favourite, *Rip Foster Rides the Gray Planet,* still inhabit a special place in my memories of my preteens. Later, more sophisticated science fiction novels (speculative fiction to the avant-garde among you) by Asimov, Clarke, Hoyle, Bova, Heinlein, Pohl and others, were a fascinating source of wonder and entertainment. Even today, spellbinding science fiction writers like Ursula Le Guin and Frank Herbert and even space farces like the movie *Star Wars,* still capture my imagination. But somehow it is just not the same. The complete escapism from reality of my youth—the wild imagination that runs completely amok—is gone . . . gone forever it seems.

This is of course not the fault of science fiction writers, but of the scientists who are steadily and relentlessly making the fantasised future come true. These scientists have been rough on the old cliches as well. You can no longer say: "He might as well reach for the moon" without sounding like an astronaut recruiter. Today one must proclaim: "The sky's certainly *not* the limit," and so on.

Novelist Norman Mailer, on the "Cruise Beyond Apollo" (S.S. Statendam, 1972), argued rather persuasively that U.S. and Soviet scientists have done a superb job of making space boring, antiseptic and hopelessly jumbled with alphabetsoup. Astronauts are said to engage in EVA, rather than take space walks. A SSUS-D is, for instance, a rocket motor. Perhaps to illustrate the point, NASA and the European Space Agency not too long ago set up a "JSLWG under a MOU to assist MSFC, ESTEC, VEN/F-ERNO and MBB to communicate." Perhaps part of the communications problem is not difficult to discover.

Yet some of the "Buck Rogers," "gee whiz," "gosh that's exciting!" aspect of space is still there if you are willing to look under the pile of acronyms, and "technicalese" that engineers spew about themselves.

Perhaps more than any single programme, the U.S. and Soviet Space Shuttle programmes, and their ultimate successors in Europe and Japan promise to open a panoply of new space opportunities of amazing scope. Space platforms, space stations and, eventually, space colonies, can be envisioned. First we will see (my guess is before the year 2000) large structures for "conventional" space applications: telecommunications, space broadcasting, earth resource surveying, meteorological and climatological applications, hydrological and geological surveying, geodetics, mapmaking and, yes, perhaps even reconnaissance and military applications.

Next we will see (after the year 2000) operational space stations that will carry on scientific research, optical and radio astronomy, material processing, space manufacturing, and perhaps energy generation and distribution. Such manned stations may assume responsibility of a part or all of the "conventional" applications as well.

Finally, we may see sometime in the twenty-first century self-sustaining space colonies. These may be artificial worlds in space or large, self-supporting communities on the moon and on other bodies such as the asteroids, Mars and, possibly, a number of natural satellites of the planets, such as Titan (Saturn), IO (Jupiter), Ganymede (Jupiter), Phoebus (Mars), etc. Indeed, Gerald O'Neill, of Princeton University, feels we will have space colonies first and large energy platforms second.

In considering possible locations for space colonies, many factors will have to be considered, such as chemical composition, amount of usable resources, etc. Surprisingly, the distance from earth is not at all the critical factor. Differences in gravity levels experienced in moving from one location to another is the most important dimension. The energy required to move from a Moon colony to a colony on Phoebus and back again is many times less than a trip to Earth and back, even though Earth is at least 100 times closer. The rules of space are frequently different from those we know on earth.

Now on a "fun, delight and whimsy" scale of 1 to 10, space colonies (about which I know little) are at least a 9; while telecommunications platforms (about which I know somewhat more) are a 2 or 3. With space colonies you can talk of flying about on wings and playing three-dimensional sports in semi-weightlessness that combine the best features of jai lai, basketball and lacrosse. The adventurous can even talk about innovative sexual techniques. Unfortunately, these are subjects best left to scientific geniuses *a la* Professor Gerald O'Neill, to science fiction writers like Robert Heinlein, or to the movie makers in Hollywood, who are at least very good at the sex angles. (I must confess some frustration under the heading of "opportunities lost" when I was not able to help my brother, the art director, when he designed the casino for *Battlestar Galactica*.)

This chapter is to address the subject of everything you ever wanted to know about space platforms but were afraid to ask.

There have been two types of proposals in recent years for space platforms. Essentially, we have had proposals for "little" space platforms and "large" space platforms—the "lisp" and the "lasp." The little space platform (or the lisp) actually isn't! By today's standards the lisp is much larger than typical-size satellites of 1,000 kilograms or less. The "lisp" would weigh many thousands of kilograms and would span distances as large as a thousand metres. Even so, the lisp would be of delicate construction, since gravity would make little demand on its structural strength. The beams forming the main structure of the platform would be of a light-weight metal latticework. Mounted on the small platforms would be large antennas and a wide variety of equipment "packaged" into separate modules. These packages or modules would be separately designed for various missions: mobile telecommunications, space broadcasting, meteorology, navigation, fixed point-to-point telecommunications, earth resource survey, geodetics, geological survey, etc. Despite the diversity of missions these packages represent, they also have much in common:

(a) the need for at least most of them to be in geosynchronous orbit (35,700 kilometres or 22,300 miles above Earth).

(b) the need for a number of antennas ranging from large to small. (This has led to the suggestion by Burton Edelson and Walter Morgan of COMSAT that such platforms be called OAF's for Orbital Antenna Farms).

(c) the need for relatively compact mass and volume.

(d) the need in many instances for the packages to be interconnected by switchable links. Also, the need for possible interconnection with other space platforms in geosynchronous orbit.

(e) the need to be routinely maintenanced and uprated to meet new requirements, but no need for full-time manned crew.

(f) the need for highly stable platform with pointing accuracy to earth of 0.01° or better.

(g) the need for electrical energy but within relatively low limits (i.e., no individual power requirement above the 5 to 10 kilowatt range and most at much lower levels).

(h) the need to minimise the cost of "leasing" space on the platform so as to achieve affordable pricing levels.

(i) the need for the platform's mass to be compatible with the lift capability of the U.S. space shuttle and other launch vehicles developed or to be developed by the U.S.S.R. European Space Agency and Japan (*i.e.*, platforms that could be built with materials logistically supplied by one to three launches).

These characteristics suggest that these packages could indeed be good neighbours to one another on a common platform. While the "lisp" would be large by today's standards, it would not be truly gigantic.

This leads us to the large space platform that could reach to gargantuan proportions! Such space platforms could weigh in the hundreds of thousands of kilograms and might span several square kilometres. In some concepts, their surface area would be as large as Manhattan Island. Such space platforms would almost undoubtedly be manned and would serve a different range of functions. These missions might include energy concentration, generation and distribution, manufacturing in space and ongoing research projects. Products manufactured in space would be those requiring zero gravity, a near-perfect vacuum, extreme temperature differentials or a combination of these. Pharmaceuticals, crystal growing, calibration of delicate pressure gauges, cryogenics, electronic equipment production and many other activities would be candidates for such space enterprises. Some have even suggested agricultural production through hydroponics, i.e., growing crops on a water and fertiliser base. Research projects might include optical and radioastronomy, medical research, high, medium and low energy particle research, materials research etc. Some day we may find the world's largest cluster of international scientists in space platforms.

The common elements of the large space platforms include the following:

(a) Ability to provide long-term lodgings for human crew members;

(b) Huge demands in terms of energy production potentially in the many gigawatts range;

(c) Desirability and possible necessity of sustaining artificial gravity at 1/2 g or more;

(d) Very high costs requiring high levels of governmental subsidy—at least initially (e.g., billions of dollars or roubles—or trillions of yen);

(e) Need to develop a heavy-lift space vehicle of much greater capacity than that of the U.S. or Soviet space shuttle or of other launch vehicles now envisioned.

The keystone of such a "lasp" project would almost undoubtedly be energy production. Energy is almost the only enterprise that could economically justify the massive investment involved without developing difficult-to-believe scenarios. Yet, there are serious and unresolved questions as to viability of solar power satellites, particularly in terms of the potential dangerous affects on the earth and other essential space application services. Two of the biggest problems are those of reflected energy that could jam space communications and "fried" airline passengers who are unfortunate enough to fly through the microwave beam at the wrong angle. In addition, there are, in more general terms, the unresolved issues of:

(i) interaction with the ionosphere by the microwave energy beam;
(ii) the affects upon the upper atmosphere caused by a large number of launch vehicle flights (the equivalent of some 1500 Saturn V launches that would be required for "lasp" might cause significant changes to the Earth's weather);
(iii) microwave biological effects;
(iv) all forms of direct and indirect radio interference;
(v) the need to achieve international agreement on frequency assignments, orbital positions, and the raising of the limits on power that can be irradiated from space.

From the foregoing, it is probably safe to conclude that the "lisp' will come first and the "lasp" will come last (i.e., not before we are comfortably into the twenty-first century). Accordingly, it is perhaps most useful to consider in detail the space platform that we will first see in operation and will first influence our lives.

To science fiction fans a functioning permanent space platform is an exciting proposition, but the skeptics' first question is why do we need it? Isn't it a needlessly expensive toy? The answer to such a question is no. Expensive, yes. A toy—perhaps to some. But it is a cost-effective answer to very real future needs. Multiple application space platforms may provide the only reasonable solution to providing vital future space services at low cost and without saturating limited frequencies and orbital space allocations. Today there are mounting technical problems in space telecommunications that cry out for immediate attention.

The cause of this problem is simply too much success! In early 1965, the INTELSAT System was the only communications satellite system in operation. By 1970 the number had grown to nearly 10. At the end of the 1970s, the number of experimental, domestic, regional, international and military communications satellite systems in operation or in planning was well over 70 and growing strong. When one adds meteorological, geodetic, reconnaissance, earth resource survey and scientific satellite systems in operation or on the drawing boards, the number is well over 100. Fortunately, some of these satellite missions do not require a slot in the geosynchronous orbit (i.e., earth resource satellites have heretofore used sun-synchronous polar orbits; the U.S. Defense Satellite Data System satellites are in highly elliptical orbits, with an apogee over the U.S.; while some of the Soviet Molniya communications satellites have been able to use similar orbits over the R.S.F.R.). Even so, the demands on available frequencies for telecommunications in geosynchronous orbit are enormous and growing.

A recent study conducted by NASA of future demand for satellite communications of the U.S. shows a potential demand of over 300 video channels, over 20 million telephone channels, and an annual data volume of 40 million tera(bits) by the year 2000. This is equivalent to the total capacity of over 100 conventional medium sized satellites such as RCA and Western Union operate for U.S. domestic purposes today. Even allowing for rapid advances in digital compression techniques and more efficient satellite transmission capabilities this would still indicate a need for 25 to 50 satellites over that portion of the orbit that must also be shared with over 40 other countries in North, Central and South America. Even if we stack satellites two abreast—one 1½° north of the orbit and another 1½° south of the orbit—there is no way we could adequately meet the overall demand.

What's more, this is not the end of the problem. The even bigger difficulty would be in interconnection of the myriad satellites that would increasingly seem like cosmic sardines squeezed inside of a geosynchronous can. In such an environment, four hop interconnections routed up and down through four different satellites might become necessary to communicate from say a radio telephone in a car in the U.S. to a business office in Manila. Signal loss, because of multiple switching, time delays of greater than a second, and an overall loss in system reliability, are only some of the things that could start to go wrong. Even with the introduction of intersatellite (space-to-space) links the problems of interconnection seem to loom large indeed.

The possible solution to these potentially severe problems are limited. There are probably only three basic options:

1. Laser-modulated satellite systems must be developed that open up major new bandwidths for telecommunications purposes (the U.S. military, in shrouds of secrecy, is spending millions in research and development in this area);
2. Future growth of satellite communications systems must become highly restricted, with fibre optic terrestrial systems providing virtually all new communications services except in the mobile and remote teleservices area (this option is not very popular with the large multinational aerospace corporations of the U.S., Japan and Europe); or
3. Development of institutional arrangements for consolidation of many satellite missions on an Applications Space Platform (ASP).

In fact, Option 1, which helps solve the frequency problems but not the interconnection problems, most likely will have to be combined with Option 3 to provide truly long-term answers. The ASP or, more precisely, a global network of five to seven of them, in the opinion of many experts concerned about long-term planning in space, is the best answer to our space application needs. The ASP is where it's at—at least technically and economically. Unfortunately, unless we can get everybody to co-operate, we still will have BIG problems.

First, let's explore the technical marvels that the underkind we will call the ASP can provide us:

1. It can conserve frequencies in two very important ways:
   (*a*) by providing wired interconnections of the various modules within the platform itself and thus avoid needless up and down satellite links to connect various systems together; and

(b) by providing a place for giant reflectors that, together with multiple telecommunications "feeds," can send tiny pencil-thin beams to individually targeted earth stations. (In this approach the same frequencies can be used over and over in each of these high resolution beams).

2. It can result in cost savings by providing economies of scale. The power supply, antenna reflectors, stabilisation system, batteries, earth and sun sensors, can all be shared. Only the small package oriented to a particular mission would have to be uniquely designed. In a way, the difference is like buying a bus ticket rather than buying a car to get to your destination.
3. It provides important operational advantages as well. The ASP will last much longer, be more reliable, allow greater redundancy and diversity of routing; yet simplify the problems of interconnecting tens and even hundreds of networks by providing "wired" interconnection of networks through switches installed on-board the platform itself. Much of the flexibility and reliability will derive from the periodic maintenance, repair and upgrading of the ASP by manned crews.
4. It may provide a number of side benefits as well. Possibilities in this regard might be the ability to conduct very low-cost, small-scale experiments, such as on the long-term affects of radiation on various materials; the conservation of scarce resources (building satellites by the thousands and launching them could eventually be very wasteful), and so on. My own personal favourite candidate for a side benefit is the possible transmission of excess energy from the ASP during nighttime and off-peak hours to earth below in order to meet the energy needs of a small city. This would, of course, not be at all on the scale of a solar power satellite but nevertheless it could still be a multi-million dollar bonus.

Recent studies by NASA have indicated hundreds of potential missions for an ASP. Indeed, in the telecommunications are in detailed technical study was done to show how an ASP with one 30-metre antenna could be used to produce 20 very high density beams of 0.16° and three more 5-metre antennas could be used to produce 193 more high-density 0.35° beams that could all together handle a total data rate of up to 100 billion bits of information a second. In terms we invented in Chapter 1, that's 20,000 TIUPILs an hour—nearly half a million TIUPILs a day. A global network of ASPs could thus digest the lifetime thoughts of millions and millions of people a day. Perhaps more to the point, such a network could handle all humanity's daily word output with less than 10 per cent of its capacity. In short, a network of ASPs will service the outputs of machines far more than it will meet direct requirements of humans. It is an eerie feeling at times to think of all those machines chattering away to one another. Yet, this certainly is the trend. My own guess is that by the mid to late 1980's over 50 per cent of all international communications will be digitally modulated machine-to-machine exchange and less than 50 per cent will be analog telephone conversations.

The specific technical design of an ASP will probably require at least another five years, but General Dynamics, Comsat Laboratories, the Aerospace Corporation and NASA have already made significant progress in this direction. The great challenges will be agreement on appropriate institutional arrangements and achieving an overall system that is truly cost-efficient.

As I will discuss in the next chapter, there is a high degree of consensus among the 80 experts who participated in the Delphi Survey conducted for this book that ASPs will become operational in the 1985 to 2000 time frame. Using the same Delphi techniques, I also found that there is a wide difference of opinion as to how this development will occur in terms of institutional arrangements.

There is an almost equally divided opinion among four basic options:

1. a technical international organisation, such as INTELSAT or an organisation like INTELSAT;
2. individual projects of governments (e.g., U.S., Japan, U.S.S.R., Germany);
3. co-operative multinational efforts among several governments in conjunction with multinational aerospace corporations (e.g., ESA, U.S., Japan); or

4. multinational corporations.

It is of course possible, maybe even likely, that several of these approaches could be taken simultaneously. Only in one regard did the experts agree, and that was that a U.N. specialised agency was consistently found to be the least likely institutional arrangement for owning and operating an ASP.

There are significant potential problems evident in this diversity of possible approaches. Some of these problems include:

(a) Owning and operating ASPs on a national basis could lead to problems of international co-ordination, of rights of non-discriminatory access by nonparticipating countries, etc.

(b) Unless there is a single entity involved in the planning and deployment of ASPs, there could be a problem of proliferation of such space platforms. This, in turn, could lead to overinvestment, technical problems with frequency-allocations, and in general, a lot of nasty feelings.

(c) The very high initial development and investment cost will tend to force the initial development of ASPs in the direction of national government projects. This could result in very expensive "gold plate" projects that would be difficult to transfer to cost-efficient commercial operations at a later stage.

(d) The natural difference of perspective represented by corporate enterprises, military projects, governmental programmes, international organisations, research organisations and universities will make it difficult to combine all applications on a single platform. It is difficult to conceive of institutional arrangements that will provide the combined qualities of political neutrality, cost-efficient and reliable operation, technical flexibility, commonality of development goals, forceful leadership and high-quality technical and operational decision-making free from "political interference".

An optimum approach is difficult to define at this stage and only the foolhardy would attempt to outline the best solution.

Accordingly, at the clear risk of appearing quite foolish a decade hence, I will outline a "success scenario" for the development of the first Global ASP network.

The First Gasp

The stage is set in November 1983. Congressman Sensible of Wisconsin, former Chairman of the House of Representatives Science and Technology Committee and a strong internationalist, is the new President-elect of the United States. He wants to make his mark as a handsome, bold leader in the John F. Kennedy tradition. Quickly, he seizes on global co-operation in space as a way to achieve a meaningful "New Horizon" for global development.

After assuming office, he devises a plan in consultation with NASA and the State Department. He then meets quietly and consults by phone with the Prime Minister of Japan, a number of European Ministers, the Secretary Generals of the United Nations, the ITU and the European Space Agency, the Director-General of INTELSAT, key U.S. legislators, and leaders of developing countries. By June 1984 President Sensible dramatically announced, at the United Nations, a new international programme called "New Horizons for Humanity in Space." In phase one, the U.S., Japan, and the European Space Agency would carry out a four-year technical demonstration programme to test construction concepts and subsystems of a multipurpose station. The U.S. might concentrate on structures and materials, as well as overall systems design; Japan on telecommunications systems, Europe on meteorological, earth resources and other application subsystems. Other countries wishing to participate in the project would be welcome subject to definition and approval of specific projects or tasks.

Second, an approved GASP design based upon the technical demonstration project would be agreed by year-end 1989. By this time, agreement would also be reached on the overall technical and financial management of the programme. The preliminary approach finding the greatest degree of acceptance was the one wherein the INTELSAT Organisation would become the "anchoring-client" for the project, with NASA of the U.S.,

NASDA of Japan, and ESA of Europe, serving as the "prime" suppliers. While there would be a number of other suppliers, all contracts would be administered through the big three space agencies that would have overall technical and administrative control of the project. Service requirements would be co-ordinated through INTELSAT, which would also seek to maintain quality standards, cost controls and deadlines.

If all proceeded well, the prototype Global Applications Space Platform (GASP) would be built and deployed by year-end 1993. After six months of testing it would become operational and the entire GASP network would be in place by the end of the 1990s.

The original suppliers (US/NASA; Europe/ESA; and Japan/NASDA) would agree to pay for their shares of the technical demonstrations and fund up to $ 125 million each for the first operational prototype and one other operational GASP platform. INTELSAT, INMARSAT and perhaps hundreds of other users would fund up to $ 125 million of the Phase 2 project. In the next and final phase the users would pay for their full share of costs. One of the biggest issues left open in the U.N. address by President Sensible was what organisations would in the longer term own, operate and lease "space" to interested customers wishing to use the GASP network.

Response to President Sensible's proposal was generally favourable in diplomatic circles and in the United Nations:

> Ambassador Tantaquip, of the Cameroon, was reported in *Paris Match* as saying: "C'est magnifique. Le Grande Machine of Internationale Co-operation 'le GASP' will aid world peace and bring the Cameroon increased prosperity as well as high quality television. We are tired of returns of *Charlie's Angels*."
>
> Foreign Minister Caliente of Venezuela: "Ole for el Presidente Sensible. He is a leader like Kennedy. Bold in his proposals. Globally concerned for his fellow mankind."

But, reactions in many other circles was, at best, divided:

> U.S. Senator Mongoose (Independent-Oklahoma), "Why

should we, as a God-fearing, right-thinking country of pioneers want to jump into bed with them "furriners." We developed the space Shuttle by ourselves. We sent a man to the Moon on our own, and even showed the world how to fly. Now we propose on global TV that we spend hundreds of millions to build tinker toys in space and that we share U.S. knowhow with them fellows overseas. Well, I'm dead set against it."

Gen. Bullmoose, retired Commander at NATO: "If President Sensible had thought this thing through more carefully, he would have seen it should have been a military project. Those bureaucrats in Washington don't realise the strategic advantage we have just lost."

Pierre Bureau, President of Multinational Conglomerate Internationale, headquartered in Paris, quoted in the *Wall Street Journal*: "This is a calculated blow to undercut the technical break-throughs that European and Japanese industries were making in conventional satellite technologies. It appears to be a share-and-share-like proposition, but the Americans will share the benefits and we Europeans, we will share the losses."

Jake Bludgeon, Australian labour leader, in *The Workers' Weekly*: "If the Japanese, the Europeans, and the Yanks want to build erector sets up there, I say let 'em—but let's not forget that while they're dreaming up expensive toys the working man has to pay for basic expenses of food and shelter. The issue for me is, are we going to get a 20-hour work week and $ 85 an hour next year or not.

Man in the street in Saigon: "But will I have more rice in my bowl?"

Man in the street in London: "Seems alright to a bloke like me."

The above hypothetical scenario highlights a number of dangers that might be encountered on the way to establishing the GASP network. These dangers include the following:

(*a*) Possible inclusion of military requirements in the GASP network.

(*b*) Possible resistance to GASP by aerospace manufacturers and others heavily involved in conventional satellite technology.

(*c*) Possible "politicisation" of technical management, rather than having a highly skilled, centralised "non-political" technical management.

(*d*) Possible proliferation of national space platforms.

(*e*) The possibility of very expensive space platforms being developed by engineers who are interested in advanced technology regardless of the cost, rather than the lower cost and less sophisticated platforms being developed to meet users' very specific requirements. (This is an almost overriding reason why an international organisation with a commercial orientation, like INTELSAT, should have a strong say, if not overall responsibility for the design and deployment of an operating GASP network.)

(*f*) The possibility of short-term individual corporate or national interests being placed ahead of longer term interests of the world at large.

The most sobering issue to consider, however, is one not addressed at all in our little scenario. This is the issue of dedicated and sincere people who feel that a gigantic centralised network for telecommunications, broadcasting and other applications would not be in the legitimate interests of the huge global population to which it would provide coverage. These critics would be concerned about loss of national cultural identity, of regimentation and universal uniformity, of opportunity for authoritarian abuse through surveillance and monitoring, of commercial exploitation of developing countries, of the devaluation of the individual human's worth, and of various manifestations of technological "future shock" in terms of new patterns of unemployment, ennui, social discontent and unhappiness.

This issue is almost unanswerable. The wise social application of new technology is of course the biggest challenge of all. Many experts feel that television has perhaps been more of a "dysfunctional" than a "functional" technology, in terms of creating more unhappiness than happiness and more discontent than contentment. The constructive uses of GASP, such as educational television, earth resource survey, telecommunications and a host of other services, is still at a very early stage of study, but the potential is enormous. The benefits of satellite technology that have accrued over the last 15 years seem large, yet when they are viewed against the entire history of mankind, they shrink to more modest proportions. The jury must remain out for at least another 50 years before we will know the answers in any truly historical perspective.

But our scientists and political leaders cannot afford to wait a half century. The time to begin planning to make these new technologies truly work for the betterment of mankind, is of course, right now. Let's hope we will have started in time. We must seek a first GASP solution—not the last GASP option.

Virtual Reality: Tele-Cities 2020

A lasting definition of a city is impossible except in terms of human context and purposes. Structures and forms shift with new human needs and new technologies. As the Greek Alcaeus said of cities in the sixth century B.C., "Not houses finely roofed, or the stones of walls well-built, nay, nor canals and dockyards, make the city, but men able to use their opportunity."[1]

The first purposes of cities were to afford common defense and a market place. Cities became possible when a chance mutation in Mesopotamia created a new wild wheat known as husked emmer sometime around 8000 B.C. This wild wheat, with 28 chromosomes, rather than the 14 of its predecessors, was fertile enough to allow productive agriculture. Thus, man was enabled to abandon nomadic hunting as a way of life and adopt an urban life-style.[2] Problems of urban renewal have been with us ever since!

New urban functions, of course, have developed over time. Cities became centres for culture, for crafts and manufacturing, for specialised labour, for communications, for storage, for distribution and a wealth of other functions—including crime and prostitution. Perhaps most significantly, this growth of functions of the city and indeed in the size of the city itself are largely linked to technology. During the period 8000 B.C. to the Seventeenth Century A.D. urban centres numbered in the hundreds or thousands. Perhaps ten cities, such as Rome, Constantinople, Peking and Sian (Changan) during this period exceeded a population of 50,000 and, in most instances, the population was typically 20,000 or less. With these populations, the city could reside within four square kilometres, or some 500 blocks. Everything was within walking distance. The city was thus on a very human and personalised scale. Everyone knew and gossiped about everyone else. The Greek concept of democracy and the city-state were based on this scale of human relationships.

The highrise, the elevator, the train, the automobile, air travel, mass advertising, electrical power networks, and cheap energy allowed cities and even urban megalopolises to grow with almost cancerous speed. This growth in recent years has been increasing horizontally and increasingly out of scale with human dimensions. In the future telecity, we will provide for husbandry of our open spaces and greater opportunity for the liberation of the pedestrian to enjoy his city again.

Today, of course the first two traditional functions of the city—defense and trade—have been discreetly turned on their respective heads in economically advanced countries. Perhaps no one was looking when these rather awesome headstands occurred.

Who can deny that the prime targets of a nuclear attack, invasion or terrorism, would concentrate on key cities, and that the survivors, if any, of modern war would likely be found in rural areas. Of the five different types of nuclear attack strategies (Countervalue, Countervalue plus Counterforce, Straight Counterforce, Counter-force plus Bonus, and Counterforce plus Avoidance), only two of them exempt urban centres. . . . So much for the protective functions of cities![3]

Who can deny that mail order catalogues (now a $ 60 billion industry in the U.S.), nationwide telephone sales (via your handy toll-free fantasy-fulfilment number) and the wholesale migration of merchandising firms to suburbia have seriously eroded the commercial retail function of the urban core city, as well as the social amenities they once offered.

The prime purpose of the core city today, although not necessarily tomorrow, is to serve as an employment centre and secondarily as cultural, social and distribution centres. These functions are increasingly daytime functions, as the nighttime city can become a hollow, ghostly canyon—the offtimes feared jungle of crime and despair.

The catalogue of ills of the modern metropolis, from Tokyo to New York from London to Cleveland, at times seems beyond reasonable solution:

- *(a)* long-term, increasing debt;
- *(b)* an eroding tax base;
- *(c)* areas with crowded, substandard and sometimes unsanitary living conditions;
- *(d)* high rates of crime and drug addiction;
- *(e)* humdrum city administration, frequently without adequate talent and imagination to seek new solutions to problems;
- *(f)* air and noise pollution and serious environmental problems, from waste management to the supply of drinkable water;
- *(g)* automobile-dependent commuters who work, but do not live, in the city. (Indeed, many commuters live 20 hours a week or more in their automobiles.) This has coincided with development sprawl and the accelerated decline of the economic and social health of the urban core; and
- *(h)* increasingly complex marketing and distribution systems, including banking, make virtually all services more impersonal.

These "urban services," it might be noted, also contribute substantially to high rates of inflation (typically 40 per cent or more of the cost of consumer products stems from such services).

Only an extreme optimist can believe that the modern city and its big brother the megalopolis can survive over the long-term without major changes. Indeed, today we do not even know the weakest link in the chain that will break first—transportation, financial solvency, water, pollution control, energy, schools or public safety.

If the city of the future is to represent a radical departure from tradition and past mistakes, it must come from a great vision—not a great invention. Technological wizardry can bring improvements, but a new philosophic concept of the city is needed to provide a long-term solution.

Arthur Erickson, the prominent Canadian architect, believes that our cities, at least in the Western World and especially in the Americas, are a direct result of the value system sometimes characterised as scientific materialism. This philosophic viewpoint, born of pioneer days, is one of man's mastery over nature.[4] It can be seen in its most brutal and muscular form in the massive U.S. dam and public works projects of the 1930s and 1940s. The so-called TVA School of Architecture. This philosophic approach, albeit somewhat refined is still very much with us today.

Jacques Ellul, the great twentieth century European critic of technology, sees scientific materialism as a predictable outgrowth of classic "liberal" democratic doctrine à la John Locke and John Stuart Mill. Ellul charges that laissez-faire democracy and unrestrained free enterprise armed with technology have had enormous destructive impacts on our environment, our cities, our lives and our sense of being. Ellul expresses his outrage by stating: "John Locke would have put billboards on the sides of the Grand Canyon."[5]

Instead, we are today wallpapering our cities with billboards, slicing apart our cities with freeways and rigid gridiron street systems and cutting off naturally occurring public gathering places that European cities are today only barely managing to retain. Lewis Mumford has expressed true concern that our modern cities will never recover from the strangulation of the automobile.

Clearly, before we can intelligently discuss the application of exciting new technologies in reforming our urban centres, there must be a new vision of the future.

The Telecity

We believe the key to the future is through the "right" use of the "right" technologies, by the "right" people. But we insist, lest we be misunderstood, there is no such thing as a single "right answer" for the new urban environment we call the 'Telecity." We will need multiple models for our Telecities—rural/industrial satellite communities; urban megastructures, linear cities, space colonies, underground cities in the desert run on solar energy, etc. Although some features, such as harmony with nature, allowance for human diversity, advanced telecommunications, electronics, and transportation systems and preservation of open space, will be common features, there can be no such thing as a single model for the Telecity. No matter how beautiful or desirable one model might be, it cannot suit the tastes and needs of all. The Telecity is, first and foremost, diversity. For our Telecities we need architects and politicians, businessmen and planners willing and able to use creatively and well new telecommunications, new computers, new transportation systems, new educational processes and new urban design concepts. Most especially, we need a new direction in public and economic policy and urban planning.

Innovative communications and transportation techniques can most dramatically redefine patterns of human relationships—to achieve urgently needed social, economic and political goals. It is thus that we have chosen to call the city of the future the Telecity. The boundaries, size—yes, even the vitality of the Telecity—will be defined electronically rather than strictly by conventional means such as physical dimension.

Let's now explore the characteristics of the Telecity of the twenty-first century.

The Telecity and the Tagot Network

A key element of the future humanised Telecity will be an integrated network designed to develop the functions of telecommunications, information processing and transportation. Sometime in the twenty-first century energy may become the fourth dimension of this network, but for the time being, we can think of it as the Talking, Going and Thinking network (TAGOT). The TAGOT network will allow the residents of the twenty-first century Telecity almost complete freedom of physical and intellectual movement. Banking, shopping, reading, studying, learning, intellectual recreating, working, corresponding, etc., will be possible within the home or a nearby service centre through a mere flick of a switch. Multi-purpose computer terminals interconnected with a telephone, video system and facsimile printer will make this possible.

Trips from the home in such an environmental will thus be increasingly oriented toward cultural, social and active recreation—and many of these trips will be accomplished on foot. Many streets could be converted to parks, recreation areas, or even vegetable gardens and farms. Nature could return to the city. With new construction technologies developed for megastructures, nature could go high-rise. Trees, gardens, even zoos, could be found for instance on the 36th floor of totally "free" urban structures.

Some streets could and should be converted to enclosed pedestrian ways, cycle ways and jogging paths. Major thoroughfares within the city will become adapted for electric car ways. These will be fully automated and thus capable of handling five to ten times as many vehicles as conventional highways. Also, there will be pneumatic tubes and conveyor belts for cargo and freight moving. Vehicles, equipment and freight may be moved at one level, while pedestrian walkways could be at another. By the year 2000 the internal combustion automobile may possibly be banned from all urban areas as being environmentally unsafe.

Schooling, government regulations, lifestyles, social patterns, even crime, will be changed by the Telecities and the TAGOT network. Education and, subsequently, work and public services, will be increasingly brought to the home electronically, rather than bringing students, workers and public servants to schools or offices. Corporations, universities, schools and even government "without walls" will become commonplace in the "information societies." Indeed, the Open University in England is today the largest university in the United Kingdom. In April 1979, the "Paperless Office" was opened in Washington, D.C. In this office all information and business services within the office are handled electronically through re-graphics facilities with nary a sheet of paper in sight. All the "partners" of this office might be next door or at the other end of a satellite circuit halfway around the world.

The potential of new electronic services are enormous. Legislative hearings, business conferences, contract negotiations, even a first "blind date," could be conducted electronically by utilising a combination of video and computer conferencing techniques. A second date would, of course, require boy-meets-girl in a close and more intimate setting. Traditional group loyalties and perhaps even cultural and national identities may well be seriously affected by such changes.

Physical distance will thus become increasingly a non-dimension in the telecity. As a side benefit, energy consumption related to transportation can be dramatically reduced. A recent study of this possibility concluded that if video conferencing were substituted for travel starting in the late 1980s, the results would tend to be dramatically magnified in the telecommunications field. Put in quantitative terms, an 8 per cent decrease in international air travel would tend to produce a tenfold increase in international telecommunications volume. Such sensitivity trade-offs could spell trouble for the world's telecommunications planners—but it portends enormous potential for the citizens of the world.

The process of electronic decentralisation will require many social readjustments. New roles will be defined, particularly as the majority of all economic activity turns to processing and handling information. The purpose of schools, for instance, will need to be clarified to determine whether schools are to provide education, babysitting services or socialisation. Social patterns will change when cheap and effective digital videophone services are established. A global network of friends and acquaintances will not only become possible, but also affordable.

The key to the architecture of the Telecity will be to create and environment where travel becomes discretionary, rather than mandatory, yet, avoid an environment where we find isolated, lonely and disoriented people locked in "electronic cells." The successful Telecity will thus be designed to sing the chorus from Cabaret: "Don't stay home alone in your room old chum. Come hear the music play. Come to the Cabaret." Certainly, cultural centres and cabarets will supply the very human dimension of the Telecity.

Telecity and Public Policy

At this point, the hardened skeptic is saying: "Fairytales,

architectural fantasy and Telecities are all very well for the addle-brained science fiction fan, but please be serious." This is a reasonable objection. The truth of the matter is that by the year 2000 our cities may well *not* resemble at all the Telecities we have described with such euphoria. They could well be ravaged with crime, auto and industrial pollution and economic depression. Indeed, to give us the necessary skepticism, it is useful to recall how the Futurama exhibit at the 1939 New York World's Fair extolled the virtues of the city of the future—the city of 1960! ". . .fresh air, green parkways, recreational centres . . . unidirectional highways on which you can surely choose your speed—100, 200 miles an hour—all the result of plausible planning and design. . . . Who can say what horizons lay before us. . . ."[6]

Unfortunately, we know what did lie beyond the horizon of 1939 and the idyllic city of Futurama has yet to arrive even two decades after 1960. The closest we have come to the city of our dreams is in Walt Disney World amusement park, where the Experimental Prototype Community of Tomorrow (EPCOT) is opening in late 1982. It would seem that some horrible moral must derive from the fact that Mickey Mouse and his friends are the only ones able to shape the future to desired objectives.

Assuming that we can be almost as smart as Mickey Mouse, let's explore how we might help bring the Telecity into being. We might start by enacting new legislation to shift emphasis away from highway construction and toward retrofitting our cities to accommodate new telecommunications, computer and urban transportation needs—the needs of twenty-first century man.

How? One priority goal must be to stimulate private investment in the city. Our city political leaders and administrators might begin by "leasing" streets, sidewalks, canals, sewers, utility conduits and public air rights to private or public concerns willing to make innovative and constructive use of these resources. Franchises could be granted to a number of industries, engaged in revitalising our cities. Indeed extension of existing franchises for cable TV systems could well lead to the creation of TAGOT systems in many cities.

Inspiration might be drawn from the Italian zoning and land-use system, where land is sold according to zoning category—a higher density means a higher price, with the proceeds going to the government. An Italian farmer rezoning his land for development must pay a stiff price before doing so. Such a system could be most effective in stemming mindless suburban sprawl in pursuit of quick development profits.

We might also learn from the experience of the Canadian city of Toronto. Toronto has avoided the madness of mandating uniform high-density development at each stop on its mass transit system, by retaining residential or existing zoning in these areas. Thus, developers wishing to provide high-rise density must offer a good plan and incentives to the city in exchange for the desired zoning. Most cities give away the high-density zoning and land-use designations and then start to negotiate. Guess what? The cities seldom win.

Our planners might begin to listen to the *Washington Post's* architectural critic, Wolf Van Eckardt, who has proposed that, as a matter of public policy, most mass transit stops should exit onto pedestrian areas, free of autos, in the form of sidewalk cafes, markets, urban parks, piazzas or squares. Such transit centres would be an assembling place for people, while high-rise structures should be located perhaps a bloc away, or even suspended several stories above these urban gathering places.

Our politicians might adopt new legislative and tax incentives (and disincentives) which would convince corporate enterprises of the desirability of creating the Telecity. We must deploy new carrots and new sticks to convince AT&T, IBM, the Detroit auto industries, Volkswagon, Mitsubishi, Fiat, Shell, ITT, Aerospatiale, TOSHIBA, NEC, Phillips and other large multinational enterprises that shape the world's economy that what is good for modern urban centres is good for them too.

Our legislators might enact strict laws with tough sanctions to protect the individual against invasion of privacy and other abuses of the new information and computer networks by large institutions, public or private enterprise.

Indeed, we might begin to think in entirely new terms of space and structure. Noriaka Korokawa's Helix City (a construction that creates "artificial land") could provide inspiration for entirely new forms of public and private collaboration in areas of transportation, utilities, taxation, etc. Such new structures should not be just for private profit, but for public profit and pleasure as well. They must be used to save energy, to create more efficient transportation, and to provide open space and to preserve historic areas. Elsewhere, we have considered the advantages of multi-use space platforms in outer space. It is now time we must also consider humanised space platforms in our reurbanised cities. Macro platforms that allow for human scale and diversity and natural beauty within them should not be beyond our comprehension.

The Telecity versus Social Inertia

The forces to resist the Telecity are everywhere—in schools of architecture, in corporate Boards of Directors, and in Western Scientific Materialism.

The importance of a physical "corporate identity" with a large, permanent building that consolidates staff and corporate power will certainly be challenged in the era of the Telecity. Eventually, this feudal (or, perhaps more accurately, futile) concept, may be discarded. Instead, we may eventually see in the twenty-first century shared-use of office buildings, with multiple clients who "time-share" headquarters. The issue of shared use is far from new. Economic optimisation through shared use of facilities or services is the basis of many businesses. We are familiar with the use of "sharing," for instance, by car rental firms, caterers, and even houses of ill repute.

Architecture, it must be recognised, is a generally conservative force reflecting society as it is, rather than as it will be. Thus it is not surprising that, architecturally speaking, the issue of sharing has arisen late in the game.

The idea of a school of architecture that operates in splendid isolation of such disciplines as transportation, energy, electronics and telecommunications, will soon have to be recognised for the anachronism that it truly is. Perhaps soon we will realise that Buckminster Fuller's thirty-five year old critique of architecture has always been on target. We would feel that we will have accomplished a most important goal if we plant the seed that eventually grows into a new School of Integrated Design Science that replaces a traditional University School of Architecture at least somewhere in the world.

This is not to suggest that the forces of innovative thinking are not already available. Eero Saarinen, the famous architect, is known largely for the beauty and grace of his buildings. But this is to grasp superficially his genius. His greatest contribution is brilliantly demonstrated in the wisdom and feasibility of shared or multiple use within a building. Dulles International Airport in Washington, D.C., is a superb example of this concept. The visitor to Dulles, impressed by its beauty, may at first miss the elegant architectural statement that it makes with regard to shared use. The airport building that serves over 3 million passengers a year is quite small. How come?

The answer is the large mobile lounges that take passengers to their planes. Since any carrier can go to any plane, a reasonably small number of mobile lounges and a few loading gates can handle a large volume of passengers. The result is small, intimate and convenient airport building where walking is minimised, along with space and energy.[7] Passengers generally love it, while the airlines generally hate it. How come?

The airlines are responding to a territorial imperative. They dislike not having their own sprawling terminal wing that is theirs—all theirs—even if it is efficiently used only a small part of the time.

Possessiveness is a wasteful but very strong and natural habit man acquired a few million years ago. Possessiveness is indeed a key element of the architecture that stems from Scientific Materialism. In the East, different patterns hold. A Japanese room has been designed for centuries to serve a variety of purposes. Thus, we may well see the first wide-scale implementation of shared-use facilities in the East rather than in the West. The Japanese Metabolism School of Architecture, drawing upon the tradition of multipurpose use of space in the Japanese home, relies heavily upon biological and scientific models, as well as upon the effective re-use of space, services and facilities in the reurbanised city. This is one of the keys to Kenzo Tange's plan for a pylon-anchored "new city" in Tokyo Bay.

Reurbanisation: Beaming Aboard the Telecity

To survive, man will redesign his cities. Form, of necessity, will follow new functions. As twentieth century cities have been shaped and squeezed into anguished bundles and strands of spaghetti by the automobile and the spurious appeals of suburban life, twenty-first century cities will be shaped by new forces—telecommunications, environmental concerns, access to food and water, preservation of open space, a steady state economy, population stabilisation, energy conservation, crime control, escape from urban ennui and anomie—and, last but not least, corporate profits.

The reshaping has already begun. Super television stations in the U.S., such as those in Atlanta, Georgia, and San Francisco, California, are connected via satellites to millions of viewers in dozens of urban areas. Canada, France, Germany, the USSR and Japan are now starting to develop and implement national television satellite broadcasting systems directly to the home. The US will be along soon afterwards. During 1985-90 the French Post and Telecommunications Directorate began a nation-wide effort to place millions of electronic Teletel terminals in the French homes.

Revitalisation of urban retail areas into pedestrian malls, construction of soaring new hotel convention centres in urban slum areas and growing consumer interest in electric cars, are signs of a coming future. Significantly, these are changes primarily related to the private sector rather than to government action except in a regulatory role.

The major changes in city designs will likely include the following:

(a) Consolidation of a central city core: This core, that may or may not be a megastructure, will be physically interconnected by pedestrian walkways, cycle paths, electric car channels. It will all be electronically interconnected with multi-channel television networks and high-quality mobile communications. The vertical city *à la* Paolo Soleri or, in more humanistic renditions, *à la* Percival Goodman, seem almost irresistible in this context.

(b) Smaller satellite cities and airports. These may be modelled after Reston, Virginia, or Columbia, Maryland, or the new towns of England. These "suburban" satellite cities and a major airport city would be surrounded by farms, kibbutzes, recreation areas

and open space. [The satellite cities and the airport would be connected to the core by high-speed (300 kilometres/hour) or 200 miles/hour transit ways].

(c) Elimination of many streets. Obsolescent streets could then be converted either to public malls, air rights development or alternative transportation modes.

(d) Long-term conversion of conventional energy supplies. New energy sources would be largely based on solar and hydrogen energy supplies. Individual homes may operate on solar energy systems and/or fuel cells, probably of the H_2—O_2 type. In general, electrical energy would tend to replace hydrocarbon combustion energy.

(e) Remote location of manufacturing processes. Such remote factories would be largely automated and largely controlled by computerised robotics.

(f) New water supply and waste management systems. These would rely heavily on recycling of resources and stored energy.

(g) Greatly increased opportunity for citizens to interlink with groups of common interests. Social groups based upon stamp collecting, computers, gourmet cooking, etc., could be established across national boundaries at extremely low cost, almost without regard to where one lived.

(h) Continued rapid growth for those sectors of the economy related to consumer services and leisure and cultural activities. These will continue to grow, with entertainment, leisuretime activities and cultural events being the prime areas of growth. Manufacturing, agriculture and hydroponics will be of great importance but claim less and less manpower.

(i) The Electronic Home of the Future. Experimental homes, experimental buildings and even experimental communities will be necessary to work out the right equations. Recent work by the Frank Lloyd Wright Foundation in Phoenix, Arizona, provides a good example of what is needed. Messrs. O'Malley and Pierce of the Wright Foundation have designed the "House of the Future." Actually, it is called the "Ahwatukee" house, literally "Shining House of Dreams." This house represents a total package of attractive architecture, advanced computer, telecommunications and energy technology, harmony with nature and, most surprisingly, reasonable cost. Key features of the house are a two-story-high atrium (called the sky lobby); low energy

consumption; and automatic computer control of doors, lights, security and appliances. The $ 30,000 worth of electronics includes aspects such as a voice synthesizer on the front door that can give a caller a polite message or, if desired, an appropriately rude brushoff to a door-to-door salesman.[8]

*(j) Education for the Twenty-first Century.*Education will likely change in several ways. Schooling will become a life-long, continuing process for most of the population—professionals may spend every fourth year taking refresher courses in order to stay abreast of new technology. Academic, technical and cultural education will become more of a diversified service (both public and private in form and frequently provided independent of a single institution or agency). It may become a service that is delivered along with library, medical, recordkeeping, entertainment, banking, mail and other related services, through new telecommunications channels to the home or neighbourhood centre, i.e., the TAGOT network. Finally, basic survival education, physical fitness, and "back-to-nature" courses may also eventually be recognised as a priority need now largely unfulfilled. Indeed, as the gap between the knowledge of an individual and the mass information society grows, there will be increased recognition of the need for survival training and reestablishing links with nature. One of the most likely results will be summer kibbutzes for children, students, retirees and adults on sabbatical. Here, young and old will learn to farm, build a fire, navigate by stars, devise basic instruments, build basic shelter, compete in sports and socialise in a truly meaningful way. Such a system could bring great social and political strengths to a high-technology society. The longer-term role of education will be to allow individuals to pursue several careers in sequence or perhaps even in parallel. Education for social improvement or as a hobby will also become more popular. Both of these results will be a logical consequence of the significant reductions in costs that the new telecommunications delivery systems will bring to education, as well as the leisure time created as a result of industrial automation. The role of the traditional public school, college and university in the twenty-first century will likely be drastically altered amid much turmoil.

Not surprinsingly the telecommunications revolution will make radically new demands on the educational system. Virtually universal typing, computer and perhaps videotaping skills will be required of the public. Such skills will be as necessary in the future as dialing a telephone and tuning a TV set is today. Effective mass teaching of such skills will be a major challenge. The educational network will need to be designed to allow effective communications at the one-to-one level, as well as in small to large groups on a flexible basis. Likely, teleconferences and "special interest" social gatherings will increase in importance as the classical classroom fades from the scene.

(k) Developing a systematic approach to the technologies of reurbanisation. Some of the more important of these new technologies are identified in the last section.

The Four Tenets of the Telecity: A Philosophy of Reurbanising the Modern World

1. *A New Dialectic for Urban Architecture (Challenge and Response).* Kenzo Tange tells us that great incompatibilities exist in the modern world: the human scale versus the city megascale; the need for individual identity versus the anonymity of the city. Tange believes, and we profoundly agree, that it is these inconsistencies that breed the vitality of the future architectural achievement. Tange admonishes us to disdain superficial or stereotyped modernisation and the naive functionalism of the Bauhaus School and the followers of Gropius. Perhaps his most important statements concern the dynamic balance between technology and human existence on one hand, and between the anonymity imposed by the super scale of the modern community and the individual need for identification on the other. This is perhaps most vividly expressed within his plan for the urbanisation of Tokyo Bay. Here, he proposed gigantic tent-like structures reminiscent of traditional Japanese roofs, only enlarged one-hundred fold. Within these structures (built on pylon stilts) he proposes that people could plan and shape their own homes, to be built within the basic platform. Diversity thus emerges from unity. As Tange explains it: "Freedom would emerge within more systematic practical structures."[9] His gigantic pylon structures provide the opportunity for individual freedom but also freedom to adapt to new technologies.

Tange's analysis of Tokyo concludes that a radial hub city begins to break down as a working unit at a population size of 10 million. At this stage, new solutions must be found. Many models are possible. Tange proposes the vertebrae of the human spine as a new model, while others of the Japanese Metabolism School suggest different biological models.[10] Soleri is perhaps most known for his proposed vertical cities, although Frank Lloyd Wright and Percy Goodman have given alternative concepts. Fuller has even proposed the floating geodesic globe city. Indeed, we have the temerity to suggest that the humanised telecity of electronic communications, internodal transportation and shared-use of space for multiple functions may eventually evolve toward structures resembling the human nervous system. The common denominator among all such analyses is the recognised need to create new forms for our great urban centres and for our rural telecentres as well. Increasingly, efficient transportation forces us toward three dimensionality, while the seeking of individuality pushes us apart horizontally. Telecommunications allows us to move in all directions, even though communication satellites help us tend toward sprawl, while fibre optics help us toward density. The most significant conclusion of all is that we need multiple models for our cities.

2. *We Must Grasp the Beauty, Nobleness, Efficiency and Flexibility of Nature in Our Cities.* Buckminster Fuller has made a lifelong exercise of talking to and learning from nature. His conclusion? Nature would never build a city or a building the way we do. Our cities and buildings are too ugly and too heavy and too costly and too inefficient. Mother Nature, who gave us snowflakes, DNA, spiral galaxies, crystals, dandelion puffs and crocuses, would never have given us New York or even modern-day Paris. Our buildings are too heavy; they consume too much materials; they are inefficiently interconnected; they are poorly shaped; and they seldom provide an effective complement to the beauty of nature.

Our new cities should be integrated as living systems.[11] Our cities should be compatible with mankind's millions of years old custom of living with and relating to nature—even if it is in radical new ways like high-rise farms (some of them may in fact be hypoponic factories). We must avoid sterile, artificial erections that guzzle energy and provide all the ambiance of chilled tapioca. In nature, form indeed follows function, but never in the grotesque, brutal and amateurish ways that misguided proponents of the Bauhaus School of Architecture have tried to lead us. Indeed, as ironic as it sounds, computers will allow us to design to achieve new flexibility, diversity, and yes even beauty. Although we may never achieve the ultimate flexibility of Mother Nature, who makes each of her delicate snowflakes in a different pattern, we should at least follow her inspiration.

If you really believe in true Functionalism, study soap bubbles and flowers—not modern architecture.

3. *We Must Forget Architecture and Take Up Arcology.* As urban megalopolises gobble up farmland, swamps, forests, marshlands and prairies, and churn forth sewage, "acid rain," noxious gases and suburban sprawl, the question must naturally arise: "Are we doing a good thing here or not?" Each year human development and industrialisation brings new perils. Oil spills in the oceans are gradually being frozen into our polar ice caps, changing their albedo or reflectivity, and thus risking their melting; the list of endangered or extinct species grows longer—indeed, man may some day be added to the list. Urban planning must envision new patterns of symbiosis between cities, farms and forests. We must plan our long-term ecology first and our cities second.

Paolo Soleri characterises the automobile as a very sophisticated machine to accomplish the "most primitive of logistics." Soleri castigates the utopian concepts of architects like Frank Lloyd Wright. Indeed, Soleri characterises Wright's proposal for Broadacres with its sprawled development concept as: "a sophisticated form of ecological butchery." Soleri feels ecological balance can be achieved through balanced horizontal and vertical growth. To him and to us, the sophisticated off springs of the escalator and the elevator, are the transportation systems of the future.[12] Finally, we must add that, while we believe in Arcology, this does not mean that we accept the uniformity, the lack of protection against sabotage and the lack of the human spontaneity that some people associate with Soleri's work. This you will see in Tenet Four.

4. *The Key to Holistic Planning is Allowance for Diversity, Change, Individuality and Decentralisation. Before We Plan a Form to Serve*

a Function We Must First Question the Value and Worth of that Function. The Goodman brothers—Paul & Percival—start out from a very useful albeit simple question. "If our cities and communities were to help us live the various kinds of lives we might find desirable, what would they be like?" Starting from this premise, the Goodmans suggest various living arrangements as diverse as:

(*a*) vertical, controlled-climate circular cities about five miles in diameter, to serve as a marketplace for goods and services and as a centre for government, culture and recreation;

(*b*) subsistence-level villages of ease and rustic minimal structure, housing; and

(*c*) sophisticated but ruralised agricultural, industrial and craft-oriented communities.

Although the Goodmans emphasise again and again the need for diversity, several general themes also recur. They suggest that it is better to move work to people—not people to work. They believe it is wrong to isolate people from nature, even in the city. (The idea of a vertical city, although an apparent contradiction, isn't. First, you can bring high-rise gardens and farms to the city. Secondly, if you conserve space, you can make the surrounding forests accessible to all.)

Finally, the Goodmans wish to create cities and communities that are free, rather than enslaved by a single precept. They reject the primacy of a single goal such as biological, economic, technological or psychological efficiency. Such flexible thinking allows nature and greenery to come to the city and factories to go to the farms. It allows jogging and bicycling to become true alternative forms of transportation; it legitimates sabbaticals from work, and even yearly carnivals of fun and frolic.[15]

If these four tenets seem grandiose, pretentious, naive and idealistic, we must confess they may well be so. While it may be prudent to always be unpretentious, low key and worldly-wise in one's philosophic approach to life this is seldom a successful way of changing the world. Unfortunately, the way of compromise, halfway measures and modest adjustments, will do little but perhaps ease the pain of an otherwise terminal patient. Our patient, the modern city, is deathly ill, and we believe more must be done than administering sugar-coated pills.

Ingredients for the Telecity

There is no hidden magic; no helpful genie simply waiting to be uncorked; no benign God waiting to throw a lifeline to a mankind which might belatedly seek help. The future we build will necessarily be built by many diverse groups—by businessmen, by technologists, by government officials, by urban planners and architects, and by involved citizens. Progress will be slow, painstaking and never guaranteed, since the essential ingredients for success are difficult to achieve and sometimes even to perceive. We need innovative and inspired leadership, revised economic incentives, and effective and humane use of new and exciting technologies—particularly in the fields of telecommunications, information processing, energy and transportation; these are the greatest needs of urban centres. The problems will likely be equally difficult for all modern urban countries, whether it be the U.S., Japan, the United Kingdom, France, Brazil, Sweden or Germany. Good and innovative urban planning is worthy of support—economically, socially and politically. The creation of a humane, attractive and economically sound urban environment requires a commitment to change, establishment of realistic social objectives for technical research and development, and innovative ways to use political and economic incentives to motivate private enterprise to create a new future.

Altruism is not enough. There must be good, sound economic incentives to stimulate effective revitalisation of urban core cities in effective and pragmatic ways.

Here's to the Future

We have briefly outlined our concept of the telecity which, if implemented in whole or even in part, could bring a great benefit to mankind. It recognises, as most urban plans do not, the existence of a high degree of interrelation among economic, social and political issues. Admittedly, we ourselves are guilty, since we have largely ignored many factors which must ultimately be weighed in effective urban planning, such as military and defense considerations, family relationships, religious needs, concerns for personal ambitions and prestige, etc.

Quite basic to the future success of urban planning as proposed here is the issue of whether individual rights and liberties and self-identification can survive in a high-technology society. If so, resistance must be extremely high to national identification numbers; universal data banks on citizens; monolithic urban plans with centralised infrastructure which can be easily sabotaged or destroyed by a single accident or disaster—one of the great failings of Soleri's designs for vertical cities. Progress which threatens basic liberties in the name of efficiency is not progress. Only wit, wisdom and diversity will show us the right way.

Another key issue is whether problems of international co-operation can be solved. The "Telecity" will be "plugged" into a global society by satellites, optical fibres and advanced economic and political systems. In this regard, impatience is man's greatest asset and worst failing. Man's impatience has brought us social evolution—a force which in the last 10,000 years has blazed a wondrous and terrible trail of war, scientific discovery and invention, and social and cultural innovation.

Given the lifetime of the sun, man has perhaps several billion years in which to evolve; indeed, he may have much longer if he colonizes other star systems. True perspective in trying to plan for the centuries and eons to come is difficult to learn—perhaps impossible for either individuals or nations. Urban planners, political leaders and certainly the public electorate, are hard-pressed to see even a decade ahead at a time. Indeed, we tend to buy our air-conditioning systems in the heat of summer, when they are most expensive and installation takes the longest. Yet, we must hope that, year by year, decade by decade, we indeed can build a future worth having and perhaps miraculously avoid designing our own destruction mechanically, biologically, socially or politically. With Man's impatience must always come technical and social innovation—and hope.

One of the most important of these hopes must be that political, scientific and business leaders, as well as citizens, will recognise the need for effective planning for the future and that this planning process must be multivariate and polyarchial in nature, rather than unified and centralised. The key to such effective planning will be the substitution of an improved quality of life for strict "economic profit" as the prime goal in life. The nexus of "need" and "greed" must find a new rapproachement. New procedures for achieving desired future objectives must be found. Consensus-forming procedures and "games," such as *Peru 2000,* are perhaps indicative of how urban planners, technologists, citizens and other movers and shakers can decide on our future courses. Other approaches, such as the Rockefeller Brothers' *Unfinished Agenda* project to define "an expert consensus approach" to solving major economic, social and technical problems must be explored. Care must be taken that such activities do not become frivolous (as some of Ms. Hubbard's projects within the World Future Society have been viewed), or achieve irrelevancy by the simple expedient of ignoring major industrial, political or economic bases of power.

Perhaps the number one problem at this point is simply one of leadership and direction. The recognition of the trends and "likely technologies" of our urban future that we have outlined in this article is not remarkably different from what other technologists or social scientists might predict for the next 50 years. The essential difference is the recognition that we need a long-term social, political and economic plan that merges local, national, regional and global needs. Will there yet be purposeful leadership? Or will we be the mere captives of vast corporate strategies? Perhaps we will simply be sidetracked into war and trivialised technological competition. There are many ways to fall short of more hopeful goals.

The need for effective leadership, to clearly identify the issues in public for a and perhaps to arrive at national and perhaps eventually global consensus is important—perhaps even essential if man is to inherit a future of hope rather than despair. If we do succeed in building Humanised Telecities and, in the process, create the economic and social infrastructure required to sustain them, a truly important beginning will have been made. If we do succeed, it will indeed have been worth the wait. As a modest estimate, it will probably take at least 50 years of painstaking effort to attain the most modest of the goals outlined herein. Anyway, check back in 2030 and let's see how we made out. Let's hope our hopes and plans turn out better than those of the Futurama exhibit of the 1939 New York World's Fair.

Developing New Technologies for Telecities

New technologies by themselves cannot create humanised telecities of the future. Strong social, economic and political actions will also be necessary to achieve these goals. Without the right technologies, however, many of the basic improvements in urban living cannot be achieved. Here is a list of priority technological needs.

Objective 1: The Urban Telenet (TAGOT)

We need universal access to flexible, interactive, wideband urban telecommunications networks—both fixed and mobile. *Targeted Implementation Date:* 2005. *Technologies:* High flux-density communications satellite systems operating from large-scale space platforms; very large-scale integration (VLSI) technology required for wrist-radio and wrist-TV capability; low-cost, light-weight, reliable fibre optic cables optimised for "wiring" cities. "Intelligent" terminals capable of digital processing of video, facsimile, telephone and data transmissions; low-cost computer/video terminal equipment. *Supportive Public Actions:* Incentives for underground optical fibre "wiring" of cities; establishment of neighbourhood community terminals for educational and other purposes; setting of technical licensing standards; and general encouragement of privately and/or publicly operated teletext, electronic mail and advanced message and packet-switched data networks; profit incentives for technological innovations in telecommunications; public research support for space applications progress, particularly larger-scale space platforms; effective international standards for all forms of electronic and telecommunications services.

Objective 2: The Triple C Car

We need a low-cost, safe, durable, low-maintenance and pollution-free car—a Cheap, Clean Car (the C^3). *Targeted Implementation Date:* 1990 *Technologies:* High-performance, reliable batteries, e.g., nickel-hydrogen batteries, traction batteries, fuel cells; and/or high energy-density fly wheels. *Supportive Public Actions:* Government funding of necessary R&D; banning of polluting automobiles from cities by 1995; incentives to oil, auto manufacturing and telecomputer energetics corporations to develop and market the Triple C car.

Objectives 3: A New Energy Order

We need to implement a new energy order based upon solar hydrogen, geothermal and fuel cell technology. *Targeted Implementation Date:* 2010. *Technologies:* High performance amorphous structure solar cells; conventional but mass-produced silicon solar cell systems installable at costs ranging from $ 0.50 to $ 1.00 per peak watt of capacity; advanced design, safe H_2—O_2 fuel cells; a safe and efficient system of distributing liquid hydrogen fuels; advanced concepts for active and passive conservation and recycling of energy, including processing of solid and liquid waste products; development and application of new geothermal energy techniques. *Supportive Public Action:* Eliminate subsides to petroleum extraction and production; halt nuclear energy bias in government-sponsored R&D; government funding of key new technologies; encourage energy decentralisation; ravamp outdated building codes, utility regulations, mortgage regulations and tax exemptions, identify new areas of profitability for large energy corporations, particularly to encourage the petroleum industries, to enter new technology fields; reduce or remove monopolistic positions in energy enterprises.

Objective 4: New Urban Technologies and Systems for the Twenty-first Century

We need to discover, invent, develop and implement new urban technologies, optimised for twenty-first century urban life. These technologies should seek to reduce or eliminate the problems of twentieth century urban living that adversely affect the quality of life. *Targeted Implementation Date*: next 10-15 years. *Technologies:* Techniques for noise reduction or abatement; for pollution control and reduction; for efficient movement of people in high-density living patterns; for recycling of materials; for new construction techniques, such as "artificial land" construction, floating cities on pylon structures—all would serve to minimise resources utilisation and to maximise attractive and environmentally sound design. Our new structures should also help in lowering crime rates and reducing violence, while preserving political and individual freedom. Over-centralisation is the greatest danger of these technologies and, thus, system studies should seek to avoid the urban beehive syndrome. *Supportive Public Action:* Public-funded design competitions and demonstrations for model cities, including satellite "new towns"; privately planned and financed renovation projects in core cities; incentives and tax credits to private enterprise to develop or demonstrate such new technologies or urban system designs; ravamping of zoning, land use, space planning processes; actively surveying the low-energy technologies of lesser developed countries for "rediscovery" in the new urban environment; development of non-lethal weapons for crime control.

References

1. *Barlett's Familiar Quotations* (New York, Permabooks, Inc., 1958), p. 7.
2. Jacob Bronowski, *The Ascent of Man* (Boston, Little, Brown & Co., 1973).
3. Herman Kahn, *Thinking About the Unthinkable* (New York, Avon Books, Inc., 1962).
4. Lecture by Arthur Erickson, Smithsonian Institution, Washington, D.C., November 8, 1979.
5. Jacques Ellul, *Technological Society,* translated by Frank John Wilkinson, New York, Alfred Knopf, 1964.
6. Richard C. Schroeder, "Quality of Life in the Year 2000," *Topic,* No. 52, 1969.
7. Eero Saarinen, *Eero Saarinen on His Work* (New Haven, Connecticut, Yale University Press, 1968), pp. 102-104.
8. Peter Marsh, "The House of the Future is in Phoenix", *New Scientist,* October 11, 1979, p. 114.
9. Robin Boyd, *Kenzo Tange* (New York, George Braziller, Inc., 1962).
10. Robin Boyd, *New Direction in Japanese Architecture* (New York, George Braziller, Inc., 1968).
11. R. Buckminster Fuller, *Utopia or Oblivion* (New York, Bantam Books, Inc., 1969).
12. Paolo Soleri, *Sketchbook of Paolo Soleri* (Cambridge, Mass., MIT Press, 1971).
13. Paul and Percival Goodman, *Communitas* (New York, Vintage Books, 1960).

8

Research Perspectives for Communication Development

Interest in communication research has paralleled our concern for communication problems in social affairs. With unflagging vigour and unyielding interest, an increasing number of researchers and scholars have been engaged in both conceptual and empirical studies bearing upon desired changes in human behaviour involving interaction and communication. In any social system, human organisations, institutions and groups exist and function to achieve certain objectives and to accomplish certain tasks in relation to specified goals. These organisations, institutions, groups, and individuals have to indulge in communication in order to exist and to perform their functions in various fields and in different areas of activities. Without adequate and effective links or channels of communication it is difficult to visualise how individuals, groups and sub-parts of the social system could interact with one another, influence others and in turn be influenced by them. But it is in this process that we are encountered with many bristling problems of communication always pointing to the gaps between what was intended to mean, and what actually was perceived to mean. Communicators at various levels and points try to influence communicatees to respond to their intended meanings, but communicatees understand and respond only partly or incompletely, but never exactly and fully. Many variables creep in this process of communication and impinge upon occurrence of communality of meaning between communicator and communicatee. In locating answers to problems of communication one has to lean towards behavioural sciences like Psychology, Social Psychology, Sociology and Anthropology which provide insights into realms of cognitive and social aspects of human behaviour. For influencing human behaviour we use language and symbols and signs as vehicles of sharing our ideas and experiences with others. Knowledge in the field of semantics and linguistics gives us insight into symbols and their meanings in different contexts and situations. And for gaining insights into operational and applied aspects of communication and human behaviour, basic understanding of disciplines like Political Science, Economics, Public Administration, Management and others is indispensable.

Essentially, problems of communication and characteristics of communication research relate to influencing efforts, so that responses given match with intended stimuli. Why humans behave as they do, and how communication can make it possible to influence them and thus change their invert and overt behaviour in the desired manner and direction, is the basic theme that has attracted behavioural researches and others belonging to different disciplines. Communication research is still drawing heavily from researches conducted in these social disciplines and is trying to piece together and integrate these research findings to infer meaningful conclusions which could shed light on the dynamic communication process. Communication science is interdisciplinary in character, and is struggling to attain its own vantage position. If it succeeds in developing a systematic body of knowledge, which can be scientifically validated, then it might, in the near future, acquire the status of an independent discipline. Conceptual and empirical knowledge in the field of communication would grow based on theoretical, experimental and pragmatic research studies and their findings. A great deal of research has been done during the last three or four decades in studying the process and effects of communication, and in utilisation of the research findings for better understanding of communication problems. Much of the research work has been done in fact, in U.S.A. in the field of communication, group communication and mass communication. Although these research studies had emanated to tackle specific problems, and had been done within the framework of single discipline, yet the implication of their findings are far reaching and, for their applications in our Indian context, could be replicated with suitable modifications. At best these studies have been fragmentary, their results sometimes contradictory, and their focus limited. Nevertheless, research work so far attempted in communication development has been quite penetrating, revealing and utilitarian in tackling some of the formidable communication problems. Emphasis on present studies is on both theoretical and applied aspects, with an eye on uses and gratification, and on need fulfilment. An overview of research in persuasive communication can be enlightening to show trends in research, gaps yet to be filled, and implications of research findings so far gathered. Whereas it would be difficult to present an exhaustive or a comprehensive panorama in a paper serving, only to orient about some aspects of communication research, a few studies might be illustratively dealt with to advantage. In attempting such an overview it might be relevant to indicate the implications of research findings in community development programmes and the need for further research in the Indian context and setting. Perhaps, one of the useful approaches, in such an attempt might be to deal with different key elements in the communication process and then to have a look at the broad and total picture that might emerge.

Research studies pertaining to source of communication have revealed that the audience, image of source affect the audience's interpretation of the communication and its persuasive effectiveness. Sources regarded as credible, trustworthy, expect high in prestige enhance persuasion. The influence of sources has been both extensively and intensively dealt with and studied by the Telecommunication Research Centre headed by Caral Hovland. There is one of the important areas in which research studies could be undertaken in India to know which are the credible sources at various levels of Community Development programmes, what are their characteristics and what effect, such sources, have on what types of audience for what types of messages. Contributions of various components of credibility such as intention, expertness, prestige, trustworthiness, and allied variables in isolation and in combination also present a rich field for investigations.

Various content characteristics have been isolated to have relationships with persuasive communication. Of these, the more widely used and discussed characteristics are mentioned. Two-sided presentation, involving presentation of arguments on both sides of the issue or question, is more effective than one-sided presentation for persuading the highly educated audience as a safeguard against later counter-propaganda. One-sided presentation is, however, more effective in persuading the less educated as a reinforcing device. There is need for further empirical evidence to test the validity of these results under varying conditions relating to other key elements in the communication process:

(i) Persuasive communication which explicitly states conclusions is more likely to be effective than those which state conclusions implicitly;

(ii) Studies are needed to disentangle the effects of pre-existing attitudes and ego involvement variables;

(iii) Communication which employs threat appeals, citing the ill consequences and dangers, is likely to be less effective as the threat becomes more extreme and intense. Recommended procedures presented through communication with minimum threat appeals are likely to be adopted more widely. Content analysis in Community Development communications might reveal interesting findings in this area of threat vs. rewards appeals;

(iv) Repetition, particularly repetition with variation, has been found to increase persuasion efficacy, particularly in campaign propaganda. Multiple and cumulative exposure to propaganda has been found to be more effective, but the results are still inconclusive, because at other occasions it has been no more effective than single exposure;

(v) Communication which presents ways and means of implementing or 'canalising.' The existing needs of the audience are more persuasive than communication which

suggests to arouse new needs and ways of satisfying them. To create new needs and then to induce, through persuasive communications, the audience to particular modes, satisfying them, is obviously far more difficult task. Research studies in India could be undertaken to ascertain, as to how far communications by extension workers, engaged in Community Development have been able to influence the villagers in canalising their needs as perceived by them;

(vi) The effects of variables such as order of presentation, emphasis, organisation, etc., have been studied through numerous studies but collations are needed to make conclusive generalisations;

(vii) Whether communication on one hand and climate of opinion and morale on the other have any relationship of cause-effect character have been studied, and the trends seem to be that for facilitating effective communication, healthy climate of opinion and high morale are the pre-requisites and not the other way normally.

Media of Communication

Several media appear to be in themselves varyingly effective as channels for persuasive communication. Besides they have been found to be differently relevant, suitable and appealing to different audiences. In real situations and in audiences which are still denied the privilege of reading and writing, informal, personal, face to face, and oral, combined with visual, communications have been consistently found to be more effective than mass media. The relative effectiveness of the mass media, in reaching mass audiences in view of the inherent characteristics of mass-ness of the mass media, varies so widely from one area to another as to defy any high generalisation. However, multi-mediated communications supplemented by interpersonal, face to face contacts, have been believed to be particularly and peculiarly effective. Certain characteristics can be attributed to each medium to make it an instrument of persuasion. But none of these characteristics has been explicitly shown by research studies to contribute to persuasion. The role and place of traditional media of communication and of both inter and intra-village and group channels of communications in developing societies like India in communicating ideas and influencing individuals, groups and communities, in creating awareness and interest in improved practices and modern ideas are believed to be singularly relevant and challenging. Yet, these media and channels have remained untapped both for operational and research requirements. The traditional or conventional field offers a vast opportunity for communication researchers to shed light on which forms of folk media are relatively more appealing and lend themselves for treatment, of which types of substance, or content of messages, and under what conditions and contexts. To what extent folk forms, tempered favourably with newer contents, could be harnessed for motivation and attitude changes.

Communication Media and Type of Audience

Audience research has been delineated into primary characteristics, psychological traits, and communication habits. Research studies have focussed attention on correlations of these characteristics together with other factors like group norms, goals, values, beliefs, attitudes and other socio-cultural sets, with responses to communication. "Diffusion of Innovations" by Everett Rogers is an illustration to this effect. Detailed studies of different segments of audiences in a caste-ridden, socially and economically stratified society, subjected to the impact of political and power influences, as obtained in India, are needed to reveal as to which types of audiences are amenable to influence by which types of communications through what types of media and channels, and by what types of communication sources.

Enough attention has not been given to the element of feedback in the communication strategies. In fact, attitude change studies have been taken mostly as feedback work. Independent research studies directed towards feedback system operative in the context of community and its sub-systems are needed to show the working of the dynamic process of communication.

The overview has been only an attempt to map out some of the important contours of the communication territory, which did not include many details and characteristics. The territory is as big, complex, and challenging as the human behaviour. Meaningful research in the field of communication is needed to enable policy makers, planners, executives, extension workers, to communicate better and with effectiveness in their endeavour towards planned social channel. Many variables operate in communication process. These have to be isolated and then given treatments gradually and systematically, till a complete and total model of communication can be worked out.

Rural Orientation of Communication

The communication process as an instrument of change beggars discussion. The theory that material changes would automatically create desired values stands impartial judgement in a democracy. A simultaneous effort towards material advancement and creation of attitudes to promote this advancement has to be adopted. For this, the content, method and channel of communication require to be perfected. Programmes of production must cater to the national needs of food production, but at the same time a cautious approach towards the farmers' preferences for cash crops is called for. Areas, which have potentialities of being developed into major cash crop areas need not be motivated to change to food crops beyond one-fourth of their total production. Similarly, the non-cash crop areas may find a greater emphasis on commercial produce as the base for national and agro-industrial production. Psychologically, the farmers in both these areas would be happy at the prospects of having their due share of rich money crops. The programme can be closely tied with nutrition education, purposefully shifting food habits to a high protein and fruit diet. This content of communication will be a double pronged drive for balancing nations food requirements and the need for industrialisation. It would also quicken adoption of new attitudes towards agriculture. Methods of communication need very little theoretical support in the presence of volumes available on the efficacy on extension methods. The dexterity in their correct use is the priority. Much more of controlled and laboratory experimentation in the field of their use would speak of the proficiency of training centres spreading over the country for community development personnel, "A study of agricultural demonstrations in Bakshi-ka-Talab Block"[1] over a period of two years attends to the lacunae in a malignant form and varying degrees in the country. The demonstration process requires constant vigilance and scientific procedures for dissemination. Village leaders will have to be trained in demonstration lay-out and the official machinery can only be the guideline. In the beginning an alternate revolving of 'farmer leadership' between the official and non official agents of change needs invitation. Ultimately, the official resources must converge on research in the field of traditional agricultural practices and the positiveness of bringing about a replacement by innovations. Many results show that pruning some of the existing practices would brighten prospects. Audio-visual media have proved a limited field use with the present resources and pockets of success in agriculture, reimburse faith in individual persuasion. Communication through modern visuals and speech pre-determine educated comprehension by the farmer and leads us to the fundamental but slow programme of adult literacy.

The Channels of Communication

The communication channel links the Central Government with the small farmer, and has shown slips of slowness and incorrectness. A recent study[2] of communications issued from the State headquarters, to the Community Development Blocks analyses partially the channel of communication. It is evident that official delays and complete non-communication of programmes are frequent bottlenecks. It highlights the heavy dependence of community development, personnel on supervision and administration at the cost of acting as a series of links in the communication channel. Majority of workers, bossing the V.L.W., continue to devote their time to office efficiency and feel that contact with the masses is partially the responsibility of the block extension workers, and solely that of the V.L.W. It is not easy to bypass the problem of heavy work-load on the V.L.W., and his inability to cope with the enormous task of reaching individuals and supervising demonstration laying from the beginning to the end. It is proposed here to discuss four case studies in the field of communication of improved agricultural techniques. These case studies are the result of our experience gained during extension work in the five adopted villages and work in B.K.T. block. These villages help the training staff in maintaining an intimate touch with difficulties encountered in the diffusion of agricultural innovations.

Introducing Wheat Seed 710 in Village Mampur[3]

The wheat area in this village is saturated with wheat seed PB 591 and it was decided to persuade a progressive farmer, who happens to be the Pradhan also, to agree to a half field demonstration for the propagation of the new wheat variety NP 710. The superiority of this variety was commmunicated to the farmer and some other village people during preliminary contacts. It was necessary to convince them that variety N.P. 710 is rust resistant, prevents dislodging, gives healthy, golden seeds and the yield per acre is distinctly superior. A field of 2/3 acres was divided equally and the two varieties—PB 591 and NP 710 were given similar treatment. When harvested the total weight of NP 710 was more than that of PB 591 but the seeds of NP 710 were inferior to that of PB 591. The result was that the total produce of PB 591, due to its superior quality fetched more price than that of NP 710. Here we find that although the per acre yield of NP 710 was more it would not fetch more money and hence the farmer would not be convinced. The matter was discussed with agricultural experts but still there is a big question mark. Here the problem is not one of effectiveness of communication but that of positive all-round superiority of a new variety which we recommend. Efforts have been made to find out the results of NP 710 in other areas, but no such reports are available. Probably, we have not reached another spot where such a demonstration to assess the two varieties was carried out. This study places importance on the soundness of research findings and their implementation in the field.

A Study of Agricultural Demonstrations in Bakshi-ka-Talab Block[4]

A study of agricultural demonstrations on Bakshi-Ka-Talab Block covered a period of two years 1959-60 and 1960-61. The objectives of this study during the first and second year were:

FIRST YEAR

- *(i)* Laying out demonstrations.
- *(ii)* Follow up
- *(iii)* Sight-seeing.
- *(iv)* Crop cutting.
- *(v)* Guidance available to V.L.Ws for this work.

SECOND YEAR

- *(i)* Planning.
- *(ii)* Part played by non-official agency in this programme.
- *(iii)* Lay out of the demonstrations.
- *(iv)* Follow-up.
- *(v)* Sight-seeing.
- *(vi)* Crop cutting.
- *(vii)* Guidance available to V.L.Ws for this work.
- *(viii)* Usefulness of the programme for the cultivators.
- *(ix)* Verification with the cultivators if they have adopted the practices demonstrated in the following season.
- *(x)* Case histories.

Block Bakshi-ka-Talab, is one and a half size block and get advantage of a cluster of important training centres in the vicinity. It is revealing to study the conclusions of the final phase of this study.

Conclusions

1. Planning of demonstrations at block level was done fairly well. Members of the Block Development Committee at the Block level and of Panchayat at village level were involved in the process of planning but their assistance in this work was limited. The major portion of the work was done by Extension Officer (Agriculture) at Block level and V.L.W. at the village level.

2. Demonstrations as an educational process were used to a limited extent. No proper sightseeing programme was organised to show the variation of growth of yield no cultivators by majority of V.L.W. Crop cutting to convince the cultivators and explain them, economic gains, was also not done for all the plots and by all V.L.Ws. Results of demonstrations were utilised

only by a few V.L.Ws and were discussed in the village Panchayat meetings to educate the farmers of their area. Extension Officer (Agriculture) discussed the results in the meeting of Block Development Committee.

3. Knowledge of the V.L.Ws about demonstrations conducted in their circle was not adequate. They should be given more guidance and training in conducting the demonstrations.

4. Only 57 per cent cultivators adopted the practices demonstrated in their fields in the following season.

A detailed study of the report confirms further the ineffectiveness of agricultural demonstrations. The normal expectations of a well laid-out demonstration are that one demonstration will disseminate the practice around the village apart from the continued adoption of the practice by the farmer on whose farm the demonstration was laid, which should be a certainty. The fact that only 57 per cent cultivators adopted the practice is disheartening, not in terms of the numerical percentage, but when we come to assess the possibilities of a scientifically laid out demonstration. It cannot be denied that a demonstration which is a failure is not only ineffective but has a negatively detrimental impact on the population. It is for this reason that if a demonstration is laid out its scientific soundness has to be ensured, otherwise it is better to avoid its organisation.

A Study of Paddy Cultivation Practices in Garur Block[5]

This study draws out the importance of leadership in the acceptance of improved agricultural practices. It also speaks of the desirable methods of individual contacts which give a fillip and motivation of village leadership as a media of communicating agricultural practices. In the hilly terrains of Kumaon, paddy cultivation envisages difficulties and primarily the acceptance of a green fodder crop (Berseem) by a progressive farmer, Jai Lal, led to increased milk production and convinced him of accepting improved methods of paddy cultivation—the programme which was in vogue with the block team. The case study gives important conclusions.

(*i*) Programmes of Community Development must vitally improve, the money income of the farmer. Only a quick tangible gain provides the base line for further acceptance.

(ii) In this case, a green fodder crop (Berseem) brought about a significant rise in the milk production.

(iii) Traditional customs and practices impede acceptance of innovations. Care has to be taken while choosing that farmer who would be willing to make a sharp departure from tradition.

(iv) A good team spirit in the block staff is an essential pre-requisite to the introduction of new agricultural practices. This team spirit must be vertical, down to the village and upto the district, and horizontal within the block team.

(v) Workers on-the-spot must be allowed initiative.

(vi) Incentives for better production must always be provided to the farmers.

Role Analysis of V.L.Ws and Result Demonstrations[6]

This is a study of 14 result demonstrations and the findings enlarge the lack of educational content in agricultural demonstrations. It says that demonstration laying is a mechnical translation of government orders and the V.L.W. neither derives nor gets technical guidance from his superiors.

The process begins with instructions from the B.D.O. who himself has received instructions from sources outside the block. The pertinent one of these are passed to the V.L.W. through the agriculture extension officer who, in turn, provides the minimum technical information, usually limited to the size of plots and fertiliser doses. No further technical help is sought or given.

As with other activities, action is taken to carry out instructions the routine way that at least fulfil minimum essentials of compliance and report. The villager is brought in the process on the lure of free supply and/or other reasons than his own needs. One control and one or two experimental plots are laid out. The crop is sowed by the farmer or his servants. A few intermittent visits are made to the plot by the V.L.W. but without specific purpose. A few neighbouring farmers, and one or two of the block staff on tour, happen to pass once or twice, but no planned explanations are given. When the crop is cut, the differences in yield are reported and generally forgotten. In five cases the crop was not even cut and weighed separately. Fresh instructions start a new but similar cycle.

The V.L.W. fails to see the demonstration as an educational activity. Much of his work consists of a series of physical activities. He thinks in the same way about demonstrations emphasising the "activity" aspect but failing to grasp or enhance the learning or educational dimensions. The pressures towards achievement and the criterion of measurement of progress in the block operations makes it difficult for him to utilise educational methods even when he serves the need for them.

The author has cited from some of the scanty number of research studies available on the subjects of communication of improved agricultural practices to the farmer. The lacunae in the communication process intermingle with social resistances by the farmer, and the situation enters a blind alley.

Official and Non-Official Agents as Carriers of Agricultural Innovations

The agents of change play the focal role in the communication of agricultural practices. Their integrity, technical know-how adaptability to varying social situations and faith in the extension process attract attention of the analyser. Fulfilment of the jobs for which they are employed has to be viewed in the context of the training they have received and the field situations they are placed in. Some of the role analysis studies of official community development functionaries give the following problems for a further probe.

(i) There is a tendency towards departmentalism; and strong attachments of subject matter specialists with their parent departments do not allow them to take an integrated view of the Community Development programme.

(ii) General administrators, who are deputed for short periods in the Community Development programme cannot make full use of either the philosophy or contents of Community Development programme.

(iii) Recent shifts on higher agricultural production devolve heavy responsibilities of acquiring knowledge of

agriculture on subject matter specialists who lack adequate training.

(iv) Faith attachment to the programme, of Community Development personnel are meagre and there is a tendency towards routinisation.

(v) There is lack of research to show difficulties of programme implementation, and for the reconstruction of a community development personality.

Farmer Leaders

The right type of non official leadership is shy and there is an emergency of power elite[7] not always in the best interests of the programme. The need of the hour is to find a chain of small farmers as leadership groups and agricultural demonstrations on their field only, will enable the majority village population to identify themselves with the effectiveness of improved agricultural practices on small farms. If the emphasis is on agriculture, as it is, the village leader training camp must be chosen carefully to convey knowledge of improved agricultural practices. The current experience is that for some reason or the other the small farmers fail to be included in these camps, and it is considered that it is they who have to become the most potent mass media of dissemination of improved practices. Their participation would ensure their own economic growth and a wide scale acceptance of agricultural practices. It would also answer the criticism[8] that the Community Development programme is yet to reach the weaker sections of the society. The power elite which monopolises the show does not depend solely on agriculture. They have other subsidiary economic and political grounds for class struggle, and occasionally, dissensions within the panchayat. The vast majority of farmers who really matter surround these resource group[9] leaders and ultimately the benefits come to the leaders and not the followers. An important bottleneck in dissemination of new agricultural technology, through village leaders, is that our training methods during leaders' camps fail to communicate the advantages of improved agriculture—not that we do not tell village leaders about improved agriculture but we often fail in communicating the total knowledge. Eventually, this failure results in the incompetence of the village leader either to practice the method on his own field or to disseminate it effectively. Village leaders who are associated with the Panchayats by virtue of having been elected, have a tendency of getting lost in the melee of statutory aspects of panchayat working and their contribution to increased production in the village is nominal. Individual psychology and built-in values in the social system are not always congenial for the promotion of the right type of attitude among village leaders which would ultimately increase agricultural production. The contemporary social values do not allow adequate feeling of pride to the village leader who lives for the sake of increasing agricultural production in the village. Even today, agricultural cultivation is of an individualistic nature and the maximum frequency of inter-change of ideas regarding agriculture among village people take the form of telling one another about the wraths of nature and failure of crops. Very few of them, nay none, discuss scientifically the factors which have been responsible for a better yield on an individual farm. Many of the farmers may wish to keep it a secret and enjoy the solitude cf better production. There is a constantly growing feeling of competition, and one fails to see universal jubilation in the event of an overall increase in village production.

It would be extremely useful to elicit opinion on the results of crop competitions, and find out the social position of the competitions in their village hierarchies. Increased crop in the field of high class village leaders does contribute to the national production, but we cannot be too sure that it also promotes the desired community feeling, for increased production, within the village community, or that it ignites a spark of new knowledge in the village community. The interdynamics of communication of improved agricultural practices in a village is of a priority importance, and to ensure a free flow of innovations the co-operative attitude in the village has to become the base. The creation of this attitude is the domain of the educator, the extension worker, and the proper village leader.

Some important areas of recommendations emerge from what has been said above.

1. Scientific and technological soundness of communicating an improved agricultural practice have to be ensured.

This includes the most important extension method of demonstration laying.

2. In order to build up village leaders, as media of dissemination of improved agricultural practices, caution has to be exercised by selecting only those who really represent the majority—socially, economically and culturally and become the focus of attention, because he is the least assertive competitor in the individualistic village society.
3. Fundamental research in agricultural laboratories must take into account the social and economic superiority of the innovation over the regional and traditional agricultural practice. This would mitigate the loss of time in breaking social barriers of tradition and long practice.
4. Role analysis studies tell us that there is a need of more field workers than supervisors and co-ordinators.
5. A recasting of community development programme can make them agricultural biased.

A Case Study

Kumaon hills in Uttar Pradesh are enshrouded in mystery, beauty, natural splendour, breath taking heights, past glory, national danger and extreme poverty. The year 1952 gave birth to one of the 55 community projects spread over the entire country. This case study of improved methods of paddy cultivation, initiated as one of the many community development programmes, is based on the present writer's experience of having worked for about two years in the Garur Block and later visiting the area again after a considerable lapse of years with the specific intention of collecting data to assess the role of rural leadership in the diffusion of improved agricultural practices. At the time of this study the Government heirarchy of community development project comprised the Deputy Project Executive Officer assisted by a number of specialised subject-matter extension officers ultimately helping the multi-purpose village level worker. The programme of community development is all pervading and each subject matter specialist in an effective link in the multi-facet approach of the programme.

The Story Begins

Garur Block, lying between a height range of 3,000 to 5,740 feet above sea level, was the bus terminus—43 miles from Almora and 110 miles from the last railway point, Kathgodam.

Agriculture is the main-stay of this area. Being a valley Garur grows excellent paddy crop. People cling to the old practices of growing this crop. When asked to adopt new improved methods you would invariably come across replies as "No let us not do it God will get angry." "Some death might occur." "Our cattle may be affected" and so on. They would only do it if they sacrificed a goat first with a view to ward off any such danger. Two instances of this mental reservation and socio-psychological attitudes can be safely cited here.

In a village a young boy, the only son of his widowed mother, agreed on the advice of a V.L.W. to transplant rice in his field as a trial. His mother and many other elders of his village discouraged him from taking on this new step. But, enterprising as he was, he laid out a demonstration of J.P.M.C. without taking recourse to the old tradition of sacrificing a goat. As the demonstration plot was showing its effect, he had to go away to Haldwani for some important work. As ill luck would have it he died of a snake-bite. Till today the villagers are allergic to any sort of innovations.

Similarly in another village a farmer planted berseem in his fields to serve as green fodder for his cattles. The crop was rich and when fed to the buffaloes increased their milk-yield. The unfortunate coincidence was that one of the buffaloes got a fractured leg and the farmer attributed his incidence to the growing and feeding of "berseem" to the cattle.

Such was the condition of this area when the community development workers had to work against these agebound social attitudes.

Thakurs constitute the majority population, and Brahmins and Harijans are in a small minority. Polygamy is economic and apart from the rather strenuous operation of tilling the soil the women (numerically more) cleverly bear the burden of other agricultural operations and tending the cattle. The comparatively free time available to the male is utilised for running small and scanty wayside shop or working as coolies. The joint family is the primary source of social security till petty quarrels (mostly among women) completely break it. Political consciousness infiltrated the area with school education higher literacy and the pre-independence national struggle. The economy of the people flourishes on agriculture and business. Indo-Tibetan border and tourist traffic ensure the latter.

Paddy and potato are the main crops and subsidiary avenues like the export of forest produce, herbs and fruits add (though meagrely) to the income of the people. The total area under paddy cultivation in Garur Block is 6249 acres out of which 2743 aces is irrigated. This case study bases findings on 800 acres of paddy growing in irrigated land. The government in 1953-54 extended a network of metalled roads which encompassed areas beyond Garur terminal and plunged into the Himalayan fastness upto the Indo-Tibetan border. Consequently, the erstwhile monopoly of Garur bus terminus dwindled and the one time lucrative shopkeepers leaned heavily on agricultural production.

The Local Leader

Jai Lal, a goldsmith by heredity turned into a farmer by choice and partial circumstances, was the intial local contact leader for the Garur Block during the early years of community development. The teething troubles of block administration were reduced due to a number of physical facilities; in the form of housing, pack animals and sundry arrangements; enthusiastically offered by Jai Lal, and in turn, a close association between him and the block administration provided the base for a largely diffused adoption of the well-known Japanese Method of Paddy Cultivation. Jai Lal's ancestors were residents of Almora; his grandfather migrated to this area in search of a lucrative business in goldsmithy. His father devoted a part of his time in small enterprises (including goldsmithy) but Jai Lal after inheriting family pursuits for a part of his early life faced crisis due to rising gold prices and lean purchases. Jai Lal owned sufficient land in the Garur valley and the block administration through a series of persuasion channels, made him agree to play the role of an innovator by adopting recommended agricultural practices. Since then, Jai Lal's interests have been varied and he has been adapting himself with the moving times and business opportunities. While he has remained religiously attached to the traditional family profession by maintaining a small goldsmith's shop, Jai Lal has been diverting his energies towards occupations promising quick profits. Today, Jai Lal clings to agriculture with the acumen of a businessman and concentrates on the prospects of winning crop competition prizes. He also finds time to take petty contracts and add to his agricultural income.

Innovator's Role—An Aid to Leadership Development

In October, 1952, the extension workers of the block team made Jai Lal their focus of attention and through a series of meetings tried to persuade Jai Lal, who agreed to try "Berseem" cultivation on a portion of his land—"Berseem" hitherto unknown in this region besides being a good green manuring crop is an excellent green-fodder for increasing milk yield. A demonstration was laid-out on Jai Lal's plot and when Jai Lal's cattle were fed on the first harvest after 45 days, the milk yield went up from 1 to 1½ seers. This interested him and Jai Lal made searching enquiries about further use of this crop which was advised to be ploughed in. During this period, usually, no cattle-fodder was available in the hills and the innovation promised brightness. Once a portion of the rich berseem crop had been ploughed into the field. Jai Lal by long and tiring stages was initiated into the adoption of transplantation of the paddy plants on the lines of J.M.P.C. Through careful nurture and advice Jai Lal grew 70 maunds of paddy in one acre of land—this soaring high production level is uncommon even in the plains and the Directorate of Agriculture were pleasantly surprised. Ultimately Jai Lal agreed to enter a series of crop competitions and became the proud recipient of a number of prizes.

The Innovation is Adopted by Other Farmers

Programmes of "Berseem" and "J.M.P.C." were thoroughly discussed in the meetings of the project advisory committee, to which Jai Lal was nominated (in view of his innovation role) as a co-opted member. The adult literacy teachers talked about the innovations in the night classes. A wide publicity was done at the time of the annual Kisan Mela. By now, Jai Lal had begun taking interest in other programmes of community development—artificial insemination, planting Bombay-green variety of banana and bringing about a change in crop rotation. In 1956-57, Jai Lal again entered the state level crop competition and won three prizes on three fields in the name of his brother and aunt. This resulted in inspiring five more farmers to enter the competition and by the end of 1961 as many as 8 farmers entered the state level competition. In 1961-62 Jai Lal failed to secure the prize which went to Pan Singh growing 114 maunds 3 seers and 11½ chattaks of paddy per acre. At the time of this study Jai Lal was hoping to break this record.

There is a regular and healthy competition amongst the farmers of Garur Block to excel each other's production. Old varieties of paddy are giving place to new. A local variety 'Thapachini' has been substituted by China 4. A latest variety known as Koesing 22 is being adopted by most of the farmers for the purposes of competitions as this is a hardy variety, the grains are weighty, the crop ripens late and does not lodge. In addition to normal manuring, Jai Lal introduced a new system of using leaves of local plant known as "Chinese tallow." This grows abundantly in the area. The foliage is rich, the leaves are soft and succulent. Many other farmers have also adopted this practice. Almost whole of the area is now sown by J.M.P.C. The practice has extended from Garur Block to other adjacent blocks. The average yield of the area has risen from 25-40 maunds per acre to 60-70 maunds per acre and one can witness an unending rush of farmers at the block office filling-up forms for the state level competitions.

Tangential Impacts of Diffusion

"People want the best cloth and most of the fine cloth is now sold to the general public" said Kishan Singh (Chairman of the Block Committee) while giving impressions about the effect of improved methods of paddy cultivation. This man, owning a cloth shop, went on to say "we do not import paddy any more, on the other hand paddy is being exported to the tune of Rs. 25,000 per year." When asked as to what other advantages had accrued on account of increased yields of paddy he explained that the farmers had adopted better techniques of cultivation for other crops also. Further he said "there is a general improvement in all walks of life." In the wake of success in one direction the mass of the people started accepting other programmes of community development. The present extension officer (Agriculture) frankly observed "Now we go to Jai Lal and other progressive farmers to seek advice in relation to paddy cultivation."

Analysis

(i) In the programme of rural development it is necessary that we start programmes which vitally touch the major section of the community.

(ii) A quick and tangible economic gain works as a spur creating a widespread effect on all walks of life.

(iii) Traditional customs and age-old practices are great barriers in the diffusion of innovations.

(iv) An integrated team spirit in the block staff is the *sine qua non* of success.

(v) The extension worker on the spot must be given enough of free scope to deal with the programme rather be asked to depend.

(vi) Incentives for good work should be provided to the extension workers and the farmers.

References

1. A Study of Agricultural Demonstrations in Bakshi-ka-Talab Block—Sharma, T.C., Orientation and Study Centre, Bakshi-ka-Talab—cyclostyled for restricted circulation.
2. A countrywide study of the time-lag in the despatch and receipt of government orders and circulars by C.D. Blocks—Ministry of Community Development for official use.
3. Case study Singh S.N., unpublished for official use.
4. A Study of Agricultural Demonstrations in Bakshi-ka-Talab Block—Sharma T.C.—cyclostyled—for official use.
5. A case study of paddy cultivation in Garur Block—Pande, B.M., Principal Orientation and Study Centre, Bakshi-ka-Talab Block, Lucknow—unpublished for official use based on the writer's

experience of working in that block for three years and a repeated study made in 1962-63.

6. Village Level Workers, their Work and Result Demonstrations, Dube, D.C. Sutton, Willis, A., and Gallup, Gladys, National Institute of Community Development, published 1960-61.
7. Unesco Study Group in Cyprus—Social Pre-requisites of Economic Growth—*National Herald*, Magazine Section.
8. Report of the committee appointed by the Government under the Chairmanship of Jayaprakash Narain.
9. Paper on Resource Groups—Sharma, K.N., Department of Sociology, I.I.T. Kanpur, unpublished but circulated for opinion by National Institute of Community Development.

9

Communication Revolution: Logical Ends

In ancient times, heroes and heroines with great regularity went to the Delphi Oracle to hear the truth about the future. With great regularity they misinterpreted the "truth" of the oracle in accordance with their own biases. With great regularity they met a bad end.

The lucky ones simply lost their fortunes, their good looks, their lovers, on their lives. The unlucky ones, like Oedipus, lost everything, including their self-respect. Melancholy fortune tellers and other bearers of bad news, ever since the days of Cassandra, have never won popularity contests or been voted most likely to succeed. Clever fortune tellers thus learned to use skilful deceit to make the bad sound good. They also hedged their bets by always using the double entendre. The Delphi Oracle was the master of this craft.

> "You will retain your present health," may mean you will indeed be healthy but you are headed for the poor farm, or it may mean you developed terminal cancer a month ago.
>
> "Great things await you afar" might mean you will be crushed by a boulder in a landslide on your next overseas trip or that a distant relative has left you a fortune. Unfortunately the attorneys will never be able to locate you and your windfall will end up in a trust

> to benefit the local animal shelter.
>
> It is thus that one can predict with certainty: "Great things await us in the twenty-first century."

Now no one truly knows what those great things are and whether they will be greatly good or greatly bad. Nevertheless, let's use some tricks of the trade to try to find out about our electronic future. Formal attempts at forecasting the future bear a kinship to what we call the social sciences. Having had formal training myself in the social sciences and forecasting, I can confidently state that both disciplines are very much a black art.

Forecasting techniques are numerous; good ones are few. There are straight-line and smooth-line projections; there are linear regression analyses; computer simulations and model-building; there are even scenario constructions and the oldtime favourite "off the top of the head guessing." Forecasts thus must be taken with large quantities of salt—a grain or two is hardly sufficient.

There is one technique that has had some limited success, at least enough that it is respectable to mention it outside the corridors of the World Future Society. This technique, the Delphi Survey, begins with a very strong point in its favour—simplicity. The procedure involves getting a group to suggest a number of possibilities for the future and then (in written or electronic text form) independently "voting" for what they expect to be the most likely outcome, sharing the results, perfecting how the options are stated, "voting again," and so on until a consensus emerges. This procedure has been proven to be more dependable than many others in predicting the future. In essence, it uses "collective" good judgment. Although the Delphi survey is typically conducted among those with special expertise, it can be used among reasonably well-informed individuals.

Although I have known about Delphi surveys since graduate school days, my first direct participation in one was at a symposium on planning the future that was being led by Frederick Pohl, the noted science fiction writer, in the summer of 1978. About 40 of us wrestled with the future for 2½ days—and produced a number of interesting results. First of all, we reached agreement that a staggering range of new technologies could be expected over the longer-term future. Only on one point did we reach a complete consensus on something we thought would *never* happen—that humans would abandon their clothing. This conclusion was not based on environmental factors or prudery—it was simply a matter of status and authority. Various forms of nudity might come or go, but some form of clothing to render status would remain.

The other result of note was our prediction of the number one news story for 1979. After quite a lengthy process, we agreed that it would be some form of a major nuclear accident! This, of course, was some nine months prior to the nuclear mishap at Three Mile Island in Harrisburg, Pennsylvania. Although the number one news story of a year is hard to judge (probably the U.S./Iranian crisis best qualifies), I do know that the TMI headlines in local newspapers in Manila, the Philippines, were captured by this story for the many days I was there while the story broke. Furthermore, the reverberations concerning the future of nuclear energy are still being felt over a year later, as global debate grows rather than slackens.

Naturally, when I began to think how to approach the subject of predicting future trends in space applications and telecommunications, my thoughts immediately focused on a Delphi Survey. I thought why not pick the collective brains of the best experts in the field in Europe, Japan, Australia, Canada, the U.S., and in the developing world? Also, it seemed prudent to make sure that the participants provided a good cross-section of government officials, scientists, corporate officials, representatives of international organisations, and of academia. Fortunately, a group of some 80 experts representing such a balance were kind enough to participate in the survey that ensued.

Rather than a lackluster recital of the results, I have decided to exercise some literary license and add a dash of embellishment here and there. The result is an apocryphal interview with Lady Cassandra, head of the newly reopened Delphi Oracle—an Oracle operating under modern-day management and utilising the world's foremost technical equipment.

An Interview With Top Management at Delphi Enterprises
Exclusive to the Future Gazette
Delphi: The Greek Isles

Skeptic Sherwin-Smithson: (First seen in an all-white, ultra-modern office building)

Hi, I'm Skeptic Sherwin-Smithson of the *Future Gazette*, the journal that provides all the news fit to be teleprinted—before it happens. I've an appointment with your boss.

Virginia Vestal, Appointments Secretary:

Just a moment. Lady Cassandra is on the videophone with the German Prime Minister. Ah, she's through. I'll show you in.

Lady Cassandra:

Welcome, Mr. Sherwin-Smithson. I was much impressed with your preliminary list of questions. They gave our staff a good workout.

Skeptic Sherwin-Smithson:

Please call me Skeptic.

Lady Cassandra:

We hope to call you "convinced" after you learn more about our operations here.

Skeptic:

I must admit I'm amazed you can run this whole operation with just those gorgeous girls in the togas out there, yourself and, of course, your computer.

Lady Cassandra:

Oh Skeptic, that's highly flattering, but almost too funny. If you want to see my staff, just look at my console over here. I need only touch the right button and I can automatically dial up any one of my eighty professional staff members on the videophone. Those two scrumptious looking receptionists out there are only our resident vestals. We do make a few bows toward traditionalism here, but not many.

Skeptic (studying videophone console intently):

Rather a good show. I see you have people from Turkey, India and Korea. Rather a diverse lot, aren't you?

Lady Cassandra:

Well, we certainly are a multinational enterprise in the good sense of the term. Although our staff of experts is largely from the U.S., with a sizable contingent from Japan, we have tried to get a good cross-section of scientific expertise from around the world. Most of our experts are on retainers for on-call duty for special Delphi projects. Their regular jobs are in industry, government and academics. We even have a few from international organisations and the Press.

Skeptic:

Very impressive. But what can your wise nabobs tell my readers about the future? For instance can you tell my readers in Europe anything reassuring about the current frenzy to deregulate the whole telecommunications and broadcasting industries in the U.S.? My readers are fearful that the Yanks are about to toss the baby out with the bath water. They are afraid that complete deregulation of U.S. communications and computers will create havoc in Europe and the rest of the world. As you know, we like to be reasonably neat and tidy in our operations here in Europe, with government monopolies pretty much in charge of things.

Lady Cassandra:

Glad you asked. Seventy-two per cent of our experts believe that there will be a major revamping of the rate base approach to telecommunications regulation within the U.S. by the year 2000, and that much greater emphasis will be placed on market competition plus profit incentives for innovations that result in better and lower-cost service to the public. The current practice of having a largely unregulated computer industry presumably will also continue. On the other hand, 66 per cent of these same experts believe that there will never be complete deregulation of the entire U.S. broadcasting and telecommunications industry. In short, it should be some time before the great unwashed electronic masses from America are completely unleashed on the world and Europe.

Skeptic:

Fascinating, I'm sure. But what's with these statistics and percentages? I thought oracles foretold the future with a crisp yes or no.

Lady Cassandra:

Oh, no! Oracles have always hedged their bets. In the old days, this was accomplished by placing a semantic jungle between future reality and the prediction. Today, we do it by including a numerical jungle within our predictions. But, we do it very scientifically. We consult with our worldwide experts—83 of them to be exact—and we ask them about the future, tally the results, give them the totals, as well as a chance to change their minds. We add up the final results and then, voila! An international masterpiece of futurism is produced. It's really the modern way. Why no self-respecting weather forecaster ever says it's going to rain today. He says there's an 85 per cent probability of rain and then we bring out the slickers. Next question, please.

Skeptic:

We keep hearing a lot about solar power satellites that will free us from our current concerns about oil shortages and nuclear energy. Is there anything to these claims?

Lady Cassandra:

Yes and no.

Skeptic:

I think I liked the statistics better.

Lady Cassandra:

Oh, but that's what the statistics say. You see, there are at least two schools of thought. There are radio astronomers and communicators and scientists who sincerely believe that solar power space platforms will irradiate such enormous power that they will royally screw up everything else. Some of these feel rather strongly that the solar power satellite is both technically and economically unworkable, as well as destructive. One of our experts summed this up rather well when he said, "I spit on the despicable persons who have perpetrated this technological hoax of solar power satellites." On the other hand, there are the aerospace and energy industry people who believe that orbiting solar power platforms are super. They say the interference problem can be solved. The need for a much larger launch vehicle is child's play, and the enormous capital investment can be proved to be economically viable. So, not surprisingly, our brain trust is firmly split. Thus, 37 per cent of our experts say oh, yes, the SPS will certainly be along by the year 2000, while 48 per cent say it will be at least 2015 and, more likely, in the longer-term future. A solid 13 per cent say it will never be a viable concept. In short, the solar power space platform is a definite maybe. Perhaps we might be more helpful on your next question.

Skeptic:

There's that chap Gerald O'Neill, the professor at Princeton University in the States, who says we will some day be living in space colonies. He makes all sorts of plausible explanations on how we can do it. Is this an elaborate humbug and, if not, when will we see the self-sustaining space colonies?

Lady Cassandra:

That's an easy one. Sixty per cent (60.2 per cent, to be exact) of our experts say a self-sustaining space colony will not be here until the longer-term future, i.e., it's at least 35 to 50 years away. Now the emphasis here is on the words "self-sustaining." Experimental space colonies on the moon, perhaps the asteroids or even one of the big planet's satellites, as well as some completely artificial ones in space, may come a bit sooner. The big question about space colonies is what will be the prime motivation for them—scientific research, space manufacturing and mining, prestige, pioneering spirit, military operations, energy production, or what have you? We have our experts looking into that very important question.

Skeptic:

I am quite a fan of that American cartoon about the police detective Dick Tracy, who has a two-way radio wrist watch that operates to a high-powered satellite in geosynchronous orbit and that allows him always to be in contact with headquarters. When will we see these little gadgets in operation?

Lady Cassandra:

Well, if you mean two-way wrist communicators for police and firemen, 66 per cent of our staff says it will happen in the time period 2000 to 2015, but such devices for the general public are in the longer-term future or maybe even never. One point your readers might find of some interest is the fact that, once you have a satellite with the power and flexibility to handle mobile service to wrist communicators, it would be a relatively easy task to shift a very benign technology into a much more sinister area—namely personal surveillance. Monitoring devices could be affixed to selected individuals or even large segments of a total population, in order that their movements or their conversations could be closely observed.

Skeptic:

Let me get this straight. Are you predicting we will have satellite-operated personal surveillance devices by the year 2015?

Lady Cassandra:

I am predicting that there is at least a 66 per cent likelihood that such devices will be technically feasible by that time. Indeed, there is some terribly sophisticated equipment already available. The Hughes Aircraft Company has just patented a clever new gadget that uses lasers and infrared imagery for seeing in the dark. This gear is mounted with a holographic lens across the front of a flight helmet to allow helicopter pilots to go lurking around at night on reconnaissance or clandestine snooping missions.

Skeptic:

That's downright scary. I may want to come to that subject before we finish. But for the time being, let's push onward and upward. Some people are talking about these big gizmoes that combine a number of individual black boxes or "packages" for TV broadcasting, fixed and mobile telecommunications, earth resource survey, meteorological applications, remote data collection, navigation and what have you. Apparently they would provide a lower cost service while helping with problems of frequency shortages and system interconnection. In a way, I guess these could be called the "ultimate high-rise condominium." Anyway, what's the inside info?

Lady Cassandra:

Mmmm. "The ultimate high-rise condominium." I'll have to note that one down. Well, at 22,300 miles (or 35,700 kilometres) up in geosynchronous orbit, you certainly could call them highrise and it is likely that the "packages" would have multiple ownership. It fits rather nicely.

Skeptic:

Thanks, but when will I see a condo in space?

Lady Cassandra:

The most likely date for an operational network of space platforms has been set at the year 2000 by just a smidgen under 69 per cent of our experts. As a prelude to such platforms, we may first see a cluster of satellites maintained in relatively close proximity to one another, with a central signalling and switching satellite in the middle to interconnect the cluster. You might liken it to a sort of a spider in the middle of the web. Anyway, the technical impetus toward space platforms, namely interconnectivity and more efficient use of frequencies, is so great that our experts are nearly unanimous in the view that we will soon see that you call "the ultimate high-rise condominium."

Skeptic:

We seem to have more and more television programming around the world and a growing international trade in television receivers. Will there come a day when we have a single global standard for television transmissions, with all receivers being more or less the same? Wouldn't this make international television relay a lot easier and cheaper?

Lady Cassandra:

Seems reasonable, but don't place any bets on it happening soon. As you know, there are three colour television standards—the French-developed SECAM system, the German-developed PAL system, and the U.S.-developed NTSC system. Each time a country wishes to establish a national colour television standard there is a "knock-down, drag-out brawl" among the backers of the three standards. This is not only a matter of prestige, but also, because of potential new markets for TV receivers and because of royalty payments. Colour television standards are among the world's most effective non-tariff trade barriers. Ergo, it will take a lot of persuasion to get everyone to agree on a single standard.

Fifty-five per cent of our experts believe that a single TV standard will come about only in the much longer-term future or never. Some of these experts firmly believe that the several standards are a good thing in terms of helping to maintain cultural diversity.

Other of our experts—about 40 per cent—feel rather differently. They believe that the digital revolution of the 1980s and 1990s may lead to the adoption of a single global television standard in the 2000 to 2015 time period. Many of these experts would agree that the prime motives would be to permit much higher picture resolution for large screens, to allow for higher levels of performance for view data, electronic mail and high-quality facsimile systems. KDD Laboratories, of Japan, for instance, has just developed a super-resolution still television picture system with 1,425 scanning lines—almost three times that of the conventional standard. Not surprisingly, it is a digital system (ADPCM with entropy coding, if you really want to know). Anyway, the new standard would not be PAL, SECAM or NTSC merely warmed over, but actually a new super quality digitally based standard. My guess is that Japan may be the one sitting in the Catbird's Seat if we eventually do see such a new standard emerge.

Skeptic:

You sure are one smart lady, but maybe we should be a little less technical for my sake, if not my readers. Could you tell me about data bases and invasion of privacy? Will they eventually have computer data bases on everyone in the world, or is this just a concern in the U.S., Europe and other such exotic places?

Lady Cassandra:

The U.S. will likely one day have either a public or a private data base on just about everyone. Fifty-five per cent of our experts think it will happen around the year 2000, if not before. Dr. Charles Jackson, the top technical staff member for the U.S. House of Representatives Subcommittee on Communications, has suggested (I believe tongue-in-cheek) that all it would take is some clever marketing. Instead of calling it a universal data bank on the American people, it might be called simply: "Who's Who In America." Thus, despite American pride in its Bill of Rights and the work of such impressive-sounding groups as the U.S. National Commission for the Review of Federal Laws Relating to Wiretapping and Electronic Surveillance, the problem of privacy is expected to get worse—at least that's what our experts say.

Nor is the situation much different in the rest of the developed countries of the world. Japan, Europe, the Soviet Union, Canada and Australia may well all follow the trend toward "bigger and better" computer data banks on everything and everybody.

There is, however, good reason to suspect that there will be increasing steps to inhibit international flows of data about people listed in local or domestic computer banks. Canada has recently moved to stop credit card companies like American Express from operating a unified U.S./Canadian data bank. International transactions of multinational banking corporations are also coming under increasing scrutiny by governments. Some banks have been sufficiently concerned already that they have moved their headquarters and computer data banks to tax and data havens in the Caribbean. Anyway, for legal, political and economic reasons, 82 per cent of our experts believe that the possibilities of a global data bank on all individuals of the world will never occur or, if it does, it will be the very long-term future.

Skeptic:

Your remarks earlier about the technical possibilities of surveillance and your predictions about computer data bases that have information about all people living in an entire country are very disturbing. What other monitoring devices from the land of *1984* and the *Tomorrow File* await us?

Lady Cassandra:

Well, there's both good and bad news on this subject. The bad news is that technically many things are now possible or will be shortly. Such monitoring devices include computer activated and controlled telephone monitors that operate on the principle of key word recognition, telephone and radio "bugs," "undetectable bugs" that broadcast on a subcarrier in order to be masked by say a television transmission, steerable and mobile closed-circuit television cameras, infrared night-time "seeing devices," etc. Why, in France, a company has issued electronic badges to its employees and has an IBM-3750 computer monitoring their whereabouts. The good news is that for the next twenty years or so anyway 71 per cent of our experts believe that an informed public and enlightened legislation will check the systematic use of such surveillance and monitoring devices. Apparently they feel that eventually efforts such as the Younger Committee on Privacy in the U.K., the various privacy commissions in the U.S., etc., will start to pay off.

Skeptic:

Since we have talked about electronic menaces in the home and in the office, perhaps we could talk about some electronic helpers as well. What hardworking new electronic gadgets will we be seeing in the next 10 to 20 years?

Lady Cassandra:

Developments and mass marketing practices in today's global economy require a long lead time. Thus, we can simply predict there will be widespread implementation of many products and services are already know about today (products that are still in experimental development). Thus, 75 per cent or more of our experts predicted the following by the year 2000.

A. Up to 25 per cent of the homes in the U.S. will have a computer/telecommunications/video centre that will provide some or all of these services: television entertainment, electronic games, schooling, bill paying, shopping, main-frame computer access, library and reference research, maintenance of household lists and files and message recording.

B. Ten to twenty-five per cent of all business communications in the U.S., Europe and Japan will be video teleconferencing services. As a consequence of this new service, businesses may very well start to decentralise.

C. Teletext or viewdata will have been introduced in a significant number of homes throughout the "developed world." The French government is actively planning to "give" all of its telephone subscribers a teletext terminal by 1992, in order to eliminate printed directories. (This French largesse only extends up to a point—using the terminal will cost money.)

D. Operational direct broadcast satellite systems for television and radio will be implemented, with the cost of receiving antennas dropping down to as low as $ 100 (1980 dollars) apiece in cost. The Nordic countries, Canada, Germany, Japan and the U.S. may be among the leaders in this field, but developing countries such as India and Brazil should not be too far behind.

Our experts also believe the videophone or picturephone will also eventually do well in homes in the U.S., Europe and Japan, but only after this service has been proven in business applications and after the bills for this service come way down as a result of the digital revolution—maybe as much as four or five times less. When this occurs the idea of telecomputing to work may also really start catching on. Anyway, nearly 80 per cent of our experts say there will be videophones in 5 to 10 per cent of the private homes in the U.S., Europe and Japan by the year 2015. Some forms of telecommuting to work will come much sooner. Workers who only need a computer or word processing terminal for their work could of course start right now. Indeed, in Chicago, on a trial programme, typists desiring to work in their homes have been given word processing terminals with an electronic mail capability. Such electronic secretaries can wake up and plug in not only their coffee makers, but also their typewriters and their offices many miles away.

Skeptic:

My gosh! You mean in the future I won't be able to go on all these junkets to visit lush resorts like the Greek Isles here and, instead, I will be stuck at home with my wife and kids doing my work by videophone from foggy ole London? Well, it's not my idea of progress. Isn't there some obstacle that could prevent all this from happening?

Lady Cassandra:

Yes. There could be some very big obstacles indeed. First of all, there is the problem of saturation of available radio frequencies in the geosynchronous orbit. A recent study of telecommunications demand sponsored by NASA concludes the U.S. will require some 20 million voice channels and over 300 video channels by the year 2000. If 30 to 40 per cent of these requirements were to be met by satellites, this could lead to a complete use of all available frequencies in the 6/4 GHz, 14/12 GHz and 30/20 GHz bands in the geosynchronous arc over the Western Hemisphere, even if we squeeze satellites into position like sardines in a sardine can. With Canada and South and Central America also planning for large demands on these same frequencies at the same orbital locations, it is not difficult to see problems ahead. Anyway, 56.6 per cent of our experts believe that all available frequencies for telecommunications and other space applications below 50 GHz may well be saturated by the year 2015. Such a growing crisis will force us both toward large space platforms and toward better co-ordination in planning of the space and terrestrial telecommunications systems, particularly the integration of space platforms and fibre optics.

Another problem that seems today remote and might even seem a "black-humour" joke in a time of serious energy shortages is the problem of thermal and electromagnetic energy pollution produced by (of all things) "excess energy." That's right—waste energy may well be a serious problem 50 years hence. Power satellites, high-powered broadcast satellites, nuclear and solar energy plants, geothermal and chemical energy sources, along with oil and synthetic hydrocarbon fuels, will help mankind to achieve incredibly high levels of energy consumption. Furthermore, strong and potentially harmful microwave radiation is also on a similar growth curve.

Although extrapolation can sometimes be a dangerous thing, projections of energy consumption levels forward, based upon the last 50 years' experience, show that we could reach the heat limit of earth some 200 years hence—and that's not taking into account such possibilities as the "Venus Syndrome," wherein a sizable carbon dioxide curtain in the upper atmosphere could create a very "hot" greenhouse effect. If, for instance, the mean temperature of the earth were to increase by as much as 100 centrigrade, we could see such consequences as the melting of the polar ice caps, flooding of all the world's sea coasts and elimination of many biological and zoological species. There are indeed a number of ways of describing in a scientifically precise and plausible manner the overheating of the world within the next century.

There are, however, only a very few ways of preventing it. Technologically, there appears to be only two important techniques—finding a way of collecting waste thermal heat and recycling it, or collecting waste heat and irradiating it outside the earth's atmosphere. Although recycling would seem the better approach, both techniques may deserve serious attention in the years ahead. While only 15 per cent of our experts believe we must have developed this technology by the year 2015, the overwhelming majority, believes we will need to do so in the post-2015 time period.

Some of our experts—I'm not sure whether they are the pessimists or the realists—foresee other problems ahead that make frequency saturation and global temperature rise seem almost trivial. These experts predict that we will see planetary space warfare in the post-2000 time period. Killer satellites, nuclear rockets launched from space platforms and laser weapons in low earth orbit are only some of the possibilities. These experts, extrapolating from the spectacular failure of the nuclear non-proliferation treaty and disarmament accords, predict a new round of arms escalation and militancy in space. In the nightmarish world of military one-upsmanship, the ultimate in "future chic" is a nuclear war in space. Should such nightmares become reality, global communications, as well as most other desirable features of life on our planet, would suffer a serious setback.

Skeptic:

Could you tell me something a little more hopeful about the future? I really don't wish to turn all my readers into manic-depressives.

Lady Cassandra:

Certainly there are some bright prospects on which the experts agree. Our brain trust believe that space applications will continue to grow in importance and to provide a wide range of important industrial and social services that should make life better and help sustain a viable world economy. Fifty-nine per cent of our experts see space applications growing from under 1 per cent of the world GNP to 3 to 5 per cent of the world's economic output by the year 2015.

The majority of our experts also foresee increasing prospects for multilateral co-operation in space. Although government-controlled space projects and privately financed corporate projects are expected to remain for some time as the prime means of undertaking space activities, multilateral projects are expected to gain in popularity as the scale, complexity and cost of such projects increase. Our experts predict that the most likely way to achieve future international space co-operation will be commercially oriented technical international organisations like INTELSAT and INMARSAT, followed by multilateral government projects and then, lastly, through specialised agencies of the United Nations. If national governmental projects are assigned an index of 100 as the most likely approach, we can compare our experts' predictions quantitatively as follows:

Likely Institutional Arrangements for Future Space Co-operation

1.	National Government Projects	100
2.	National Commercial Projects	98.5
3.	Commercially and Technically Oriented Projects of International Enterprises (e.g., INTELSAT)	89
4.	Multilateral Government Projects	78.5
5.	U.N. Specialised Agencies	46.5

Such multinational projects might be undertaken for a wide range of possibilities: lunar colonies; solar power stations; space industrial and resort stations in earth's orbit; and perhaps, in the nearer term, with space platforms for telecommunications and other services.

Skeptic:

A final question, Lady Cassandra. What do your experts feel will be the social consequences of all the impressive new technology that they have predicted? Will it, on balance, be a better world?

Lady Cassandra:

Social predictions are much more murky than technical predictions. Machines and technical designs are far more likely to behave in a consistent and regular manner. People and national policy are indeed more like random Brownian motion. Certainly, our social scientists have a long way to go before we can project mankind's behaviour the way we predict the future path of technical development. Most of our staff are technologists and we, as a matter of policy, do not project the social future. The small number of social scientists on our staff do feel great concern about whether our technology will prove socially functional or dysfunctional.

Let me share with you some widely disparate views—one pessimistic (particularly with regard to the U.S.), and another that is much more hopeful. The first view is from a Korean mass media expert—the pessimist. She says:

"By the 2000 to 2015 time frame, the United States will become almost completely mechanised, with human beings increasingly perceived as a part of these mechanisms. This will lead to complete atomisation of humankinds with increased apathy toward everything. This will, in turn, lead around 2020 to entirely new approaches to education, socialisation and human relationships, as well as a wide range of choice among value systems.

In the twenty-first century, Asia, particularly China and Japan, may well rise to a dominant power position, as the superiority of oriental philosophy is recognised within an increasingly technological world.

The 'rationalism' of advanced technology will undermine the rigid belief systems of socialism/ communism within the U.S.S.R. This should lead to a breakdown of socialist philosophy within the U.S.S.R. and independence for East Europe.

Economic and technical pressures will ultimately lead to the creation of a united Europe, at least within industrial organisations, but probably politically as well.

The developing world will become more integrated in the world technically and economically, at least up until the year 2000, but new and subtle forms of control will then be exercised by the advanced information societies to create sophisticated new forms of neocolonialism. If this does not occur, the alternative will likely be overt north-south hostilities."

The second prediction is from an American political scientist, Dr. Wilbur Blume, who predicts the following: "We will see the emergence of a global inventory, marketing and distribution system, largely based on satellite and telecommunications systems. This will allow a stronger global economy and more equitable distribution of the world's resources. We also see the development of a global information telenet available to all countries. This will be a key ingredient in the struggle of developing nations to achieve parity with the more advanced states. The global inventory and marketing system and the global information telenet will have several important social impacts. One will be a heightened level of expectation on the part of all people, as well as a further confrontation between traditional values and those of modernisation. A second important development will be diminished nationalism, as people increasingly identify with a region or a particular aspect of the new integrated global economy. Multinational enterprises will likely command increased allegiance. Conflicts in such an environment will more likely be resolved economically, rather than militarily. The same economic and technical focus will lead to a blurring between socialistic and democratic political philosophies.

These shifts in economic trade and intellectual access, coupled with the great flexibility provided by personal communications systems, will serve to reshape our cities, change our commuting habits, restructure our socialisation patterns, and make possible significant economic growth—perhaps ultimately, even global wealth. All sources of traditional authority and belief systems will be challenged, i.e., the nucleus and extended family, religion, political dogma, nationalism and cultural beliefs. People will no longer be remote, even though they may wish to remain so. Tremendous freedom and flexibility will be technically possible, perhaps well beyond what is socially desirable."

These are, of course, only two speculations on the future amid a myriad of other possibilities. Despite the many differences between these two forecasts, the basic conflict of traditional beliefs and structures against modern ones is there. One expert sees the struggle as having largely negative consequences, and the other sees a generally favourable balance. My personal bias is that the balance will be about 45 per cent good, 40 per cent bad, and 15 per cent starkly indifferent. It's not much of an advantage on which to stake our whole global civilisation, but then we really have no choice. We passed that milestone with fire and the wheel.

Skeptic:

Lady Cassandra, you can call me a "believer." Can I take you to dinner this evening?

Lady Cassandra:

Thought you would never ask.

10

Information System for Administration: Public Service Applications

In addition to support of online data bases and remote online searching, microcomputers have been used in a number of public service applications. This chapter reviews circulation control, reserve book room systems, media booking systems and interlibrary loan applications. The first three have obvious similarities, with each requiring some specialised fields of information. While some libraries have evolved their own systems for these applications, the more comprehensive systems have been developed by commercial vendors for multi-library use. Interlibrary loan procedures have also been analysed for microcomputer support; at present there are few customised systems, although the use of general electronic mail messages for requesting titles is common.

This chapter describes various micro systems for these public service applications. Different sized systems are reviewed to show a range of capabilities and to offer new ideas for libraries contemplating in-house development of a system or evaluating commercial systems.

Also included is a brief overview of public access micros and the use of micros for computer-assisted instruction.

CIRCULATION CONTROL

Circulation support was one of the earliest applications of computers in libraries. Circulation is a repeatable and generally predictable operation. It is a labour-intensive task requiring many hours of clerical assistance. Additionally, it is usually the most visible operation in a library. For these reasons, circulation has often been the first service to be automated.

As microcomputers began to appear in libraries, a number of micro-based circulation systems emerged. Because of the built-in limitations of microcomputers, three factors have dictated the type of micro used in a given operation and the type of circulation system developed. The first is circulation volume. Most smaller micros are single-user systems and require a slow and steady flow of transactions in order to be effective. Size and complexity of the record make up the second governing factor. The smaller micros usually cannot accommodate the full MARC record, but they have been used effectively for circulation material with simplified records. The third factor is whether there is a need for a true inventory control system. If a library needs to maintain records of only the items actually in circulation at a given time (an absence system), a small micro may be effective.

The larger microcomputers are multiple-user systems, capable of supporting hard disk storage, and can support all of the functions typically found in a circulation system on a large computer. The only limitations are the number of concurrent users (presently about four) and the amount of storage that can be accessed (about 256 million characters on a hard disk).

Microcomputers have also been used effectively to support circulation-related functions. As a backup system when a larger mini or mainframe system is down, microcomputers can perform limited data collection functions so that materials can continue to circulate until the larger system is restored. Micros have also been used as "front-end" devices. In this capacity, they perform specific tasks in a circulation system such as handling the user interface or collecting transactions while the larger computer is busy with other operations. Micros can serve as interface devices between larger circulation systems and networks. In addition, several peripheral devices on larger systems, such as light pens, touch screens, intelligent terminals and disk controllers, are controlled by microprocessors.

The systems described in this section illustrate each of the functions noted above. They are no necessarily the best systems available in each case but show what may be done using microcomputers for circulation control.

A Large-capacity System: The Integrated Library System (NLM)

The Integrated Library System (ILS) designed by the Lister Hill National Centre for Biomedical Communications at the National Library of Medicine (NLM) is an example of a system running on a machine at the upper limit of microcomputers. As the name suggests, the system is an integrated one, with several functional modules operating on a common data base of MARC records. Development was begun on the system in 1978 with funding from the Army Library at the Pentagon, and the circulation module was installed in the Army Library in 1980. The entire software package includes the master bibliographic file, a circulation module, a serials checkin module and limited online searching capabilities. Full serials control, acquisitions, cataloging, authority control, network access and a full patron-level interface are under development. The software is available from the National Technical Information Service (NTIS) for a licensing fee of $ 2000. ILS is also marketed by Avatar Systems, Inc. and Online Computer Systems, Inc.

The system was designed to run on a variety of machines that support the Meditech Interpretive Information System (MIIS), an operating system supplied by Medical Information Technology, Inc. (Meditech). The microcomputer that will operate the system is the LSI 11/23, manufactured by Digital Equipment Corp.

In this section, only the circulation module of the ILS system will be described. Other modules are described in related works. The circulation module's features are comparable to any circulation system on any size machine, and it can handle the circulation requirements of large libraries. The software is largely table-driven, meaning that system parameters such as loan periods or fine rates may be changed easily according to local needs. The terminal control subsystem is also table-driven to allow a variety of terminals to be used. Help screens prompt new users. Checkin and checkout modes use light pens, with manual overrides to allow keying of data if desired. Code 39 bar codes were selected since they offer upto three lines of eye-readable information. Extensive error checking and verification are built into the checkin and checkout modes but also may be overriden if desired.

The system provides for recalls, holds and renewals according to various user-prescribed parameters. An interesting renewal feature is the ability to automatically renew all items for a given patron with a single command. Another unusual feature is the "cart" function. Items checked in are assigned to a cart to await shelving. The shelves can, by a single command, change the location field on all items to the proper shelf location when the cart has been emptied.

The patron file allows online entry of new patrons and patron inquiry by name or identification number; it also maintains usage statistics by patron. The item file is tied into the master bibliographic record and is copy-specific for monographs and issue specific for serials. It may be accessed by identification number, author, title or call number. The master bibliographic file can also be accessed by International Standard Serial Number (ISSN), Library of Congress Card Number (LCCN) and subject.

The system provides standard circulation system outputs such as recall notices, overdues and fine billing. It also can produce bibliographies or selective dissemination of information (SDI) reports on request. It maintains usage statistics for each item and each patron. Regular reports produced include item and patron status reports (such as overdue items or delinquent borrowers), usage analysis, collection analysis and new acquisition lists.

An interface to the Online Computer Library Center (OCLC) is provided to allow users to capture bibliographic information directly from an OCLC 100 or 105 terminal. Storage requirements depend on record size, authority file support, type of access desired and the indexes for separate and dictionary catalogs. The library can reduce storage requirements by limiting the system capabilities.

Medium-capacity Systems

The Library Circulation System

The Library Circulation System, designed and marketed by Futura Computer Products, Inc., runs on various microcomputers that use the CP/M operating system and are based on the Z-80 or 8080 microchip. A typical configuration is a Vector Graphic, Inc. microcomputer with either 5¼ or 8-inch floppy disks or 14-inch hard disks, 1 cathode ray tube (CRT) terminal with light pen and a dot matrix printer. Depending on the disk configuration chosen, the system costs from $ 15,000 to $ 30,000, including software. The smaller system can handle 1720 patron records and 2,380 circulation records while the larger system can handle 32,000 patrons and 32,000 circulation records. From 300 to 1,000 transactions can be kept online, again depending on the disk system chosen.

The system uses standard bar code labels for checkin and checkout with the ability to key in directly if the bar code is missing or unreadable. The user interface has two levels, one with helps and prompts and the other with an abbreviated command structure for the experienced user. Where possible, operations are triggered by a single keystroke. Many of the system parameters such as loan periods are table-driven and easily changed. Patron information is kept online, with usage data, fines and delinquency indicators dynamically updated. The overdue and recall modules are custom written for each institution purchasing the system.

Nonesuch Circulation System

The Nonesuch Circulation System, offered by Ringgold Management Systems, consists of a microcomputer with 64K of memory (any CP/M-based micro or the TRS-80 Model 11 or Model 16), both floppy and hard disk storage units, a bar code reader and a printer, at a cost of about $ 39,000. It can accommodate up to 50,000 titles and patrons. It supports separate files for titles, patrons, charges and holds.

The system supports the following functions in an online mode:

* Charge
* Discharge
* Renewal
* Place hold
* Inquiry about item
* Inquiry about patron
* Block patron charging
* Patron registration

Additional functions are run in a batch mode:

* Overdue notices
* Recall notices
* Backup/recovery
* End of term notices
* Item master lists
* Physical inventory
* Statistical summaries

Libra

CTI Library Systems, Inc. has developed a range of circulation systems based on the Apple microcomputer. CTI's first product, introduced in 1979, was the Library Backup System (described in the next section). The stand-alone circulation systems it now offers include the Libra systems for micros.

The CTI Libra systems have most of the same capabilities as CTI's Esprit system, an integrated system for minicomputers. The low-end Libra system, on an Apple II +, uses either 5¼-inch floppy disks or 5 to 10-megabyte hard disks and will support 5,000 to 10,000 patron records, 800 titles per diskette and an annual circulation of 80,000. It sells for between $ 5,000 and $ 7,000. The higher end of the Libra series includes up to 20 megabytes of hard disk storage and uses the Apple III. It will support 10,000 patron records, more than 55,000 titles and an annual circulation of from 80,000 to 1,00,000. The price is about $ 15,000.

Libra systems support the following features:

* Item search update: the bibliographic file is searchable by author, title, multiple subjects, bar code number and call number
* Patron search/update
* Checkin/inquiry: uses light pen or keyboard entry
* Checkout/renewal: uses light pen or keyboard entry
* Overdue notices
* Library specific variables: loan periods, grace periods and item checkout limits can be set by the library
* Day-end backup

Small-capacity Systems

Online Circulation System

The Online Circulation System is one of several software packages available from Richmond Micro Software for the Apple II + microcomputer. The programme costs about $ 500. It will support up to 65,000 titles and 3,000 user records with appropriate Apple peripherals. The hardware, which must be purchased separately, would cost about $ 10,000 for the maximum configuration. The system uses bar codes and light pens for checkout and checkin. Automatic overdues are generated and printed by the system. It also permits on-the-shelf inventory of the collection using the light pen. Missing item lists are automatically compiled and printed by the programme.

LSC Circulation System

The Library Software Co. has developed the LSC Circulation System, an inexpensive software package for libraries with 100 or fewer transactions per day. The programme, selling for $ 125, can run on an Apple II or a Radio Shack TRS-80 Model III and requires 48K of memory. Transactions are keyboarded online. Automatic overdues and bills are printed on request. Reports can be printed alphabetically or can be grouped—for example, by home-room. The system would be ideal for a school library.

A Backup Circulation System

An example of a microcomputer used as a backup for a circulation system running on a mini or mainframe is the one developed on an Apple II at Brigham Young University. The system is marketed by CTI Library Systems, Inc., and can be used as a backup to CL Systems, Inc. (CLSI), Geac Computers, Inc. and CTI minicomputer systems. CTI packages a standard 48K Apple II micro with diskette, communications card, colour monitor and Integer BASIC for about $ 3,200. The software costs an additional $ 1,500.

The system provides the regular light pen, laser or command checkin and checkout that the larger system provides. Return charges and renewals are also collected on the micro. Transaction counters and signals to indicate full diskettes are built into the system. When the larger system is running again, all of the transactions are sequentially uploaded into it from the micro. The micro also can be used for bookmobile charges; transactions from the bookmobile are read into the central library system at the end of the day. Since data are stored on multiple floppy disks, there is no limit to the number of transactions that can be stored. When not being actually used for backup, the micro can be used as a terminal to the host system, or it can be programmed for other applications within the library.

A Front-end Processor System

A system that not only uses a microcomputer as backup but as a front-end pre-processor for a large system has been developed and implemented at Oberlin College. (The Oberlin system was modified from a Bucknell University system.) The micro system runs on the college computing centre's SIGMA-9 mainframe computer and was designed for use when the SIGMA is down and for handling end-of-semester peak loads. The microcomputer, an Intel 8080, sits under the circulation desk. It monitors all use of the system and performs specified tasks that the mainframe system does not have to process.

The microcomputer handles traffic management for six terminals in the library through a single communications line into the mainframe computer. The user prompts, error checking of input and driving of the bar code readers are all done by the microcomputer. The micro also formats all data for storing in the mainframe. Upon retrieval of a record, the microcomputer does all of the formatting for display on the screen. Actual storage and retrieval of data is handled by the SIGMA 9. When the mainframe is busy or goes down, the microcomputer stores the data on floppy disks until the mainframe is available. The micro then sends the data automatically.

System Interfaces

Microcomputers have also been used as interfaces between circulation systems and bibliographic utilities. An example is the TPS-400 interface designed by TPS Electronics. Based on either an Apple II + or an Apple IIe, it serves as an intelligent buffer memory between online cataloging systems such as OCLC or Research Libraries Information Network (RLIN) and online circulation systems such as CLSI. It connects directly it to the printer port of a terminal for the host cataloging system and reformats the data to be read into the end-user circulation system. Full MARC formats or any specified subset may be used. The system sells for $ 8,995 for a single cataloging terminal; up to four terminals can be supported.

The TPS-400 can be used with the TPS-300 interface, which has a customised micro-processor for scanning bar code numbers for a direct transfer to the OCLC or RLIN terminal records. The bar codes can be placed in any field by positioning the cursor. The interface is available for $ 1,995. The TPS-450 is a spine label printing system that can be attached to the TPS-400 for producing spine labels for the cataloging records. The price is an additional $ 1,500 with the TPS-400 or $ 6,500 for a stand-alone Apple-based system used for label printing.

RESERVE BOOK ROOM SUPPORT

Reserve book room (RBR) systems are rarer than circulation systems since most public libraries do not use them. Many of the requirements are similar to those of circulation systems, with a few features that are unique. An RBR system uses the same type of bibliographic file and user file as does a circulation system. Other features common to both are charging and discharging with a light pen, recalls, overdues and holds. RBR systems must be able to accommodate the additional requirements of shorter loan periods (often as short as one hour), fine schedules based on the clock rather than the calendar and the need to place holds on all copies of a title. Often many copies of a given title will be placed on reserve, and 15 people may be waiting for five copies. Therefore, more sophisticated queuing algorithms are required than are typically needed for circulation.

Often nonlibrary material, such as personal copies or reprints of articles may be circulated, requiring flexibility in the construction of the item records. Additional access points to the records, such as course number or professor's name, may be needed. Other desirable features are the ability to add and delete items by course list and the ability to save a course list online for a later academic term.

As of early 1983, all of the programmes known by the authors to handle reserves are locally produced, and none of them are full reserve systems. Given the speed of development, by the time this book is published, several of the circulation system vendors may be offering a reserve module as well.

Southern Illinois University at Edwardsville

The Lovejoy Library at Southern Illinois University at Edwardsville was one of the pioneers of microcomputer use in the library, using Apples for many applications. One is the printing of a reserve book catalog using a programme called Magic Window from Softape Art-SCI, Inc. Several other catalogs are maintained by the same programme.

East Carolina University

The Health Sciences Library at East Carolina University in Greenville, NC, has implemented a reserve control system on a Radio Shack TRS-80 Model II. It was developed in-house and handles reserve checkout, checkin and recall. (The library also uses a number of commercial packages such as Radio Shack's Scripsit for word processing. Profile for inventory control and VisiCorp's VisiCalc for statistical reports.)

MEDIA BOOKING PROGRAMMES

Media booking has a number of requirements that are common to other modules. Like circulation, it requires both an item file and user file. Like a reserve system, it must handle short loan periods and be able to queue users. Media booking also has some unique design requirements. A complete booking system will not only schedule the "software," such as films, tapes or slides, but also the equipment. This requires a dual but co-ordinated reserve system. Often schedules are very tight, with minimum set-up times available between uses, particularly in school or university environments. There may be a further need to schedule set-up personnel and operators; this requires a three-level reserve system and very sophisticated scheduling.

Unlike reserve and circulation, which usually operate on a first-in/first-out type of queue, booking systems need to be able to reserve future dates and times and must be able to display open times in the schedule. It is often desirable to schedule months in advance, particularly in an educational environment, where an entire term may be scheduled at one time. A desirable feature is the ability to schedule backup titles in case the desired one is not available.

A total media system should also contain a parts inventory for bulbs, cables and other equipment. It should have an alert feature to signal recorder of disposable parts before the supply is exhausted.

Because of the complexity of the system requirements and the fact that there are fewer media centres than libraries, full automated media systems have been scarce, even on mainframe and minicomputers. However, several commercial micro-based systems have emerged. As with other applications, a number of institutions have implemented single features of a media booking system on a microcomputer, and many of those may be available to other libraries.

STC Film Booking System

The Software Technology for Computers (STC) Film Booking System is available from Nolan Information Management Services. It uses an Apple II with two disk drives, 48K and a

132-column printer. It is a menu-driven system written in assembly language and Applesoft II.

STC Film Booking can handle up to 850 media software items, 20 customers and 1500 transactions. The file structure allows for almost instantaneous retrieval. Data entry is screen-prompted with built-in error checking. It features complete sorting and searching capabilities. Algorithms allow for easy scheduling, built-in travel days and receiving material. Standard reports from the system include bookings on both a daily and a year-to-date basis. A list of films not available can be printed, as well as a complete customer utilisation report.

The media file records include title, run time, type of media, school grade level, cost, purchase data, inspection date, subject code, producer code, distributor code and condition. The customer file includes name, address, city, state, zip, travel days and routing information.

The software diskette and manual can be purchased for about $ 500.

AMI

Research Technology International has had a media booking system for minicomputers for several years. Its new microcomputer system is called AMI (Automated Media Information) and features a preservation programme, booking searches, title searches, information reports, cancellation reports and production of shipping forms.

The AMI system permits bookings up to one year in advance. Alternate late and alternate title assignment are built-in features of the system. Inventory management, catalog production and automatic checkin are also standard features. Variable booking periods are available, and subject indexing allows customers to browse the file by topic to find related films.

Media Equipment Control System

Media Equipment Control System (MECS) was written as a demonstration system by the Graduate School of Library and Information Science at Indiana University, Bloomington. It is written for the Vector Graphic, Inc. machine. The system is basically an equipment inventory and is meant to demonstrate for library school students some possible uses of a microcomputer in a media centre.

St. Luke's Methodist Hospital

The Health Sciences Library at St. Luke's Methodist Hospital in Cedar Rapids, IA, uses an Apple II + for audiovisual inventory control. The software was locally developed.

INTERLIBRARY LOAN SYSTEMS

The needs of an interlibrary loan (ILL) system are very similar to those of a circulation system. In this case the patron is another institution. Usually fines are not involved. Since most transactions are done by mail. Telex, telephone or a link to a utility such as OCLC, more paperwork is typically involved than with a simple circulation transaction. Because the activity represents an extra service in the minds of many librarians and administrators, detailed statistics are usually kept, such as classes of libraries served, geographical areas served or type of material sent.

While the systems offered by OCLC, RLIN and other networks have been heavily used by larger institutions, most smaller libraries have relied on totally manual systems for interlibrary loan.

Design features for a computerised interlibrary loan system usually include a name and address file. The institutions included in the file represent both those to whom materials are being lent and those from whom materials are being borrowed. Thus, the function of the file is rather like a combined user and vendor file. Usually a sophisticated system would not only contain all of the information required to communicate with the other institution but would also include counters to keep track of total number of items borrowed, lent or recalled as well as unfilled requests.

The bibliographic file is typically built at the point of transaction and in that sense is similar to an absence system for circulation. Ordinarily an entire collection need not be represented in the bibliographic file since typically only a small percentage of the collection goes out on interlibrary loan.

Some automated ILL systems handle only a single feature of the whole operation, such as the production of standard American Library Association (ALA) interlibrary loan forms, the handling of ILL statistics or a simple checkout system for the materials handled. A complete system would certainly have to include communications capability, usually through a modem and a connection to a phone line. Sophisticated systems would have auto-dial capabilities and auto-answering for receiving loan requests. If standard phone lines and regular long distance rates are the only communications available, the system will be expensive to run and probably only justified if time were at a premium, as might be the case in a special or corporate library. Where free or blanket charge phone networks are available, the automated system is an option for any library.

Several interlibrary loan activities have been implemented with microcomputers. Probably the simplest is the use of electronic mail systems to communicate requests.

L*O*A*N

Computerland, a nationwide chain of computer stores, offers the Library Online Automated Network, or L*O*A*N. The turnkey system includes an Apple II microcomputer with 48K of memory, 5¼-inch dual disk drives, a monitor, a modem, upper and lower case, printer interface and the L*O*A*N software, and sells for about $ 7,300. A printer is extra. (The package also includes software for assessing. The Source, a consumer-oriented online data base system from Source Telecomputing Corp.) The L*O*A*N software may be purchased separately for $ 2,500.

The system features automatically completed ILL forms for books or journals. An automatic bulletin board, which is displayed at log-on time, allows each library to customise its welcome message. An automatic mail feature notifies the user of waiting messages; the "help" function explains system commands and can be accessed at any time during the programme. The system can store messages and loan requests and forward them in batch mode to reduce line charges. Numbers can be dialed directly from the keyboard to save dialing and switching

A system log keeps track of all users with date, time, name, address and phone number. Each message or ILL request is assigned a number so it can be referenced later. The system automatically logs off if there is no user activity for five minutes. Since the system includes auto-answering, it is a true 24-hour system. It need not be attended to receive loan requests.

Montana State Library

In Montana, a microcomputer network has been established to facilitate interlibrary loan operations between the State Library and six regional libraries: Bozeman Public, Parmly Billings, Miles City Public, Glasgow City-County, Missoula City-County and Great Falls Public. The libraries use Apple II + micros with Microcourier software from Microcom, Inc., for communications. The interlibrary loan requests are prepared daily and stored on 5¼-inch diskettes for later transmission when nighttime telephone rates are in effect. A dot matrix printer is used to produce forms on multi-part paper.

The Microcourier software can also be used to communicate using On Tyme-II, an electronic mail system from Tymshare, Inc. This extends the potential network beyond libraries that have Apple microcomputers; libraries with any terminal that can access On Tyme-II can communicate interlibrary loan information.

MICROS AS INSTRUCTIONAL TOOLS

The use of microcomputers as instructional tools is growing rapidly in libraries. The greatest boom is in "public access" micros, with libraries throughout the country offering microcomputers for patron use. Another, though much less prevalent, micro application is computer-assisted instruction (CAI). These applications will be described briefly in this section.

A discussion of the microcomputer invasion of schools and colleges is beyond the scope of this monograph and will not be included here. It should be noted, however, that virtually every school in the U.S. is expected to own micros by the end of the decade. The population will become increasingly computer literate, with profound implications for library collections and services.

Patron Use

A 1983 survey by *Advanced Technology/Libraries* indicated that nearly two-thirds of the 83 public libraries responding owned at least one microcomputer. (This compared with 47 per cent of 85 responding academic libraries and 28 per cent of 106 responding special libraries.)[1] Many of the public libraries make the machines available for patron use. Most also provide a collection of programme for use with the micros and some instruction in their use.

Among libraries with active patron access micro programmes are the Chicago Public Library, the Columbus (OH) Public Library, the Baltimore County Library System, the Queens Borough (NY) Public Library, the San Francisco Public Library, the Scottsdale (AZ) Public Library and the Nashua (NH) Public Library. Some libraries allow patrons to borrow machines, much as they borrow other instructional materials. Among them are the Albany (NY) Public Library, the Portsmouth (NH) Public Library and the Cloquet (MN) Public Library.

Libraries often cite lack of funds as the chief obstacle to owning public access micros. Many libraries have solved the funding problem by appealing to local groups such as "Friends of the Library." A popular alternative has been to use coin-operated microcomputers, supplied free by the equipment vendors. The coin box accepts tokens, which the patron buys from the library. Typical charges are $ 3-$ 3.50 per hour. In some cases the library can collect a small percentage (typically 5 per cent) of the revenue.

One vendor that supplies coin-operated micros is Micro Timesharing, which also offers a variety of business, educational and game programmes at no cost. The company provides publicity, including paid advertising and Press releases, to promote the use of the micros. The equipment consists of Apple II + microcomputers with 48K of memory, a disk drive and a printer.

Maxwell Library Systems (MLS) offers a no-coin "coin-op" microcomputer system. Instead of coins, issues a plastic card which has time upto 15 hours magnetically encoded on it. The card is purchased at the library desk and when inserted into a slot at the microcomputer turns on the monitor so the machine may be used. When the time is expired, only the monitor is turned off so data are not lost. The CARD-Op mechanism alone can be purchased for about $ 1,400 from MLS. A full system from Maxwell costs about $ 3,500 for an Apple II + with 48K, two disk drives and a desk to which the equipment may be secured.

Gaylord Bros., Inc. offers the Compuvend system, which comes in three models that can accept quarters, dollar bills or tokens. The library can adjust the charge per unit of time. A steel desk provides security for the equipment. The system includes a vendoverride staff key to enable use of the system without depositing currency.

The Chicago Public Library has logged some interesting statistics on its public use micros. The average time spent per visit was 1.5 hours. Fifty-eight per cent of the users were beginners. Only 22 per cent of the users had ever taken a computer course. The micros were used for playing games by 48 per cent of the users, for business applications by 47 per cent and for educational programmes by 35 per cent.

A number of libraries have become involved in organised computer literacy programmes such as Computer Town, USA (CTUSA), which began in Menlo Park, CA, as a grass-roots, volunteer literacy project. CTUSA soon found its way into the public library's meeting rooms where it could use the several micros that had been donated by an interested manufacturer. By late 1982 there were more than 70 Computer Town projects in the U.S., Canada, Great Britain and Germany. A monthly news bulletin is published by the People's Computer Company, P.O. Box E, Menlo Park, CA 94025.

Some libraries have encountered problems with public use micros. Libraries that had offered free use of micros and subsequently introduced pay-as-you-go machine experienced a sharp drop in their use. Several libraries have had equipment stolen. Vandalism is a continuing problem if the micro is placed in a remote area of the library.

Other problem issues that must be resolved are monitoring the use of the micros, preventing illegal copying of library-owned software, deciding what kinds of software to provide and establishing that the library is not liable for lost data.

Computer-assisted Instruction (CAI)

Computer-assisted Instruction (CAI) has been available on larger computers since the 1960s and is now being developed for micros. CAI systems typically display a paragraph of information and then ask a question based on the data presented. If the user responds correctly, it leads him to the next logical paragraph. If not, it coaches him and redisplays the data and the question. Sophisticated CAI systems such as PLATO, developed by Control Data Corp. (CDC) use graphics terminals and displays that include both text and diagrams. PILOT, one of the popular CAI languages, allows an instructor to compose a CAI course without requiring a knowledge of computer programming.

As a personal, single-user machine, the microcomputer is ideally suited for CAI. CDC has announced a version of PLATO that will run on an Apple II +, Apple IIe. IBM PC and the Texas Instruments, Inc. home computer. Most of the PLATO courseware, which has been developed by CDC over a period of 20 years and at a cost of $ 900 million, will eventually be available in the micro version.

The International Institute of Applied Technology, Inc. has offered PILOT-plus, a micro version of PILOT, its CAI programme. PILOT-plus runs on CP/M-based micros, including the Apple IIe (with Z-80 chip), TRS-80, North Star, Altos, IBM PC, Xerox and Hewlett-Packard. Enhancements available include a colour monitor with touch screen and interfaces for video discs, digital voice output and high resolution graphics. The basic system includes the course software, a statistical package that monitors student use and a data base management system to maintain courseware.

The University of Louisville uses a locally designed CAI system that runs on Cromemco Z2D microcomputers. The system is housed in the Health Sciences Library and logged nearly 100,000 users in 1979, its first year of micro-based operation.

Library schools are experimenting with the use of microcomputer-based simulations for teaching online searching and for illustrating the concepts of computer technology. Online searching of remote bibliographic data bases has received particular attention for computer-assisted instruction.[2-4] Initial developments centred on software for larger machines, but this interest is now being transferred to microcomputers. One of the major reasons for using simulations, for which micros are generally well suited, is the high cost of actually using remote vendor systems for training and demonstrations.

Another advantage of a simulated search system on a local machine, whether microcomputer or larger machine, is greater control. There are likely to be fewer technical problems, such as system problems or communications interference, which would prevent the demonstration or instruction. There are no royalty costs or communication charges either. However, there are some problems. The large search systems have sophisticated software that is difficult to simulate totally, given the storage constraints of microcomputers. Such simulations must also be revised each time the vendor system is enhanced. Even more of a problem is the data base. Most training files are relatively small, especially on a small micro system. Thus students cannot learn one of the more critical aspects of online searching—the manipulation of large files of information. Nonetheless, micros are still effective in demonstrating the retrieval and manipulation capabilities of online systems.

While there has been some work toward specialised packages for instruction on using library tools such as the card catalog or a particular index, these have been slow to evolve. Most efforts seem to be coming from individual libraries rather than the publishers of the printed tools. This most likely reflects the publishers' need to develop systems with large market potential.

Newberry College in South Carolina has developed a library instruction computer game that teaches students to create a bibliography on specified topics. Players must find the citations from an abbreviated version of the *Reader's Guide to Periodical Literature.* The game begins with screens of instructions and interpretations of cross-references and citations. Once the game is begun, a clock tracks the amount of time required to complete the bibliography. Developed initially on a Digital Equipment Corp. PDP minicomputer, the software is being translated into Applesoft for use with Apple microcomputers.[5]

The National Bureau of Standards Library has developed software packages to instruct staff in various procedures. Initially CAI was introduced as a means of teaching deaf technicians to work with serials. Programmes have also been developed for training student staff to understand the Library of Congress classification scheme. The programmes, based on the Bell and Howell Genis software, allow a number of attempts before providing the correct answer. The system monitors students' performance and provides a score at the end of the training session.

SUMMARY

Microcomputers have been used successfully in many different public service applications. Although a large research or public library could not rely on present stand-alone micro systems for circulation support, a small or specialised library may find a microcomputer excellent for this application. Many systems include modules for other applications, which can further help to justify their cost. As of this writing, no complete reserve book room support programmes are available for microcomputers although several locally developed systems are in use. As with circulation, media booking systems have been offered commercially as well as developed locally. The relatively low level of transactions for interlibrary loans makes this an application well suited to micros, although there are special communications needs to be considered. Better commercial software packages can be expected for most of these applications in the very near future, and some of the successful "home-grown" systems may also be made more widely available.

Microcomputers for public access will be found increasingly in all kinds of libraries. Computer-assisted instruction, once the province of larger machines, is under development for micros, although progress in this area is relatively slow.

References

1. "Public Libraries Lead Microcomputer Boom; Academics, Specials Lag Behind," *Advanced Technology/Libraries,* 12(3): 1-3 (March, 1983).
2. Meredith Gillette, "The Use of Microcomputers for Online Demonstrations and Instruction," *Online '82 Conference Proceedings,* (Weston, CT, Online, Inc., 1982), pp. 341-345.

3. Frances E. Wood, "Online Teaching Aids from the Department of Information Science, University of Sheffield, England," *Online Review,* 5(6): 487-494 (December, 1981).
4. R. Frederick Guy, J. Andrew Large and Christopher J. Armstrong, "Microcomputer Simulations of Online Bibliographic Systems for Teaching Purposes," *Proceedings of the 1981 National Online Meeting* (Medford, NJ, Learned Information, Inc., 1981), pp. 261-270.
5. Arie C. Kolewyn and Katherine Corby, "Citation: A Library Instruction Computer Game," *RQ* 22(2): 171-174 (Winter, 1982).

Index